Pennsylvania Association of Nonprofit Organizations'

The Pennsylvania Nonprofit Handbook

5th Edition

Gary M. Grobman

White Hat Communications
Harrisburg, Pennsylvania

Published by White Hat Communications.

Copies may be ordered from:

White Hat Communications
PO Box 5390
Harrisburg, PA 17110-0390
(717) 238-3787 (telephone)
(717) 238-2090 (fax)
http://www.socialworker.com/nonprofit/nphome.htm

The material in Chapter 4 and Chapter 16 of this publication was authored by Michael Sand, and is reprinted with permission from the author. The author gratefully acknowledges the contributions Mr. Sand made to the material that comprises Chapter 15. The material in Chapter 6 and Chapter 7 was authored by Gerald Kaufman, and is reprinted with permission. Some of the material in Chapter 20 is based on the book *The Non-Profit Internet Handbook*, authored by Gary Grobman and Gary Grant. The material in Chapter 25 was authored by Dr. Pam Leland of Seton Hall University, and is reprinted with permission.

This publication is intended to provide general information and should not be construed as legal advice or legal opinions concerning any specific facts or circumstances. Consult an experienced attorney if advice is required concerning any specific situation or legal matter.

The opinions expressed in this publication are solely those of the author and contributors and do not necessarily reflect the opinions of the Pennsylvania Association of Nonprofit Organizations, its board, staff, or members.

Contact the author in care of White Hat Communications, or by e-mail at:
gary.grobman@paonline.com

Printed in the United States of America.

Editing: Linda Grobman, John Hope
Proofreading: Judy Margo

ISBN: 0-9653653-1-X

Table of Contents

Foreword by *Joseph Geiger*, Executive Director, Pennsylvania Association of Nonprofit Organizations

Introduction
Advantages and Disadvantages of Incorporation
Nonprofits and Private Benefit

Introduction to Incorporation
Choosing Incorporators
Choosing a Corporate Name
Choosing Corporate Purposes
Choosing to Have Members or No Members
Additional Provisions
Corporate Dissolution

Introduction to Preparing Bylaws
Legal Requirements of Bylaws in Pennsylvania

Board Formation
Organization Officers
Getting Good Board Members
Keeping Good Board Members
Board Responsibilities
How Boards Function Effectively
Holding High Quality Board Meetings
Relationship Between Board Members and Staff Members

Introduction
Purpose of Strategic Planning

Foreword

Joe Geiger
Executive Director
PA Association of Nonprofit Organizations

Congratulations! You have decided to be a part of the fastest growing segment of business development in the United States. You are considering joining, or have already joined, hundreds of thousands of other nonprofits in the United States. They come in all sizes, shapes and colors. The nonprofit sector's heritage includes helping in an emergency, encouraging the human spirit, educating and shaping values and goals and being the first to offer a hand.

You have chosen to be a vital link in developing the fabric of the community. From the time our ancestors landed on Plymouth Rock (or staffed the Welcome Wagon that greeted those who did), people have worked together in formal organizations to better the human condition. The nonprofit sector has always been in the forefront of improving our society and the human condition.

Today, the nonprofit sector is in a very challenging period. Nonprofits are experiencing ever-growing scrutiny and demands for accountability. Service demand is increasing. There is more competition for charitable dollars. The public and government both are demanding that nonprofits improve their efficiency. This book will help you respond to these challenges.

As the chief executive officer of PANO, I am pleased to be a part of *The Pennsylvania Nonprofit Handbook*. Every week, callers to PANO ask questions: Should we start up? Should we merge? Should we go out of business? I am pleased to have a practical tool that can help answer these questions. This book will help you keep on track. It is also an extraordinary resource for those who already manage or serve on the boards of nonprofit organizations. With practical advice on fundraising, communications, lobbying, personnel management, grantsmanship, and scores of other issues, it is a must for every nonprofit executive to have.

This book has been revised and expanded since the 4th edition was published back in 1996. There are new chapters on mergers, change management, quality, and the Year 2000 problem. And, this edition also includes a chapter devoted to the significant developments affecting nonprofits that have occurred since the previous edition. Here, in one place, is a useful summary of the seismic events of the last year or so—from enactment and implementation of the *Institutions of Purely Public Charity Act* to passage of the state lobbying reforms, from publication of the IRS intermediate sanctions regulations to enactment of the Volunteer Protection Act.

As you work through the process of establishing your organization, remember that PANO is here to help you. PANO is the statewide organization bringing together the best resources to guide, train, and help your organization to be the best that it can. *The Pennsylvania Nonprofit Handbook* is at the top of the list of essential tools to have on your bookshelf. And, I must add, membership in PANO is a complimentary tool as well. Please join today; we are only as strong as our membership, and the effectiveness of PANO's voice in serving the interests of Pennsylvania's nonprofit community is directly proportional to our numbers. See the back of this book for more information about PANO, and how to join.

In summary, *The Pennsylvania Nonprofit Handbook* is must reading. While it will have value as a reference tool to be consulted when needed, I highly recommend that you read the book cover-to-cover to familiarize yourself with the panoply of issues facing the modern nonprofit in Pennsylvania.

J.M.G.
April 1999

Introduction

Americans of all ages, all stations in life, and all types of disposition are forever forming associations. There are not only commercial and industrial associations in which all take part, but others of a thousand different types—religious, moral, serious, futile, very general and very limited, immensely large and very minute. Americans combine to give fetes, found seminaries, build churches, distribute books, and send missionaries to the antipodes. Hospitals, prisons and schools take shape in that way. Finally, if they want to proclaim a truth or propagate some feeling by the encouragement of a great example, they form an association. In every case, at the head of any new undertaking, where in France you would find the government or in England some territorial magnate, in the United States you are sure to find an association.

—Alexis de Tocqueville
Democracy In America
1835

Little has changed about the American propensity to form benevolent associations in the 164 years since de Tocqueville wrote the above words. The modern charitable institution, however, may bear little resemblance to the typical charity of the 19th century. Burgeoning demands for services, increased government regulation, keen competition for funds, the advance of technology, demographic changes, and the public's change in perception of our institutions have all worked to increase the challenge to those in leadership positions with nonprofit organizations.

Virtually every Pennsylvanian is touched in some way by the services of the commonwealth's nonprofit organizations. Organizations such as churches and synagogues, civic groups, hospitals, day care centers, libraries, colleges, symphonies, art museums, the Red Cross, Salvation Army, and the American Cancer Society work in partnership with government and the public to improve our lives and those of our neighbors.

The nonprofit sector's participation in the American economy is impressive. According to Thomas McLaughlin, writing in his 1995 book *Streetsmart Financial Basics for Nonprofit Managers*, nonprofits account for at least 6% of GNP and employ 7% of the workforce. In January 1999, the Internal Revenue Service released a study indicating that after adjusting for the effects of inflation, assets and revenues of nonprofit tax-exempt organizations more than tripled, to $1.9 trillion and $.9 trillion respectively, between 1975 and 1995.

Pennsylvania's nonprofit sector accounts for approximately 10% of total state employment and has estimated total budget revenues of more than $33 billion, according to a 1991 study by the Western Division of the Pennsylvania Economy League. There are more than 75,000 nonprofits registered in Pennsylvania with the Department of State's Corporation Bureau, and this number is growing at the rate of about 2,500 each year. Many of these have not been active for decades. Of those that are active, more than 29,000 nonprofits in Pennsylvania have 501(c)(3) tax-exempt status, according to the IRS, and that agency's Master List has records of more than 54,600 tax-exempt organizations operating in Pennsylvania. In fiscal year 1997, there were 692,594 organizations in the United States with 501(c)(3) status, and 141,776 with 501(c)(4) status.

Most Americans recognize the value of nonprofit organizations in society. Of 120.4 million individual tax returns filed nationally in 1996 by individuals and couples, 31.6 million claimed a tax deduction for charitable giving, totaling more than $86 billion in deductions, according to the IRS. Many more billions of dollars were donated by persons who do not itemize, or who do not bother to declare the value of their charity on their tax returns. The business community also donates billions of dollars each year to charitable institutions.

According to the latest (June 1998) annual report of *Giving USA*, published by the American Association of Fund-Raising Counsel Trust for Philanthropy, total charitable giving by individuals, corporations, and foundations increased by 7.5% in 1997 over the previous year, to an estimated $143 billion. This represented the largest annual increase since 1989. Additionally, billions of hours annually are volunteered to nonprofits. According to the latest (1995) statistics on volunteering compiled by Independent Sector, 93 million Americans, half of all adults, volunteer an average of 4.2 hours each week with nonprofits. This totals 15.7 billion hours in volunteer time. The dollar value of this amount is an estimated $201.5 billion, based on a 1995 estimate of $12.84/hour of value (which has been revised to $13.73/hour for 1997). As those who volunteer can attest, the value to society, such as the relief of human suffering, far exceeds the dollar value.

It is difficult to foresee and anticipate all of the barriers that stand in the way of a nonprofit organization's creation and survival. One thing is certain—there will be barriers. Forming and running a nonprofit corporation, or any corporation, is a major challenge. Yet it is proven that the accomplishments such organizations can achieve far exceed what any single person, operating without an organizational structure, can achieve alone.

Starting and running a nonprofit corporation in the 21st century requires political acumen, immense technical skill, vision, physical and mental stamina, and, perhaps most of all, luck and a sense of humor.

In the fall of 1984, the Internal Revenue Service, because of a computer glitch, lost $300 million in federal tax withholding payments of 10,000 companies. Even after the snafu was discovered, thousands of the companies received curt letters threatening that the government would seize their property and bank accounts if the tax payments were not made within 10 days. As a nonprofit executive who was on the receiving end of one of these letters, I can certify that "maintaining a sense of humor" was not easy at that time. Yet in the years since that IRS debacle, several more calamities beyond my control afflicted the nonprofit I ran.

There were times when running a nonprofit was no picnic. And then there were times when it was the most fun I ever had. I would like to think that if a publication such as *The Pennsylvania Nonprofit Handbook* had been around when I first started, my job would have been easier.

Purpose of the Handbook

As one might expect, a plethora of laws, regulations, court decisions, and other government policies apply to nonprofit corporations. Until this book was published, no single source of information on the legal requirements of forming and operating a nonprofit corporation in Pennsylvania had been available.

The purpose of this handbook is to provide answers to questions such as:

1. What does one have to do to form a nonprofit corporation?
2. What are the advantages and disadvantages of incorporating?
3. How does a nonprofit organization qualify and apply for 501(c)(3) status?
4. What kind of paperwork is involved in typical nonprofit operations?
5. What should be in a nonprofit corporation's bylaws?
6. How does a nonprofit organization qualify for discount bulk mailing privileges?
7. How does a nonprofit organization qualify for a state sales tax exemption?
8. Can a nonprofit organization engage in unrelated activities that generate income?
9. Will the tax-exemption of a nonprofit organization be at risk if it engages in lobbying?
10. What steps need to occur to merge with another nonprofit corporation?

This handbook cannot purport to answer every conceivable question, but it does attempt to provide sources for answers to many of the questions posed by nonprofit board members and staff. It also provides primary source material on important state and federal laws and regulations, sources for some of the most useful government forms, and sound advice about many nonprofit management issues. The 5th edition also provides the addresses of useful Web sites where additional resources may be found.

Who Can Use This Book

This handbook will be a useful reference to—

a.   Those who are considering forming a nonprofit corporation.

b. Those who need to keep up-to-date on laws, regulations, and court decisions that affect nonprofit organizations, including executive staff and board members of existing nonprofit organizations.

c. Those who will benefit by the advice included in this handbook on running a nonprofit organization, such as fundraisers, lobbyists, public affairs consultants, staff and leadership of funding organizations, and government officials, in addition to those who serve as the staff and board members of nonprofit organizations and their associations.

This is the fifth edition of this publication. Every effort has been made to make this *Handbook* as useful as possible, and free from errors. It is the intent of the author to seek corrections as well as suggestions for improving this publication, and to incorporate these contributions in future editions. A survey/order form has been included in the appendix to provide feedback to the author and the publisher.

Acknowledgments

The author gratefully acknowledges the contributions of scores of individuals and organizations to the first edition of *The Pennsylvania Nonprofit Handbook*. Among them are Michael A. Sand, Kathleen Steigler, and Linda Grobman, all of whom edited various editions of the *Handbook*; Mr. Sand, who wrote the chapter on boards as well as the chapter on applying for grants which appeared for the first time in the fourth edition; Bob Mills, Esq., who completely rewrote and expanded the sections on volunteer and staff liability; the Nonprofit Advocacy Network, which published and distributed the first and second editions; and the Hospital Association of Pennsylvania, which subsidized the printing of the first edition.

Thanks are due also to those who reviewed and edited specific chapters of this edition and previous editions of the *Handbook*, including Richard Utley, past Director of the Department of State's Bureau of Charitable Organizations; Karl Emerson, the current Director of the Bureau; Terry Roth, Esq.; W. Barney Carter; George Bell, Esq.; Bill Knoll, Classification Reform Instructor for the U.S. Postal Service; Otto Hofmann, Esq.; Phil McKain; Jim Fritz, Esq.; Gerald Kaufman; Bob Mills, Esq.; Frederick Richmond; the late Steve Zneimer; Jim Redmond; Elizabeth Hrenda-Roberts; Ron Lench; Christine Finnegan; Joan Benso; Dick Shelly; John Briscoe; and Ken Wickham. The Pennsylvania Department of State; the Pennsylvania Department of Revenue; Independent Sector; Jon Maiden of the Internal Revenue Service's Statistics of Income office in Washington, DC; and Joan Shafer of the Internal Revenue Service Public Affairs Office in Philadelphia cooperated in researching this publication. The author also thanks the staff of the United Way of Pennsylvania, particularly Deborah Foster and Norma Sheets, who worked diligently to publish the third edition.

I am also appreciative of the contributions to this publication which were made by Gerald Kaufman, a nonprofit consultant from Philadelphia, whose essay on governance of nonprofit charities and chapter on nonprofit ethics deserve to be shared with every board member and staff person who is affiliated with a Pennsylvania charity; and Dr. Pam Leland of Seton Hall University for her thoughtful chapter on how to respond to property tax exemption challenges. Joel Cavadel, an attorney from York, Pennsylvania, made many contributions to the section on Mergers and Consolidations, for which I am most grateful. Some of the material in the chapter on change management was adapted from material on outcome-based management jointly written by Frederick Richmond and me, and from material on large group intervention that Gerald Gorelick and I wrote together.

John Hope did his usual thorough and professional job of editing and proofreading, and additional proofreading of this edition was provided by Judy Margo and Linda Grobman. The index for this fifth edition was prepared by Judy Margo.

Finally, a word of thanks to the Pennsylvania Association of Nonprofit Organizations, particularly to its executive director, Joe Geiger, for participating in the fifth edition. PANO is fast becoming the single address for charities without their own state-wide associations to turn to for information, products, services, and training.

G.M.G.
April 1999

Chapter 1
The Decision to Incorporate

Synopsis: Among the advantages of incorporating an organization are limits on liability, lower taxes, and increased organizational credibility. Among the disadvantages are loss of centralized control, increased paperwork, and the time and expense of running a corporation.

Introduction

Pennsylvania law (15 Pa. C.S.A. §5301) lists the types of purposes for which incorporation as a nonprofit organization are permitted. These purposes include, but are not limited to—

"athletic; any lawful business purpose to be conducted on a not-for-profit basis; beneficial; benevolent; cemetery; charitable; civic; control of fire; cultural; educational; encouragement of agriculture or horticulture; fraternal; health; literary; missionary; musical; mutual improvement; patriotic; political; prevention of cruelty to persons or animals; professional, commercial, industrial, trade, service or business associations; promotion of the arts; protection of natural resources; religious; research; scientific and social."

Generally, there are three classes of nonprofit corporations:

1. Funding agency (e.g. United Way, Jewish federation, private foundations)

The primary purpose of these organizations is to allocate funds, either those solicited as private donations or those already accumulated in an endowment or private fortune, for other agencies that provide actual services. Many of these organizations restrict their grants of funds to groups that provide a narrow range of services of interest to the funding organization. A Jewish federation is likely to make contributions solely to Jewish-affiliated organizations or others that principally serve the Jewish community. The United Way generally provides funding to social service agencies. Some foundations restrict their contributions to organizations promoting services for women, health-care related studies, or arts and humanities agencies.

2. Membership organizations (e.g. Common Cause, the Sierra Club, League of Women Voters)

These organizations exist principally to provide services (such as advocacy, information sharing, and networking) for their members, usually with a specialty of expertise.

3. Service agencies (e.g. hospitals, schools, day care centers, family services)

These organizations exist to provide specific services to the public. They often charge fees on a sliding scale for their services to fund the bulk of their budgets.

Each type of organization operates differently in many significant ways.

The decision to incorporate is a mere formality for most leaders who envision a large organization with employees, contracts, offices, property and equipment. Corporate status in general, and nonprofit corporate status in particular, provides many advantages. Maintaining an unincorporated organization with annual revenue and expenditures comfortably in five figures is cumbersome at best, if not impossible. It is at the low end of the scale where the decision to incorporate poses a dilemma.

It would be ludicrous to consider incorporation for the Saturday morning running group get-together, which collects two dollars from each of its eight members to pay for the refreshments after the run. Yet, when the group expands to three hundred members, dues are collected to finance a race, the municipality demands that the club purchase insurance to indemnify against accidents, and the club wants a grant from an area foundation to purchase a bus to transport its members to area races, then incorporation is clearly the option of choice.

Advantages of Incorporation

1. Limited Liability. Of all the reasons to seek corporate status, this is perhaps the most compelling. Under Pennsylvania law, the officers, directors, employees, and members of a corporation, except under very limited and unusual circumstances, are not personally liable for lawsuit judgments and debts relating to the organization. Thus, the personal assets of the organization's executive director or board members are not at risk in the event there is a successful suit against the corporation, or in the event the organization goes out of business while owing money to creditors. Assets of an organization may be minuscule, while the individuals running it may have substantial assets. Corporate status protects those personal assets. Many people won't even consider participating in the leadership of an organization unless their personal assets are shielded by incorporation.

The PA General Assembly has enacted laws (Act 1986-57, Act 1986-145, and Act 1988-179) to expand the liability protection afforded to nonprofit boards of directors and volunteers. These laws are discussed in more detail in Chapter 9.

2. Tax Advantages. In the absence of incorporation, income accruing to an individual running an organization is subject to federal, state, and local taxes at the individual rate (see pages 75-76), which is substantially more than the corporate rate. In the case of nonprofit incorporation, organizations can be exempt from many taxes, depending upon the type of organization. For organizations that are charitable, educational, religious, literary, or scientific, 501(c)(3) tax-exempt status is particularly attractive (see chapter 8). Pennsylvania law exempts all nonprofit corporations from state corporate income tax. Certain types of charities may be exempt from Pennsylvania sales and use tax and local property taxes as well. Many types of charitable institutions, such as colleges and hospitals, which have substantial property holdings, would be taxed beyond their ability to operate if they were denied tax exemptions. Many funding sources, such as government, foundations, and the public as well, will not make contributions to an organization that is not a 501(c)(3), since this status provides a tax-exemption to the contributor, and assures that there is at least some minimal level of accountability on behalf of the organization.

3. Structure, Accountability, Perpetuity, and Legally Recognized Authority. When people and organizations interact with a bona fide corporation, they have confidence that there is some order and authority behind decision-making of that entity. A reasonable expectation exists that the corporation will continue to honor agreements even if the principal actor for the organization dies, resigns, or otherwise disassociates himself or herself from the organization. They know that there is a legal document governing decision-making (as detailed in the bylaws), succession of officers, clear purposes (as detailed in the Articles of Incorporation), a system for paying bills, accounting for income and expenses, and a forum for the sharing of ideas on policy and direction from the corporation's board members. So long as the necessary papers are filed, the organization will continue in perpetuity regardless of changes in leadership. This gives such organizations an aura of immortality that is seen as an advantage in planning beyond the likely tenure of an individual board chairperson or an executive director.

4. Ancillary Benefits. Nonprofit incorporation can provide cheaper postage rates (see chapter 22); access to media (through free public service announcements); volunteers, who would be more hesitant volunteering for a comparable for-profit entity; and the so-called "halo effect," in which the public is more willing to do business with a nonprofit because of a real or perceived view that such an organization is founded and operated in the public interest.

5. Strength of Collegial Decision-Making. Decision-making in an autocracy is clearly easier and more efficient than in an organization run as a democracy. Yet, there is a value in making decisions by building a consensus among a majority of members of a board. Members of a board often bring different experience and talents and provide information that would otherwise not be available in making decisions. Issues are often raised that, if otherwise overlooked, could possibly result in disastrous consequences for the organization.

Disadvantages of Incorporation

1. Loss of Centralized Control. Many organizations are formed and run by a charismatic leader with a vision of how to accomplish a particular task or mission. Decision-making is enhanced without the distractions of the scores of issues that relate not to the actual mission of the organization but to the organization itself. The very act of forming a nonprofit corporation can be draining—preparing and filing Articles of Incorporation, negotiating bylaws, finding quality colleagues to serve on a Board of Directors, hiring qualified staff if necessary and dealing with the myriad of personnel issues that emanate from hiring staff, preparing budgets, raising money, and preparing minutes of board meetings. Even finding a convenient time and place where the board can meet to assure that a quorum can be present can pose a troublesome and potentially overwhelming problem at times.

Incorporation is a legal framework that trades off the advantages addressed earlier in this section with some serious disadvantages. Decisions can no longer be made in a vacuum by one person without oversight or accountability, but are legally under the purview of a board of directors. Decisions have to withstand scrutiny of *all* persons on the board, some of whom may be hostile or have personal axes to grind. By definition, boards of directors are committees, and committees often make compromise decisions in order to mollify members with divergent viewpoints and competing interests.

For those used to making quick decisions "on the fly," and who revel in not having one's decisions subject to second-guessing, modification, or otherwise being meddled with, incorporation can be a shackling experience and can dilute one's control over the organization.

2. Paperwork, Paperwork, Paperwork. Even in the smallest nonprofit corporation, the paperwork load related to corporate status can at times be overwhelming. There are deadlines for virtually every filing. Keeping ahead of the paperwork wave requires discipline, commitment, and a sense of humor. Forms get lost in the bureaucracy, misfiled, or lost in the mail.

Failure to handle this paperwork can result in criminal penalties, in some cases. There are penalties for missed filings (e.g. failure to file a timely 990 federal tax return results in a $20/day penalty, up to a maximum of $10,000, or 5% of the agency's gross revenues, whichever is smaller—and $100/day up to $50,000 for organizations with annual gross receipts exceeding $1 million). As soon as the first employee is hired, the paperwork wave accompanying that accomplishment almost requires the hiring of a second employee to file all of the federal, state, and local government forms relating to employment.

In the first year, the filings can be intimidating, time-consuming, and frustrating. A new corporation must develop a bookkeeping system that is understandable to the accountant who will perform the audit and prepare the financial reports, pass resolutions and file forms to open up corporate savings and checking accounts, order checks, file tax returns and pay taxes (and there are many federal, state, and local taxes that each require their own filing at different times of the year), reconcile savings and checking accounts, prepare board meeting announcements and minutes, devise a system to pay bills, establish a process for the reimbursement of expenses, file forms to protect its corporate name, prepare an annual report, adopt a personnel policy, purchase office equipment, rent an office, prepare budgets, write fundraising letters, and find and retain board members.

The only consolation is that after a few years, one becomes familiar with the required filings and they become routine and just a minor nuisance.

Few of these tasks have a direct impact on the actual work of the agency, but typically they will consume more time during the initial year after incorporation than the actual mission of the organization.

3. Expenses in Money and Time. Significant resources are required to establish a corporation and run it efficiently. No law prohibits running a corporation from one's home with volunteer staff. Legally, the only monetary requirement for running a corporation is to pay $100 to the Pennsylvania Department of State to file Articles of Incorporation. Yet doing so often sets off a chain of events that dramatically increases the organization's complexity. Opening up corporate bank accounts, doing expense reports, filing taxes, and doing the paperwork described above are difficult to accomplish solely with volunteer labor. Raising the funds necessary to hire a person to do all of this work (in addition to coordinating the actual work involved in the purpose of the organization) adds to this burden, and requires even more filing and paperwork.

Many of these tasks would be required even in the absence of a decision to incorporate. But one can avoid much of the "wasted" time and energy by keeping "small." By keeping small, however, there is a substantial limit to what one can accomplish. Experiencing the disadvantages of incorporation is the cost one incurs to receive the substantial benefits.

Nonprofits and Private Benefit

Nonprofit corporation status provides many advantages over comparable for-profits. Yet this status is not conferred without a cost. Generally, nonprofits must operate differently and with different motivations than their for-profit counterparts. There is a general legal doctrine that prohibits nonprofits from acting in a manner that results in "private inurement" to individuals, i.e. the transfer of earnings or profits from the corporation to its "owners." The basic principle at work here is that a for-profit is intended to benefit its owners, whereas a nonprofit is intended to further a purpose.

There is nothing illegal or unethical about nonprofits selling goods and services and generating income. In the 1990s, nonprofits are becoming more sophisticated in finding new revenue sources to supplant the loss of government funds (see Chapter 23). In fact, nonprofits are specifically permitted by Pennsylvania law to generate a profit (see below). Yet nonprofits are delineated from their for-profit counterparts by the destination of any profit.

Pennsylvania law specifically prohibits private inurement. Section 7309 of Title 15 of the Pennsylvania Code includes:

> *"Any nonprofit corporation, the lawful activities of which require the receipt and payment of money, including among other things the charging of admission fees, tuition or other school fees, and fees for the handiwork of members of the corporation, shall have the right and power to receive and collect such moneys to the extent necessary for the accomplishment of the purpose or purposes for which it is organized, and, in so doing, may make an incidental profit. All moneys so received or collected by any nonprofit corporation shall be applied to the maintenance and operation or the furtherance of the lawful activities of the corporation, and in no case shall the moneys be divided or distributed in any manner whatsoever among the members of the corporation."*

Section 5551 of Title 15 also includes the following section:

> *"§5551. Dividends prohibited; compensation and certain payments authorized.*
> *"(a) General rule.—A nonprofit corporation shall not pay dividends or distribute any part of its income or profits to its members, directors, or officers...*
> *"(b) Reasonable compensation for services.—A nonprofit corporation may pay compensation in a reasonable amount to members, directors, or officers for services rendered.*
> *"(c) Certain payments authorized.—A nonprofit corporation may confer benefits upon members or nonmembers in conformity with its purposes, may repay capital contributions..."*

Section 5730 of Title 15 (Compensation of directors) authorizes a nonprofit corporation board of directors to "fix the compensation of directors for their services as such, and a director may be a salaried officer of the corporation." Pennsylvania law does not preclude the board of directors from serving as the nonprofit corporation's employees, provided they are not compensated unreasonably for their services. Yet there is a clear prohibition against the income received by the organization being distributed to these directors in a manner other than as "reasonable" compensation for services.

The term "reasonable" has been generally defined by the courts as compensation that is not excessive compared to individuals with similar expertise and responsibility in the same or similar community. Internal Revenue Service regulations (see pages 261-263) have been promulgated to place restrictions on compensation. However, there is no legal precedent for a doctrine that suggests individuals who work for charities or nonprofits should be paid any less than their for-profit counterparts.

Chapter 23 includes a list of many of the important differences between nonprofits and for-profits.

In the 1989 text *Starting & Managing a Nonprofit Organization*, author-attorney Bruce R. Hopkins provides a useful chapter on the issue of private inurement in nonprofits.

Tips:

- Review Pennsylvania nonprofit laws and decide whether the organization is willing to be subjected to the limitations and accountability required by these laws.

- Avoid incorporating if it is essential to maintain complete control of the organization, and if it is possible to keep the scale of operations small.

- Contact someone who runs a nonprofit corporation of similar size and type envisioned for the organization. Ask questions about paperwork requirements, office equipment, rental space, and the benefits and pitfalls of running such a corporation.

- If leaning toward incorporation, identify potential incorporators/board members who are—

    a. Accessible, and not spread too thin among many other competing organizations

    b. Potential contributors to the organization

    c. Experienced fundraisers

    d. Knowledgeable about the issues of concern to the organization

    e. Respected and well-known in the community

    f. Experienced in legal, accounting, and nonprofit management issues.

Chapter 2
Steps to Incorporation

> Synopsis: Organizational leadership must file the appropriate forms with the Pennsylvania Department of State's Corporation Bureau to incorporate an organization. Among important decisions to be made are choosing the corporate name, choosing whether to have members, and choosing corporate purposes.

Introduction to Incorporation

While incorporation is a legal procedure, it does not require the services of a lawyer. However, lawyers with training and experience in Pennsylvania nonprofit law can be useful in reviewing, if not preparing, Articles of Incorporation and bylaws that are consistent with both statutory requirements and with the purposes of the organization. In 1988, the PA General Assembly enacted legislation (Act 1988-177) codifying its laws relating to associations and corporations. The provisions of more than 200 laws, enacted since 1838, were reorganized within a single document. Organizations should review the state laws applying to nonprofit corporations. There are several sources for the text of these laws.

The first is the 400-plus-page 1988 codification itself. It can be found in county law libraries, some public libraries, and many university libraries.

Of particular interest is Subpart C, Article B (Domestic Nonprofit Corporations Generally), sections 5301-5989 (pages 1652-1676). One should be aware, however, that the full text of some sections of current law that were not changed by the enactment of Act 1988-177 are excluded from this version.

Law libraries have copies of the Purdon's *Pennsylvania Consolidated Statutes Annotated.* Pennsylvania nonprofit law is codified in Chapter 15. Make sure in researching current law to refer to the most up-to-date supplement for use in the current year. This supplement will include all changes to laws made since the books were printed.

Choosing Incorporators

Incorporators are the persons legally responsible for forming the corporation. It is legal and common for one person to serve in this capacity, although several persons may sign the Articles of Incorporation form as formal incorporators. According to Section 5302 of Title 15, "One or more corporations for profit or not-for-profit or natural persons of full age may incorporate a nonprofit corporation under the provisions of this article." According to Don Kramer, an attorney who specializes in nonprofit law for the Philadelphia firm Montgomery, McCracken, Walker and Rhoads, "natural persons of full age" means an individual who is at least 18.

Incorporators frequently play a more active role than solely being a name on the Articles of Incorporation filing. If they act to promote the interests of the new corporation (e.g. raise funds, recruit personnel, negotiate leases or purchase property for the organization), their legal status is augmented by the responsibility of serving in a fiduciary capacity. This legal status confers on them the duty to take actions in the best interest of the corporation rather than in their own personal interest, and to disclose any conflicts of interest that may occur in their business dealings on behalf of the corporation.

By law, the incorporators make agreements on behalf of the corporation while it is in the process of legal formation. These agreements have no legal effect until they are approved by the corporation's Board of Directors once the corporation legally exists. As a result, incorporators who do make these agreements must make it clear to the other party that the agreement is not binding until the corporation exists as a legal entity and its board ratifies the agreement.

Once the Articles of Incorporation are filed and the Department of State approves them, incorporators have no formal status, with one exception. They are invited to be present at the organizational meeting required by law, at which the Board of Directors is selected.

It is a common practice that the incorporators include members who will be serving on the first Board of Directors. Thus, care should be taken as to the qualifications of incorporators, as they may continue their association with the corporation as directors (see Chapter 4).

Choosing a Corporate Name

One of the most important and basic decisions in forming a corporation is deciding on a corporate name. This name will be the organization's corporate identity, and the image it creates provides the first impression of those outside the corporation. "Short and descriptive" are two desirable characteristics in a corporate name. Many nonprofit organizations choose a name that gives the connotation of helping, or otherwise doing charitable activities in the public interest, rather than implying a for-profit motive. If the organization plans to apply for 501(c)(3) status, avoid names that would be suitable for organizations whose activities are clearly not eligible for this status. The organization may wish to consider suitable acronyms comprising the first letter of each word of its name, but cute or frivolous acronyms often give an unprofessional impression.

The process of having to change a corporate name after incorporating and operating as a nonprofit often results in time-consuming and costly activities, such as changing the logo (see Chapter 22); reprinting stationery, business cards, checks, and brochures; and changing all of the legal forms relating to Articles of Incorporation, bank accounts, and contracts.

For obvious legal reasons, the name must be unique, although it is also legal to adopt a name similar to another existing corporation after receiving permission from that corporation and filing the necessary forms to do so (see below). Pennsylvania law states that the name can be in any language, but requires that it be expressed in English letters or characters. The name cannot imply that the corporation is a governmental agency of the Commonwealth or the country, a bank or savings institution, a trust company, an insurance company, or a public utility. For more information about the limitations on corporate names, consult section 5303 of Title 15 of the Pennsylvania Code.

Organizations should perform a name search with the Department of State to ensure that no other corporation, active or inactive, is using an identical or similar name. The department will provide a name search over the telephone at no charge. Call (717) 787-1057 for this service. The department will provide this information in writing for a $12 fee. For a fee of $52, the department will reserve a corporate name for 120 days.

Many corporations also do a national name search and take steps to register their names with the United States Patent and Trademark Office as trademarks. This can be done only for those organizations that will be marketing goods and services interstate. The fee is $245, which provides registration for 10 years, assuming the owner certifies that the trademark has active status.

For more information or to obtain the correct forms, contact the Patent and Trademark Office:

Patent and Trademark Office
Trademark Assistance Center
U.S. Department of Commerce
Washington, D.C. 20231
(703) 308-9000
(703) 308-7016 (fax)

A pre-addressed postcard for obtaining this information is included in the back of this book.

Choosing Corporate Purposes

It is generally advisable to state broad corporate purposes in a manner that permits the corporation to grow and change direction without requiring its Articles of Incorporation to be amended. The purposes should be specific enough to permit the corporation to be eligible for 501(c)(3) status, if this is expected. Research similar organizations and review their Articles of Incorporation to obtain ideas on framing Articles of Incorporation.

Choosing to Have Members or No Members

In general, it is desirable to complete item six in the standard form of the Articles of Incorporation by filling in "The corporation shall have no members." This will assure that all power and authority will be maintained by the Board of Directors, and will avoid the difficult legal problems of expelling an individual member should that occasion arise. Outsiders, including those who would pay dues in exchange for participating in organizational programs and activities, can still participate in the activities of the nonprofit corporation without being legal members who are entitled to vote on the affairs of the corporation.

As with almost every issue, there are exceptions to this. Many organizations will find it desirable for each participant in the organization's programs and activities to have an equal voice in the internal governance of the organization.

Additional provisions

Item 10 on the form permits additional provisions to be added to the Articles. Many corporations that wish to qualify for 501(c)(3) status add a provision that will facilitate tax-exemption approval. One such provision is a statement forbidding the corporation from engaging in partisan political activity on behalf of a candidate or substantially engaging in lobbying. The language for this provision can be adopted from 501(c)(3) itself:

> "No substantial part of the Corporation's activities shall consist of carrying on propaganda, or otherwise attempting to influence legislation (except in accordance with Section 501(h) of the Internal Revenue Code). The Corporation shall not participate in any political campaign on behalf of or in opposition to any candidate for public office."

Another provision to add is applicable to organizations that wish to qualify for an exemption from the state sales tax (see Chapter 24). Paragraph 5(c)(4) of Act 55 of 1997 (see page 220-224), the *Institutions of Purely Public Charity Act*, provides statutory requirements for charitable exemptions. Among the requirements is that organizations must have in their legal governing document a provision relating to the use of surplus funds available in the event of a sale or dissolution. The Pennsylvania Department of Revenue advises organizations to use the language of Act 55 in their Articles of Incorporation:

> "In the event of a sale or dissolution of the Corporation, it is prohibited to use any surplus funds for private inurement of any person."

A pre-addressed postcard is included in the back of this book for obtaining the Articles of Incorporation filing form (DSCB:15-5306) and other forms referred to in this section. In addition, these forms may be downloaded from the Corporation Bureau's web site at http://www.dos.state.pa.us/corp/forms.htm. One original should be mailed along with accompanying documents to:

Department of State
Corporation Bureau
308 North Office Building
Harrisburg, PA 17120-0029

A $100 filing fee, made payable to the "Department of State," should be included with each application. Accompanying the application should be:

- Three copies of the docketing statement (form DSCB:15-134A)
- Copies of form DSCB:17.2 (Consent to Appropriation of Name) or form DSCB:17.3 (Consent to Use of Similar Name), if necessary
- Any required approval forms.

The department requires an actual street address or rural route box number. It will disapprove applications if a post office box is listed as the corporate address. It is acceptable to provide the address of a commercial registered office provider.

The incorporators are required by Pennsylvania law to advertise their intention to file Articles of Incorporation or the actual Articles of Incorporation in two newspapers of general circulation, including one legal journal, if there is one for the applicable county. Most counties have a legal journal. In Dauphin County, for example, incorporators must publish an advertisement in the *Dauphin County Reporter,* a publication of the Dauphin County Bar Association. The names and addresses of legal journals from other counties are listed in Appendix D. You may wish to check with the department's Corporation Bureau to verify this address. Contact that office at (717) 787-1057.

The department will send a confirmation of the filing of the application only if it receives a self-addressed, stamped postcard or envelope with the filing information.

Applications for Articles of Incorporation take about a week to process, not including mailing time. A copy of the application will be returned with the date noted and the Secretary of State's signature in the upper right hand corner of the Articles of Incorporation. This is the only confirmation organizations receive. The original will have been microfilmed by the department, and copies of it or any other Articles of Incorporation can be ordered from the department for a photocopy charge of $12 plus $2/page.

Once the Articles of Incorporation are filed and approved, be sure that all actions taken on behalf of the corporation will clearly indicate that they are actions for the corporation and not on behalf of individuals. Otherwise, such individuals may be personally liable for fulfilling the terms of contracts and other agreements, such as paying rent, staff salaries, telephone installation costs, and so on. One way to indicate that persons are acting on behalf of the corporation is to explicitly sign legal contracts and other documents as follows:

(corporate name)
By (individual's signature)
(individual's corporate title)

Corporate Dissolution

Pennsylvania law (Title 15, §5971-5998) provides for procedures to voluntarily dissolve a nonprofit corporation, and the legal requirements affecting nonprofits that are involuntarily dissolved by government authorities.

In the event that a voluntary dissolution is desired *even before* a nonprofit corporation begins its operations, Articles of Dissolution may be filed with the Department of State, using form 15:5977. A pre-addressed postcard for obtaining this information is included in the back of this book. The Articles of Dissolution must be ratified by a majority of the members (if the corporation has members) or incorporators, and include—

1. The name and address of the corporation;
2. The date of incorporation and the law under which the corporation was incorporated;
3. A statement that the corporation has not received any property in trust, and has not commenced business;
4. A statement that membership dues, other than the amount already expended for necessary expenses, have been returned;
5. A statement that all liabilities of the corporation have been discharged, or that provision has been made to discharge corporate liabilities; and
6. A statement that the majority of the members or incorporators have elected to dissolve the corporation.

In the case that business of the corporation has already commenced, the procedures become quite complicated.

Dissolution can be proposed by a majority of the Board of Directors "or other body," or through a petition recommending voluntary dissolution from members entitled to cast at least 10% of the votes that all members are entitled to cast. The question of whether the corporation should dissolve is then required to be voted on at a regular or special meeting of the members or Board of Directors. Written notice of the meeting must be sent to all members. The resolution shall be considered adopted upon approval of a majority of members who cast their votes or, in the absence of members, a majority of the Board of Directors. The action can be rescinded using the same procedure prior to the time that Articles of Dissolution are filed with the Department of State.

The Board of Directors has full authority to wind up the affairs of the corporation, which include mailing by certified or registered mail dissolution notices to all creditors, claimants, and municipalities in which the corporation has a registered office. State law then requires the corporation to "as speedily as possible" collect sums owed to it, convert its assets into cash, and discharge its liabilities. Unless the bylaws provide otherwise, remaining assets shall be distributed to the members on a per capita basis. The only exception to this is that the assets of a dissolved 501(c)(3) corporation must, in most cases, be distributed to another 501(c)(3) organization. Section 5977(b) of Title 15 requires the nonprofit to seek approval of a court before it disposes of property committed to charitable purposes. When the nonprofit seeks this court approval, it must first notify the Office of Attorney General of Pennsylvania, Charitable Trusts and Organizations Section, 14th Floor, Strawberry Square, Harrisburg, PA 17120, so that this office can participate in the proceeding. For additional information about this requirement, call the Charitable Trusts and Organizations Section of the Office of Attorney General at (717) 783-2853.

The legal requirements for the involuntary dissolution of a corporation are much more complex. Nonprofits that face legal notices concerning involuntary dissolution need to seek immediate legal advice. Codified Pennsylvania law relating to involuntary dissolution may be found in Subchapter G of Title 15 (Sections 5981-5998) of the Pennsylvania Code.

Tips:

- **Review the legal requirements of Pennsylvania nonprofits (Sections 5301-5998 of Title 15 of the PA Code) to make sure the organization can and is willing to comply with them.**

- **Have a lawyer review, if not draft, the Articles of Incorporation.**

- **Include in the Articles of Incorporation additional provisions to enhance the prospects for achieving the appropriate federal tax status (e.g. 501(c)(3)) if such status is desirable (see Chapter 8).**

- **Choose a short and descriptive corporate name.**

Chapter 3
Bylaws

Synopsis: Bylaws provide general policy guidelines for non-profit corporations. There are statutory provisions that go into effect automatically in the absence of comparable bylaw provisions.

Introduction to Preparing Bylaws

Pennsylvania non-profit law requires each corporation to have a set of bylaws. Pennsylvania statute (15 P.S. §5309) provides that the incorporators must schedule a meeting of initial directors (or the incorporators, if the directors are not named in the Articles of Incorporation) for the purpose of adopting bylaws. State law requires that at least five days' notice be given for the organizational meeting.

The term "bylaws" is defined in law to be "the code or codes of rules adopted for the regulation or management of the business and affairs of the corporation irrespective of the name or names by which such rules are designated."

Perhaps the best advice in formulating organizational bylaws can be found in the publication *Robert's Rules of Order Newly Revised,* published in 1991 by Scott, Foresman, and Co. (ISBN: 006275002-X). The 706 pages in the book contain an invaluable wealth of knowledge not only on parliamentary procedure but on organizational leadership. This book provides guidance on drafting certain bylaw provisions, and includes a sample set of bylaws. A more recent, 160-page edition of the book was published in 1993 ($8.95, Berkley Publications, ISBN No. 0-425-13928-X).

Certain provisions must by law be included in bylaws of Pennsylvania non-profit corporations. Beyond legal requirements, corporate bylaws are a necessary and important document, and great thought and care should be exercised as to what will be included in them.

Typical bylaws include provisions governing the following internal procedures and policies of the non-profit corporation:

1. The purposes of the corporation, consistent with any federal tax law limitation or state laws governing lobbying or other activity
2. Limitations of liability of directors, consistent with PA law (see 15 P.S. §5552)
3. Types of officers
4. Terms, powers, and succession of officers
5. Location of principal office
6. Whether the corporation will have members, or whether all powers will be vested in a board of directors
7. How directors will be selected, and how vacancies will be filled

8. How many directors there will be
9. Length of, staggering of terms of, and limits on consecutive terms of the board of directors
10. Terms under which a member of the board of directors can be disqualified
11. Conditions under which the Annual Meeting and other regularly scheduled board meetings are held
12. How unscheduled meetings of the board can be called
13. Terms under which notice of board meetings must occur
14. What constitutes a quorum for the transaction of business
15. How many directors are required to approve an action
16. Whether actions of the board can be ratified through the mail or by conference call, or require directors to be present at a meeting
17. Power of the Chairperson (or President) to appoint committees, and to provide for rules, powers, and procedures of such committees
18. Whether alternates can be empowered to represent directors, and who selects them
19. Who is responsible for preparing board meeting minutes and for storing and using the corporate seal on official documents
20. Who is responsible for keeping and reviewing the corporate books, and dispersing corporate funds
21. How amendments can be made to the bylaws
22. Terms and conditions regarding compensation, if any, paid to directors
23. What committees are authorized, and what powers and duties they have
24. The terms under which the corporation will be dissolved

Legal Requirements of Bylaws in Pennsylvania

Pennsylvania law provides for some minimum standards with respect to bylaws of non-profit corporations. For example, every Pennsylvania non-profit corporation must—

- Have a President, Treasurer, and Secretary (or officers who perform comparable duties). A single person may hold all three offices. The President and Secretary must be citizens of legal age. The Treasurer may be a corporation, or an individual citizen of legal age.
- Not have meetings organized for the transaction of business unless a quorum is present.
- Not expel a member of the corporation "without notice, trial and conviction, the form of which shall be prescribed by the bylaws."

Pennsylvania statute provides rules on many of the above bylaw options in the absence of explicit directions in the non-profit corporation's bylaws. Thus, it is important to place provisions in the bylaws that will be intended to supersede these statutory legal guidelines, if the directors feel that the guidance provided in law is not acceptable to the corporation.

Among the provisions of bylaws that deserve the highest consideration and thought are the following, with some comments about the issues they raise:

Quorum Requirements

A quorum is the minimum number of members or directors required to be present for a meeting to be held for the legal transaction of business. The purpose of a quorum requirement is to assure that actions are taken by a representative number of duly authorized participants rather than by an elite few. Unless the bylaws provide otherwise, a quorum is by Pennsylvania law a majority of the directors in office. The bylaws can provide that it can be higher or lower. Standard advice, in the absence of relying on the statutory requirement, is to set the quorum at the minimum number of people who will be expected to attend a meeting, considering emergencies, adverse weather conditions, or conflicts with competing meetings. If the bylaws permit it, board members may participate in meetings and be counted as part of a quorum if they are in communication by speaker phone or by conference call.

Since actions cannot be taken legally at board meetings without a quorum present, it is best to begin with a conservatively low quorum requirement. Then change the bylaws to increase that number as appropriate. Otherwise, it is possible that the corporation will never have a quorum for its meetings, even if the sole purpose of the meeting is to have a change in the bylaws to decrease the number of directors constituting a quorum.

Voting Rights

Boards need to vote to formally demonstrate that they have taken actions. Many organizations can be effectively run by consensus rather than formal voting, but even the most congenial and tolerant boards will eventually face issues that will divide them. In the absence of a provision in the bylaws, action may be taken at a board meeting with the approval of a majority of directors who are present at the meeting. There is nothing to prohibit a two-thirds vote being required to assure that actions are closer to forming a consensus. A two-thirds vote may be suggested for changing bylaws, or for changing membership dues requirements. Generally, a majority vote is sufficient for most routine board decisions, and avoids the inability to take positions and action that can occur as a result of a two-thirds voting requirement.

Selection of Officers

Many organizations are attracted to the democratic notion of offices being opened to all. With such a policy, any director can run for an office, ballots are prepared, and the winner is selected by the majority (or plurality) of voters from the Board of Directors or the membership at large. Other organizations feel that democracy puts at risk an orderly succession and threatens the existing power structure. Orderly succession can be accomplished by providing for a Nominating Committee, appointed by the Chairperson, which selects a slate of officers. This slate is then perfunctorily approved by the full board. Both systems have their advantages and disadvantages.

Some organizations utilize a third alternative that combines the two. The Nominations Committee recommends a slate of candidates, but the procedures permit other candidates to run as well.

Executive Committees

Board meetings may occur at regular intervals, but issues arise in the interim that demand immediate attention. In such cases, it is valuable to have a mandated procedure for taking legally legitimate actions in the absence of board meetings. The mechanism to accomplish this is the executive committee, provided for in the corporate bylaws. While the executive committee typically is comprised of the corporation's officers, Pennsylvania law (15 P.S. §1531) authorizes executive committees comprised of one or more directors appointed by the board. By law, the executive committee has all of the power and authority of the full board with the following exceptions:

- The executive committee cannot fill vacancies on the board.
- The executive committee cannot adopt, amend, or repeal bylaws.
- The executive committee cannot have powers inconsistent with the resolution passed by the board establishing it.

A sample set of bylaws that could be sufficient for many newly-formed, small non-profit corporations is included in Appendix B.

Tips:

- **Review Pennsylvania law with respect to corporate bylaws. Identify which provisions are required, which provisions apply only in the absence of a different provision in the bylaws, and which act to pre-empt the statutory guideline.**

- **Give careful consideration to the more important bylaw provisions, such as—**

    - **Quorum requirements**
    - **Succession of officers**
    - **Powers of the Executive Committee**
    - **Voting by the board of directors**

- **Have an attorney review the bylaws to assure that they are in compliance with state law, and to ensure that the organization's desires with respect to internal decision-making will be consistent with efficient operating procedure.**

- **Schedule an organizational meeting to approve the bylaws, and distribute a draft of proposed bylaws before this meeting.**

- **After a final version of the bylaws is approved, provide a final copy of the bylaws to all members of the board of directors.**

Chapter 4
Nonprofit Boards of Directors

> Synopsis: It is a critically important function for nonprofit organizations to find and retain qualified, experienced board members and officers. Board meetings generally have a routine order of business and provide the forum for making organizational policy.

One important requirement of a nonprofit organization is the formation of a board of directors. The board has the responsibility to set policy for the organization in accord with the applicable laws and to see to it that the policies are implemented.

Board Formation

The size of the board should depend on the needs of the organization. If the board's role is strictly policy-making and the policies are implemented by a qualified staff, a small board might be more appropriate. However, if extensive board time is required for fundraising or implementing programs, then a much larger board would be in order.

The number of board members is set in the bylaws. One effective technique is to set a minimum and maximum number of board members and to allow the board to determine its size within these parameters. Then the board can start small and add members as the need arises.

The term of board members must be included in the bylaws. Board members should have fixed terms of office. One common practice is for all board members to have three-year terms, with one-third of the members being elected each year. In this way, board continuity is assured. Some boards allow their members to serve unlimited terms; other boards wish to limit the number of terms to assure new members with fresh ideas.

The election process should also be spelled out in the bylaws.

Most organizations have a Nominating Committee that is responsible for recommending new board members to the full board. Additional candidates for board membership can be nominated either in advance or from the floor at the election.

The titles, duties, length of term, and process for the election of officers should be spelled out in the bylaws.

Organization Officers

The elected officers of most organizations are similar:

Chairperson, Chair or President

He or she leads the meetings of the organization, appoints committee chairs, and either signs checks or delegates this duty to another individual.

Vice-Chair

The Vice-Chair assumes the duties of the President or Chair in his or her absence, or upon his or her death or resignation. In many organizations, he or she is given specific responsibilities either in the bylaws or by vote. In some organizations, the Vice-Chair automatically becomes the next president.

Secretary

The Secretary either takes minutes at the board meeting or approves the minutes if taken by another individual, and is responsible for all official correspondence.

Treasurer

The Treasurer is responsible for finances of the organization, usually makes financial reports to the board, and signs checks.

In some organizations, the officers are elected by the full membership. In others, the board of directors elects its own officers. Many organizations elect their officers to two-year terms, although one-year terms are quite common. Some limit the number of terms of officers.

Getting Good Board Members

Many organizations are finding it more difficult than ever to get excellent board members. This is due to factors such as the proliferation of nonprofit boards, the increasing number of women in the work force, and the fact that upwardly mobile professionals often relocate.

To assure excellence, many nominating committees are meeting several times during the year to search for potential board members rather than just once. One effective technique is to strive for a diverse board, and to list the types of characteristics desired. Some might be:

> *Expertise*: Some board members should have personnel management, fiscal, or legal expertise.

> *Ages*: It is helpful to have older Americans represented, as well as youth and individuals in-between.

> *Races and Religions:* All major races and religions in the community should be represented on a diverse board.

> *Backgrounds:* It would be helpful if some board members had corporate backgrounds, some were government leaders, and others served on the

boards of other nonprofit groups.

Users of the service: Many boards include representatives of the client population being served.

The Nominating Committee or Board Development Committee searches throughout the year for individuals with these characteristics.

Each board should have a list of board member responsibilities. These might include attending board meetings on a regular basis, serving on at least one standing committee, and participating in fundraising. This list of duties should be provided to each prospective board member, and no board member should be elected who will not agree to meet these responsibilities.

Keeping Good Board Members

One technique for keeping good board members is to require all new board members to participate in an orientation program before they attend their first board meeting.

The first step in the process is to receive and review materials that all board members should have received previously. These include the following:

- Articles of Incorporation
- Bylaws
- Funding applications
- Personnel, fiscal and other board policies
- Annual reports
- Names, addresses, phone numbers, and biographical sketches of other board members and key staff members
- List of committees and committee duties
- Minutes of the last several board meetings
- Audits, budgets, and recent financial statements

The second step is to hold a meeting with the board chair and the executive director. This provides an opportunity to ask questions about the materials received, visit the staff offices and programs, get an update on current issues, and review board member responsibilities.

Other steps to encourage productivity of board members include the following:

- Give board members specific projects. A board member who serves as chair of a committee or who has specific fundraising responsibilities is more likely to stay active.
- Keep board meetings interesting.
- Thank board members for their work.
- Have social events periodically, in addition to formal board meetings.

One other technique is to remove unproductive board members quickly and then replace them with new and productive ones.

This includes the following:

- Having a policy in the bylaws that missing a specified number of board meetings without a reason will result in automatic dismissal.

- Re-electing only board members who have been meeting their responsibilities.

- Calling board members who have not been active to ask them if there are any problems. In some cases, the Chairperson should ask for their resignation if they do not agree to meet board responsibilities.

Board Responsibilities

Members of boards of directors have the following duties:

Personnel
The board hires the Executive Director. This is the board's most important responsibility. It then makes assignments to the Executive Director and monitors the Executive Director's performance. It is appropriate for the board or its Personnel Committee to do a formal performance appraisal of the Executive Director at least annually. The board approves salary scales and job descriptions for the other staff members who are hired by the Executive Director. The Board approves the Personnel Policies for the organization.

Finance
The board approves budgets for the organization. No funds are expended unless they are included in a budget approved by the board. The board approves spending reports that are submitted to them on a regular basis.

Fundraising
All applications for funds are submitted to the board before being submitted to funding sources. The board also approves plans for special event fundraising, and board members are expected to participate in fundraising events.

Planning
Board members approve short- and long-range plans for the organization. They then monitor the effectiveness of the agency's programs to see if they have met the goals outlined in the plans.

Board Development
The board selects new board members and adopts procedures to see that excellent board members are selected and continue to serve.

Public Relations

Board members are aware of all of the organization's activities and encourage participation in appropriate activities by the community.

Advising

Board members advise the Executive Director on policy implementation as requested.

How Boards Function Effectively

Boards set policies only through a majority vote of their members at board meetings, unless the bylaws provide otherwise. For boards with staffs, one effective method of policy making is to ask the staff to draft proposed policies. These policies are then sent to a board committee for review.

The chair of each committee should be a board member appointed by the board president. Members of committees are usually selected by the committee chair and may include non-board members.

All committees are advisory (except that the bylaws may permit the Executive Committee to act on behalf of the board between board meetings). Once a committee has approved a proposed policy, it is submitted to the board for approval.

Board members who wish a policy to be adopted begin the discussion by making a motion that a policy be approved. If another board member seconds the motion, discussion can begin; if not, the motion fails.

Once a motion is seconded, the Chairperson opens the floor for discussion. Members are recognized by the Chairperson before they may speak, and they can discuss only the motion on the floor. When the discussion has ended, the Chairperson announces that a vote will be taken.

The easiest way to vote is by a show of hands. The Secretary can then record the vote. If more than a majority approve a policy, it becomes the board's policy (unless the bylaws provide otherwise). It is the responsibility of the Executive Director to implement that policy.

The Executive Director receives instructions from the board at a board meeting. It is improper for individual board members to give assignments to any staff member without prior board authorization.

Holding High Quality Board Meetings

One key factor in getting and keeping excellent board members is the quality of the board meetings. If board meetings are unproductive, board members tend to be unproductive. An important technique for improving board meetings is to do as much planning *before the board meeting* as possible.

This might include:

- Sending a notice of the date, time, and location of the meeting to the members several weeks before the meeting. Even if the board meets the same day of each month at the same place and time, a reminder notice is important.

- Giving the board members the telephone number of the individual (usually the Chairperson) to call if they cannot attend the meeting. In this way, the Chairperson can get input on important items from individuals who cannot attend the meeting. Also, if a quorum will not be present, the meeting can be canceled in advance.

- Notifying members of important items to be discussed at the meeting. For major items, information or issue papers might be included in the meeting notice packet.

- Including as many written items as possible with the meeting notice rather than distributing them at the meeting. This includes the minutes of the previous meeting and the Treasurer's report, for example. Members then have an opportunity to read items before the meeting, and members who do not attend the meeting are kept up-to-date more effectively.

- Developing a preliminary agenda before the meeting. Committee chairs who will be asked to report at the meeting should be notified. Background reports should be developed for important issues.

The board meeting should start on time. Once the members know that every board meeting starts on time, it is much more likely that they will be prompt. Each board meeting should start with the distribution of a written agenda. The agenda should be as detailed as possible, listing each separate item to be voted on.

Once the Secretary announces that a quorum is present, the Chairperson asks all those present if there are any additional items for the agenda. Thus, there will be no surprises and the Chairperson can run the meeting more effectively. The Chairperson has the option of referring new items to committees or postponing items until future meetings.

The order of business at most meetings is as follows:

- *Approval of the minutes of the previous meeting.* A formal vote is needed to approve the minutes. Minutes should be distributed to all members and should not be read aloud at the meeting.

- *Chairperson's Report.* The Chairperson should state before each item which items are informational and which require board action. The Chairperson should remind the members that only policy-making recommendations require board action.

- *Executive Director's Report.* This report should be in writing. If it is lengthy, it should be distributed before the meeting. The Executive Director should then highlight important aspects of the written report and take questions.

- *Committee Reports.* Committee reports should be in writing unless they are very brief. After giving the report, the Committee Chair should make specific motions when board action is required. Only policy items require board action; no board action is required when the committee chair is simply providing information.

- *Unfinished Business.* The only items belonging in this section are ones raised at previous board meetings. The Chairperson should remind the members when the item was raised originally and why it was postponed.

- *New Business.* Major items of business are discussed as part of the Chairperson's Report, Executive Director's Report, or Committee Reports. At the beginning of the meeting, members are asked if they have additional agenda items, and the Chairperson has the option of placing some of these items under New Business.

- *Good and Welfare.* Many organizations provide an opportunity for members and guests to make short announcements, raise issues to be discussed at future meetings, or to comment on items of interest.

- *Adjournment.* No formal action is needed. The Chairperson announces the date, time, and place of the next meeting, reminds the members of steps to be taken before the meeting, such as committee meetings, and adjourns the board meeting.

After the board meeting, the minutes are sent to board members for their review. The minutes must include a list of attendees and the motions made and votes taken. Additional information may be included at the pleasure of the board. Many organizations include only the minimum required, and the minutes do not include individual comments made at the meeting. While the minutes need not be taken by the Board Secretary, they should be distributed under the signature of the Board Secretary.

Relationship Between Board and Staff Members

The board of directors sets policy for the organization. Several examples of the types of policies set by the board are provided above. The only way policy can be set is by a majority vote of the board at a board meeting (unless the bylaws provide otherwise).

The executive director (or the chief executive officer of the organization) attends all board meetings, and is responsible for implementing the policies set by the board. The executive director hires other staff members (whose salary levels and job descriptions have been approved by the board) to assist in implementing these policies.

When an item arises at a board meeting, the Chairperson rules whether the item is a policy matter. If so, a vote of the board is required in order for action to be taken. If the item is not a policy matter, no board vote is taken. The purpose of the discussion is to provide guidance to the executive director on non-policy matters.

The executive director researches sources of funds and writes grant applications. Before a grant application can be submitted to a funding source, it should be approved by the board.

Certain types of communications between board members and staff members are not appropriate. For example, individual board members may not give assignments to staff members. Assignments are given to the executive director by vote of the board at a board meeting. The executive director is responsible for assigning tasks to other staff members. Staff members should not complain to individual board members about programs, assignments and policies. Complaints should be made according to specific procedures established by the board. When a board member volunteers to help out in the office, that person must be treated as a staff person and no longer wears the "board hat." The executive director remains the person to make assignments to that person.

TIPS:

- **Develop a list of typical decision areas that are likely to arise in the course of routine corporate operations and reach a board consensus on whether the decisions should be made by—**

  a. **The executive director alone.**
  b. **The executive director, in consultation with the board.**
  c. **The executive director, in consultation with the board chairperson.**
  d. **The board alone.**
  e. **The chairperson alone.**
  f. **A committee of the board.**

  Review, revise and update this list annually.

- **Consider adopting a policy on the responsibilities and privileges of board members, and include a conflict-of-interest policy.**

Chapter 5
Strategic Planning

> Synopsis: Formal strategic planning is not for every organization. All stakeholders must be committed to successfully develop and implement a strategic plan. Although such plans require a major investment in money and time and have other institutional costs and risks, the benefits include enhancing the agency's ability to respond to internal and external threats.

Introduction

Strategic planning is a formalized process by which an organization makes a study of its vision for the future, typically for three years or more from the present. A strategic plan is an important management tool for agency leaders to consider the effects of advances in technology, changing markets for its services, the effects of government funding cutbacks, or the emergence of other organizations (both for-profits and nonprofits) that provide similar, competing services.

Agency CEOs often are so involved with putting out fires and responding to the exigencies of day-to-day operations that it is a luxury to set aside time to think about the position of the organization even a year in the future. An agency's board is often ill-equipped to consider changes in agency structure and operations in the context of a regular board meeting.

Purpose of Strategic Planning

In his 1994 book *The Rise and Fall of Strategic Planning*, Henry Mintzberg lists four reasons organizations do strategic planning: to coordinate their activities, to ensure that the future is taken into account, to be rational, and to control. Strategic planning is designed to suggest remedies for agency problems before they blow up. Deep cuts in government grants, changes in markets, advances in technology, competition from for-profit businesses, and changes in demographics in an agency's service area all crystallize the need to change the basic way an agency does business.

Virtually all successful large for-profit businesses engage in a formal strategic planning process. The conventional wisdom is that businesses that do so, regardless of whether they are for-profit or nonprofit, are more successful than those that do not over time. However, Mintzberg cites scores of academic studies that show mixed results as to the benefits of strategic planning in business and industry, and concludes that the value of strategic planning is nebulous at best.

Putting that aside, a periodic strategic planning process provides the framework for a long-term assessment of emerging threats, and the opportunity to develop creative strategies to respond to them. The intent here is not to encourage or discourage nonprofits to engage in a formal strategic planning process; rather it is to raise issues to consider in the event that this endeavor, for whatever reason, is under consideration.

Strategic planning requires the diversion of both money and time. For most nonprofits, both are scarce. Thus, it is important that agency leaders systematically evaluate whether the benefits of preparing, updating, and implementing a periodic strategic plan outweigh the costs. Strategic plan preparation often involves the hiring of an outside consultant, plenty of meetings, and the involvement of board members, agency staff, and other agency stakeholders for an extended period of time.

The strategic planning process is fraught with danger. The contents of a final strategic plan often are totally at odds with the vision of the agency leader who first suggested preparing one. The planning committee dynamics are often uncontrollable by the people who provide the agency with leadership. Agency leaders may be uncomfortable sharing the agency's dreams and aspirations, its "dirty little secrets," and proprietary financial projections with a professional outside consultant, and may be even more reticent with community members of the planning committee. Yet many agencies that successfully complete a strategic planning process improve their performance. Participating board members feel a renewed connection and bond to both the agency and their colleagues. Agencies that don't plan for the future, whether in a formalized process or informal board retreats, often suffer the consequences.

Strategic planning in the for-profit sector has been popular for several decades. In the for-profit world, strategic planning has the advantage of having each member of the committee, virtually by definition, already in agreement on the basic mission of the organization that is, in short, to make as much profit as possible. There will be differences, of course, as to the methods used to accomplish this. In a nonprofit, there is not always agreement on the mission from the outset. In a hospital situation, for example, some planning committee members may view the mission as providing quality health care to the community. Some may feel it is to teach medical students, advance life-saving technology, increase "market share" by gobbling up other health care institutions, or serve populations not served by other institutions.

In a for-profit setting, the outcomes are easily measurable—net profit and market share are statistics easily compiled. In the nonprofit sector, consumer satisfaction, community benefit, and image in the community often are considered more important than bottom-line net revenue, and are difficult to measure satisfactorily. In the nonprofit sector, board members may actually be concerned if the institution is making too much net revenue and not providing services to sectors of the market that would clearly result in revenue shortfalls. It is the nature of nonprofits that the institution is not motivated by private profit motive and, in theory, this can create conflicts. As one commentator wryly suggested in response to President Bush's *Thousand Points of Light* program, it's all right to be one of the "thousand points of light" and do good deeds, but someone still has to pay the light bill. As a result of government cutbacks, tensions are mounting within nonprofit boards as they wrestle with difficult decisions concerning how to ease the financial crunch while maintaining historical markets.

Making the Decision to Develop a Strategic Plan

The motivation for initiating a strategic plan comes from many sources:

Board members. Board members who have participated in successful strategic planning as a result of their service on other nonprofit boards are often the source for initiating a strategic plan. Board members who run their own businesses or work for for-profit companies that routinely develop strategic plans also may raise this issue. Many who serve on nonprofit boards see strategic planning as a management and governance tool equal in importance to budgeting, and cannot imagine an organization that doesn't initiate a formal process to look inward at least once every half-decade.

Funders. Some funders require the development of a strategic plan before they make grants to nonprofit charities. These funders want evidence that their contributions will be used prudently and cost-effectively, and will influence the direction of the organization. A strategic plan developed as a result of such a requirement by a funder would obviously highlight changes in the organization's programs that are the direct result of the contribution.

Retirement of a long-term CEO. Many nonprofits were started by visionary leaders who ran the organizations from the seat of their pants. This "old school" of doing business may no longer be valid. New agency leaders, many with MBAs, believe that nonprofit organizations are businesses, and the same management techniques they learned in business school are applicable to the philanthropic sector. The new school recognizes that the bottom line remains the principal concern of the agency, whether or not the bottom line is interpreted as the net revenue at the end of the year or the number of satisfied clients served. The old school agency executive is often skeptical, if not fearful, of strategic planning. Perhaps his or her vision of the agency has never been challenged, and a formal process to evaluate the agency from top to bottom, from the mission statement on down, is a threat to executive autonomy. In some cases, that skepticism is justified.

Once a new generation assumes the mantle of leadership, there is motivation to rebuild the agency from the ground up, starting with the mission statement, and proceeding, in some extreme cases, to changing the model of the copying machine. A strategic plan is often the vehicle for the new leadership to assert its authority and provide a mechanism for a higher level of executive accountability.

Agency Trauma. More often than not, it is an organizational crisis that triggers the decision for a strategic plan when an agency has no regular process to prepare one. The resignation or firing of a CEO is a traumatic event for any nonprofit. Sometimes, this event has occurred because of underlying unresolved issues and problems that may have developed and been inadequately addressed over many years. In the case of the involuntary separation, the organization's leadership has the opportunity to reshape the organization before a new executive takes over and molds the direction of the agency. Other traumatic events that may trigger the initiation of a strategic plan are the loss of a major funder, the establishment of competition from another nonprofit or for-profit, major damage or aging of the agency's physical plant, liability suits, or quantum advances in technology that call into question the future demand for services by the agency.

Benefits of Strategic Planning

1. It permits discussion of issues in a proactive rather than reactive mode. Usually developed in an atmosphere that encourages creativity and brainstorming, the strategic plan may not only include concrete directions, but also provide an institutional set of core values. In a typical board meeting, there is simply no time to engage in a meaningful discussion about the long-term future of an agency, unless the board governance model recommended by Gerry Kaufman in Chapter 6 is followed. Many nonprofits are operating on the edge of financial chaos, often one failed grant application away from having to lay off staff or fold entirely.

2. It requires an action plan to solve real problems faced by an agency. The action plan is a template that the staff can use to implement the policies and desires of the board. Many CEOs complain that the board helps with solving problems, but fails to provide direction on the core values of the agency. A strategic plan explicitly includes those core values, and assists the CEO in creative strategies for solving current problems and anticipating future ones.

3. It provides a formal mandate for the reallocation of resources to respond to changing conditions, and the means to obtain additional resources if required. A successful strategic planning process that develops an aggressive plan to attack problems often energizes a moribund board.

4. It builds inter-board relationships that might not otherwise exist, and creates a partnership among the board chairperson, board members, staff, funders, and other stakeholders. Each has a role that is defined in the plan and, if bought into, the added responsibilities increase the available resources of the agency. The social contact that occurs at many board retreats, particularly those designed in bucolic settings away from the hustle and bustle of the agency, cement personal relationships among participants. This improves the bond between the agency and its leadership.

5. It provides a mechanism for the board, staff, and agency stakeholders to become more informed about the activities and problems faced by the agency. It promotes, in many cases, a frank discussion by the agency executive of problems that might not be shared in a conventional board meeting context. Many CEOs welcome the process in that it takes a burden off their shoulders and shares it with the agency's "owners" and constituents.

6. It provides an opportunity to focus on the forest rather than the trees. As a CEO, it is easy to become lost in the mundane issues of personnel, budgeting, office management, board relations, and public relations, and virtually ignore issues relating to the actual purpose and mission of the nonprofit.

Costs of Strategic Planning

1. **Money.** Serious strategic planning costs money, a scarce resource for most nonprofits. Many nonprofits recognize that it is useful to have a trained, dispassionate consultant to assist in the planning process. There are costs to schedule planning meetings and travel to those meetings. Many organizations recognize the value of eliminating outside distractions to aid brainstorming, and thus schedule planning meetings at staff retreats held at attractive, isolated camp grounds, conference centers, business resorts, or hotels. There are costs of photocopying and printing all of the planning documents. There are opportunity costs, as well, because staff and board resources are diverted from other duties.

2. **Time.** Any realistic strategic planning process requires the allocation of precious staff and board resources. Meeting preparation, meeting attendance, minutes, preparation of draft and final strategic plans, and hiring a consultant all take time. It is not uncommon for a strategic planning process to take more than a year.

3. **Potential bad will.** As with any process, things can go wrong. Bad group dynamics can result in painful meetings and destructive outcomes. It is not unusual for a group to spend an entire four-hour meeting arguing over trivial words in a mission statement. This can be painfully frustrating for committee members more interested in developing an action plan to solve agency problems. Strategic planning may bring board factions into collision, and meetings can degenerate into a test of wills. This may be healthy in the context of a committee rather than having a drag-out fight at a board meeting, but it means that to have a constructive planning process, personal baggage must be dealt with first. If the final strategic plan is not implemented, board members who participated may feel that the agency wasted their time, and may not be as likely to participate in future efforts, or even may resign from the board. Current staff members may feel threatened that their jobs are at risk, and may look for other employment.

4. **Loss of Agency Initiative.** A formal strategic plan may diminish an executive's initiative and quick response to changing conditions, because the preferred course of action is not in the strategic plan. The strategic plan may become outdated quickly and stifle a more appropriate response to changing conditions that were not anticipated in the plan. In addition, strategic planning often involves the board not just in setting objectives and outcomes, but also in determining the methods that should be used to achieve those objectives and outcomes. Many feel that this is the role of staff, not the board, and takes away the flexibility necessary for executive staff to function effectively.

A Sample Strategic Planning Model

The intent of this chapter is to give a cursory review of what a strategic plan is, its costs and benefits, some advantages and disadvantages, and some issues that often arise when nonprofits consider initiating a strategic plan. It is recommended that other specific resources be consulted when exploring the need for a strategic planning process, and several excellent sources are included in the bibliography. The following is one model for developing a strategic plan, and is a hybrid put together from several theoretical models.

Step 1. Decide whether to develop a strategic plan.

Consider the costs and benefits mentioned earlier in this chapter, and also consider the following questions:

- Is there enough time and money to allocate for this planning process now?

- Is the agency prepared to implement whatever plan eventually is approved, or will it sit on the shelf?

- Do we have a commitment from the agency's executive director, board chairperson, board members, and other stakeholders to develop a plan, or will we just be going through the motions?

- Are the agency's short-term problems so overwhelming that the agency is wasting time planning for the future when its continued existence is seriously threatened by current problems?

Step 2. Build the infrastructure necessary to develop a plan.

a. Appoint a planning committee of the board. Include creative board members, funders, the CEO, chief financial officer, clients, and opinion makers from the community. Consider that any committee of more than 10 becomes unmanageable. Some strategic planners recommend that the entire board serve on the committee.

b. Compile and distribute articles and related material on strategic planning to the entire board. (For information on reprints or rights to photocopy this chapter or other copyrighted materials, contact the publisher of the material.)

c. Decide on whether the facilitator/consultant will be a board member or private paid or volunteer consultant. A board member already knows a lot about the organization, its strengths and weaknesses, its personnel, and all other members of the committee. On the other hand, that board member brings with him or her prejudices about colleagues and staff, and often has a point of view or hidden agenda that is not held at arm's length. A private strategic planning consultant has the experience to keep the discussion focused and follow the agenda. There are many consultants who have experience working with nonprofit agencies in designing the planning process itself, participating in orientation sessions for the planning committee, serving as a referee for dispute resolution, helping the committee reach consensus when that is desired, neutralizing oppositional or disruptive participants, and providing technical assistance.

A good consultant can organize the process and provide logistical support so that the agency board and staff will not be absorbed by the planning process mechanics. On the other hand, a bad consultant may influence the process beyond what is desirable, and constrain the participation of committee members. One must be careful to assure that the plan, if written by the consultant, is not a tepid re-write of the plan the consultant developed for a previous client, which may have only minimal relevance to the current client.

It is good advice to informally survey comparable organizations to check out potential strategic planning consultants. Statewide associations such as the Pennsylvania Association of Nonprofit Organizations (PANO) and the Pennsylvania Society of Association Executives (PASAE) may also be helpful in identifying consultants. Of course, it is vital that any contract between the organization and the consultant spell out exactly what services are required, the timetable, and the level of participation required by the consultant.

Step 3. Decide how many years the strategic plan will cover.

In general, small nonprofits choose a shorter time frame than larger nonprofits, perhaps 2-4 years for smaller agencies, compared to larger institutions, which prepare 5-year plans.

Step 4. Put in writing the timetable and the process.

This includes the steps that are required and who is responsible for accomplishing each task. Among the tasks are:

- appointing the committee
- hiring a consultant or facilitator
- leading the orientation of the planning committee
- picking the meeting site
- scheduling the meetings
- writing the first draft of the plan
- providing the procedures to review and revise the draft
- writing the final plan
- developing the process for the planning committee to approve the final plan
- formulating the review and the process for the full board's approval of the final plan.

Step 5. Prepare a memo on what is expected out of the strategic planning process.

This memo to the planning committee should highlight the major problems that are to be resolved by the strategic plan, such as reviewing and updating the mission statement, how to respond to potential cuts in government funding, how to respond to the location of a for-profit competitor, how to deal with a change in the demographics of the people in the area served by the agency, and so on. The memo should note whether the planning report should be a consensus document (that does not meet unanimity) or rather majority rules after all points of view are heard.

Step 6. Have the agency board endorse the planning process, and allocate funds necessary for it to proceed.

Step 7. Appoint the committee, appoint or hire the facilitator/consultant, send out orientation materials, and schedule the first meeting.

The first meeting

The first meeting is usually an orientation session, which includes some of the following components:

1. A review of the purpose of the committee, the timetable, future meeting schedule, meeting the facilitator.

2. A review of the agency's current mission, history, short-term problems, long-term threats, staff resources, programs, activities, strengths and weaknesses, major successes and failures, core values of the organization, financial status, future commitments. The agency's CEO and CFO should be present to answer questions from the planning committee, and ask questions of the facilitator to establish ground rules for the planning process.

3. An analysis of the needs of the stakeholders, including those currently receiving service, and scenarios about how those needs may change. For example, is the population served by the agency changing demographically? Is government funding likely to drop? Is the community becoming poorer, limiting future fee-for-service revenue and requiring more non-fee revenue?

4. An analysis of institutional limits: population served by geography, age group, income level.

5. An identification of what in the above can be changed by the organization as a result of strategic planning and what is the result of forces beyond the control of the agency.

The second meeting

The second meeting begins the brainstorming of the committee. This meeting examines the mission statement, and reviews potential changes to that statement which, in some cases, could have been unrevised for decades. The facilitator may list various problems on the horizon of the agency, with the planning committee serving as a focus group—such as funding problems, changes in markets, competitors, outside threats from changing social, economic, political, technological conditions, or demand for services. The planning committee is given a homework assignment to come to the third meeting with suggestions for solving these problems.

The third meeting

The third meeting consists of brainstorming on action strategies that will solve the problems identified at the first and second meetings. The facilitator lists each strategy, and includes a table that includes the costs and benefits of each, the probability of success, and the pros and cons. Each strategy for each problem may be ranked based on the committee's assessment as to the value of the strategy.

The fourth meeting

The committee develops an action plan, including a timetable for implementation, which includes coming up with the resources necessary to implement the action plan. The plan also includes a procedure to review the progress made in implementing the plan.

In the above model, a draft strategic plan can be accomplished with four three-hour meetings.

In *Managing a Nonprofit Organization*, Thomas Wolff outlines six levels in the linear model of strategic planning. In the linear model, the planning committee considers one level before proceeding to the next. This contrasts to the integrated planning model, which provides for many of these levels to be considered simultaneously, recognizing that the end result is interdependent upon each of the earlier levels.

Level 1. The planners consider the mission statement, which describes the purpose the organization is trying to achieve.

Level 2. Agency goals are developed, providing the general direction in which the organization intends to go.

Level 3. Objectives and targets are set, indicating the outcomes the organization hopes to achieve.

Level 4. Strategies are formulated to meet the objectives and targets. These are the methods and ways the organization plans to achieve those outcomes.

Level 5. An action plan is developed to implement the strategies.

Level 6. An evaluation is performed after implementation, to review whether the outcomes were achieved and whether the strategies were successful.

For example, a hypothetical nursing home might have a planning document that, in an abridged form, is as follows:

Level 1. To provide quality long-term care services to the aging population of Anytown, PA, for the purpose of improving the quality of life for those who need institutional care.

Level 2. To reduce the operating deficit and become the long-term care institution of choice in the community by improving quality of care.

Level 3. Increase non-fee revenue by 50%, and improve the cash-flow situation by taking advantage of accounting productivity. Improve government reimbursement by 25% within three years.

Increase private pay residents from 30% to 50% within the next five years.

Level 4. Issue charitable gift annuities and hire a development staff member.

Hire a lobbyist to assist the statewide association to advocate for continuing the Medicaid intergovernmental transfer program.

Hire a marketing associate to place advertisements in publications read by active, upscale middle-aged persons whose parents may be in need of long-term care services.

Level 5. Investigate the legality of charitable gift annuities, and hire a consultant by July 15 to develop a program for residents and their families.

Aggressively go after accounts receivable, delay accounts payable for an additional 30 days, eliminate programs that are not profitable, increase fee-for service; increase fundraising; become entrepreneurial by selling subscriptions to a newsletter.

Place an advertisement in the PaSAE Bulletin to hire a registered lobbyist.

Hire a marketing associate by June 15, and use endowment funds for seed money, and assume the new staff member will generate at least enough income to finance his or her salary.

Level 6. One year after final approval of this report, require the executive director to prepare a progress report on whether the goals outlined in level 2 are being achieved, and what mid-course corrections to Level 5 are required in order to meet the targets of Level 3.

The process of planning each level can be discussed and refined for 2 hours or nine months. The parameters differ, obviously, for a hospital with a half-billion dollars in gross revenue compared to a charity with $50,000 in gross receipts.

The actual plan may be written by the facilitator, the chairperson of the planning committee, or staff in consultation with the board and facilitator. In every case, the planning committee should review a draft of the plan before submitting its final version to the board. The board reserves the power to approve, disapprove, approve with changes, or send the plan back for revision.

Some of the changes that may be recommended by a nonprofit agency strategic plan are:

1. a mission change
2. a change in the character of services provided
3. a plan to expand or downsize staff
4. a plan to expand or sell capital equipment and/or physical plant
5. a plan to expand fundraising
6. a plan to retrain staff
7. a plan to move the agency's location
8. a plan to seek a merger with similar organizations
9. a communications plan to improve or renovate the agency's public image
10. a plan to hire a lobbyist, or form a statewide association representing agencies with similar problems or uncertainties
11. a plan to establish a for-profit subsidiary
12. a plan to seek, or refuse, government grants
13. a plan to liquidate the agency
14. a plan to professionalize the agency, or deprofessionalize it—e.g. a decision by a hospital to substitute nurse aides where registered nurses were used formerly
15. a plan to change the governance of the organization—increase or decrease board membership, change quorum requirements, change voting requirements, change committee structure, change the powers of officers
16. a plan to change the compensation structure to reward and improve productivity
17. a plan to change the agency's market niche
18. a plan to change into a for-profit
19. a plan to modernize the name of the agency

Some components of a strategic plan may be:

1. a five-year projection of staffing patterns
2. a five-year projected budget
3. sources of revenue to implement changes called for by the plan
4. a marketing strategy
5. a schedule for periodically updating the strategic plan
6. a schedule for evaluating whether the plan is being implemented effectively and whether the strategies provided in the plan are successful
7. a physical plant/equipment plan
8. yearly updates to the plan

| Pennsylvania Association of Nonprofit Organizations

Chapter 6
A Transforming Model for
Nonprofit Board Leadership
By Gerald Kaufman

Overview

The nonprofit sector in the United States has undergone substantial changes over the past 20 years. There are many factors that are responsible for this change. The nonprofit sector itself has grown enormously over the past decade, fueled by the tremendous increase in fees and government funding. The nonprofit sector's funds are no longer predominantly from charity; only 18% of the revenue of the sector, excluding religion, came from philanthropy in 1990. The remainder came from fees (51%) and government (31%).

Society now relies on the nonprofit sector to deliver health and social services, participate in economic development, build housing, feed the hungry, educate and protect children, provide art and culture experiences and convey many other services. The sector no longer primarily dispenses charity, but rather provides essential services to all people, regardless of their income level.

Increased government funding has brought with it all of the trappings of bureaucracy: rules and regulations regarding internal management and financial accounting; program operation manuals governing all aspects of client treatment; and a strong emphasis on reimbursement for a detailed defined set of services, often overshadowing the organization's original mission, and narrowing the vision.

Providing services to individuals, although essential, does not translate into building strong, safe communities. The rise in numbers and importance of community development corporations and the resurgence of the settlement house movement may be vehicles for some community building.

Boundaries between the nonprofit sector and government and the for-profit sectors are eroding. Many parts of the nonprofit sector are becoming quasi-government. Large corporations and nonprofits are forming partnerships to solve community problems or to enhance the corporate image. This trend challenges the responsibilities, independence, and traditional values of the nonprofit sector.

Individual nonprofit organizations have become larger and more complex, often requiring sophisticated, professional management. An increasing number of them are using the most modern technology and marketing tools to raise money, attract clients, and influence public policy. In this climate, small community-based organizations have difficulty competing.

One result of the growth in size, complexity, and importance of the nonprofit sector is increasing scrutiny by the press, the public and governments at all levels. Public officials are raising questions about whether nonprofits are being operated in the public interest or for private gain. Challenges to tax exemptions, particularly in Pennsylvania, are occurring in many jurisdictions. The IRS is increasing its auditing and oversight of nonprofit, tax-exempt organizations.

Disclosures of one well-known major charity's excessively high salary and perks for its executive director and similar scandals have led to the lessening of public confidence in the nonprofit sector, according to a recent Gallup poll.

Current Board Functioning

In many instances, boards of directors continue to operate as if change of this magnitude had not occurred. Too often, as one author put it, boards "... fall into trivia, short term myopia, meddling in staff work, and other failings. They do so even when composed of intelligent, experienced, caring members."

Professionally staffed, large, complex organizations tend to pursue funding without too much regard to mission. In these situations, boards often evaluate executive directors on the basis of the fund balance at the end of the year, rather than the accomplishment of the mission.

Ideally, the essential role of boards of directors is assuring that nonprofit organizations are mission driven, governed by a board of citizens responsive to the community that they serve, based on the values of altruism, community and diversity, operated in an ethical and prudent manner, and providing citizens an opportunity to participate in the civic life of the community.

When one observes boards and board committees or reads minutes of meetings, one sees that much time is spent listening to reports. Committees meet to listen to appropriate staff members report on the subject matter under the committees' jurisdiction.

These meetings typically involve several telephone calls between the staff and the committee chairpersons, resulting in preparation of a report and the agenda by the staff. The meeting might take several hours of discussion and, as a result, some minor changes might be made to the report. The same process is repeated at board meetings, with many or all of the committees reporting. In addition to committees, the executive director and treasurer also make reports.

The line between board and staff roles and decisions is blurred. Too often, when the board is asked to take some action, it is of a trivial nature that should have been made by the executive director, such as: what kind of computer to buy, what insurance agent to use, what color the invitations should be for the fundraising dinner, what the sign-in and -out requirements should be for employees, and on and on. Some boards get involved in more weighty administrative decisions such as hiring staff, signing all checks, and approving grant proposals. In these instances, although much time is involved, seldom are the recommendations of the executive director not followed.

All of this activity gives many board members a sense that they are doing important work. But much of it is rubber stamping at best, or destructive interference in responsibilities of staff at worst. Others, however, frequently complain about the mind numbing details that occupy board meeting time. As a result, board attendance is frequently low and quorums hard to assemble. What these activities largely amount to is reviewing what has already occurred, and they have little relevance to what are uniquely the board's responsibilities.

A major complaint of many executive directors is the enormous amount of staff support that these board activities require, and a feeling that much of it is meaningless. Another point of conflict often is around fundraising, with the executive director's expectations of the board seldom being fulfilled.

Boards also do some important work, such as composing the mission statement or engaging in strategic planning. Here, too, boards often defer to executive directors and give pro-forma approval to executive directors' efforts. However, some boards engage in strategic planning over extended periods of time, even as long as a year, involving themselves in the minute details of program operation.

Most board members receive little or no training as to their role or what is expected of them, other than being told that they "make policy," approve budgets, and have a fiduciary obligation for the fiscal integrity of the organization and for fundraising. This often translates into: routine approval of the annual plan and detailed financial reports prepared by the staff, receiving and reviewing the annual audit, and selling a few tickets to the annual fundraising event or helping to arrange a silent auction.

Another function performed by many board members is to act as volunteers in some aspect of the organization's programs. Although this is a worthwhile activity, it has nothing to do with board members as governors of the agency.

There is often tension between boards and executive directors concerning access to information. Boards spend so much time on trivia because they have not articulated what is important to them. They may look at anything and everything because they are not sure what they are looking for. Boards complain that they don't get enough information, or they get too much and don't know what to do with it. Executive directors complain that boards demand information and then they don't read it.

If the nonprofit sector is to be the strong value and mission driven sector that the public expects and its history and role in society demands, strengthening and emphasizing the centrality of boards of directors is essential.

A New System of Board Governance

If we are to transform nonprofits into much more effective and accountable organizations, we must redefine the role of board governance. In this new world, we need a model of board governance that will assure that nonprofit organizations will be operated with vision on behalf of the community they serve, in an ethical and prudent manner, producing results that justify the costs.

John Carver, the father of this model of board governance, in his book, *Boards That Make A Difference*, defines board governance as follows:

> *Board leadership requires, above all, that the board provide vision. To do so, the board must first have an adequate vision of its own job. That role is best conceived neither as volunteer-helper nor as watchdog but as trustee-owner. Policy Governance is an approach to the job of governing that emphasizes values, vision, empowerment of both board and staff, and the strategic ability to lead leaders.*

The concept of trustee-owner is central to this new system of board governance. Every nonprofit exists for the benefit of the "moral" owners and the board functions as trustees on their behalf. The board's job is to define who those moral owners are. In the case of a legal services agency, the owners might be all low-income people living in the community that the organization serves. For a low-income housing development group, the owners might be, at one level, all of those needing decent low-income housing; but, at another level, the owners are all residents of the city, because a healthy society is one in which everyone is housed decently.

Every nonprofit exists for those who would benefit from the realization of its mission in its broadest sense. Boards of trustees operate nonprofit organizations in trust for these moral owners. The *primary* responsibility of boards then is not to support the staff, but rather to assure that the organization fulfills its fiduciary obligation to the owners.

Board members may also act as volunteer-helpers but they do that as any non-board member would, not as trustee-owners. The board has certain, defined watchdog functions, but that should not take up the majority of its time as it does now in so many organizations.

While everyone in an organization makes policy at some level, the question is what policies are the board's? Policy is defined as, "The values or perspectives that underlie actions." The following is a short summary of the four areas that define the board's job and for which written policies are required:

1. Ends or Outcomes. The board must determine how the world will be different as a result of the activities of the organization. To do that, the board must decide what human needs will be met, for whom, and at what cost. The board should formulate these ends policies starting at the broadest level—the mission statement—and continue from the next broadest formulation to a point where they are willing to stop and delegate the balance to the executive director.

The mission statement is a statement about outcomes. Outcomes are not activities; they are the results expected from the activities of the organization. Under this model, boards are concerned with results or ends, and their obligation as owners of the organization is to assure the production of worthwhile ends.

Practices, methods, activities are means, not ends. Boards should stay out of staff means, except to say what means are not acceptable, which will be discussed below.

A typical nonprofit mission statement might be that it provides "high quality services to the mentally retarded" or "shelter and supportive services for the victims of domestic violence." These are statements about activities, not about outcomes. Boards must decide what they expect the agency to accomplish, and what results are expected from these high quality services.

An example of a results-based mission statement might be to prepare the mentally retarded for "independent living in the community." In that instance, the board might further specify that independent living includes job readiness, household maintenance, knowledge of community resources, and other skill areas that the board believed were necessary to enable the clients to live independently in the community. What means the staff put in place to achieve the ends should not be a matter of board concern.

Private and government funders often dictate staff means by requiring very specific programs, activities, and methods. Under these circumstances, if boards are clear about ends, then staff can negotiate with funders about means. If staff believes that programs prescribed by funders will not achieve the results or ends determined by the board, then the organization should refuse the grant or contract or the board should revise the ends policies.

Such an approach will counteract the seduction for nonprofit agencies to pursue whatever funding is available, whether or not the funding will accomplish the reason for the organization's existence.

In the area of domestic violence, for example, there are studies that show that if police are trained to intervene strongly with an abuser, the repetition of domestic violence can be substantially reduced. However, most domestic violence agencies are paid to provide only shelter and treatment for the abused partner.

Under this model, boards would grapple with the question of what outcomes the organization is expected to achieve and would regularly monitor the agency on that basis. Outcomes might include reduction of abuse, independent lives away from their abusers, temporary respite, or preservation of families.

The formulation and reformulation of ends policies will occupy much of the board's time and, to perform that role, much of a board's attention will be focused outside the organization. The board will need to inform itself of community needs and how those needs are changing, whether there are other organizations it should be collaborating with, how changes in public policy are likely to affect the mission, and whether the organization should merge with other groups to better accomplish the mission.

2. Executive Limitations. These policies articulate the board's values regarding how the executive director manages the organization. Executive limitations policies are proscriptive; that is, they are expressed in negative terms, and state what the board will not permit in the following areas: treatment of staff and volunteers, financial planning (budgeting), financial condition, asset protection, board awareness and information. These are the usual areas of board concern with the means the executive director uses to manage the organization.

Under this model of board governance, boards do not get involved in the program activities as governors of the organization, other than to assure themselves that the activities are achieving the desired ends. (Board members may get involved in the activities as volunteers working under the supervision of the appropriate staff person, and in those instances they are not acting in their board member/governor capacity.)

If boards determine the ends to be attained and then ordain the means of attaining them, it is not reasonable to hold the executive director accountable for the outcomes. Executive limitations narrow and define the board's involvement in staff means.

Under traditional board operations, boards prescribe from time to time how the executive director is to operate the organization. A typical example is the formal adoption of a set of personnel policies. At other times, board members suggest what kind of telephone system to install, how often the newsletter should go out, fundraising ideas, marketing strategies, or even how to run a staff meeting.

Board actions or suggestions are scattered through the minutes over the months and years, often forgotten. The executive director may not be sure whether the board is directing the executive director to take some action, or merely offering suggestions, and many of these ideas and suggestions just float out in limbo. On the other hand, some board members may interpret a suggestion as a board directive and later criticize the executive for not complying.

Executive limitations place the responsibility for operational details where it belongs, on the executive director, other than the values of prudence and ethics that the board has identified as important limitations on the executive's authority. These policies regarding executive limitations normally can be written in five or six pages and provide the basis for clearly defined and targeted monitoring of executive director actions.

Boards, under this approach, free themselves from the operational minutiae and the impossible and endless task of monitoring all details of programs and management. With executive limitations in place, the board will have identified what is really important to it and confine its monitoring accordingly.

Thus, instead of boards drafting or even approving personnel policies, executive limitations would state what it would not allow in the treatment of personnel. For instance, board-drafted personnel policies normally include a detailed grievance procedure for employees. Executive limitations would simply state that the executive director shall not fail to have a policy permitting employees to submit a grievance to the board.

Other examples of value laden executive limitations are prohibiting discrimination regarding hiring or promotions, sexual harassment, and making purchases over a certain amount without competitive bids. Boards should not concern themselves with matters that do not involve their values, such as what holidays the staff has off, whether the organization has flex time, or other details of staff operation properly in the province of management.

Executive limitations policies free the board for the much more important and exciting work of defining the organizational ends, of envisioning the future. The staff, in turn, has much more time to do the work necessary to reach the vision.

3. Executive Director-Board Relationship. This set of policies describes what is expected of the executive director (achievement of ends policies and non-violation of executive limitations), and how and when the policies of the board will be monitored. The executive director is evaluated on the performance of the agency, not on individual performance.

A fundamental principle is that a board monitors only against criteria previously set. The board monitors against these pre-set criteria in one of three ways, depending on which criterion is being monitored: executive director's report regarding ends and executive limitations; external report, such as an audit; and direct inspections of documents or locations. A monitoring schedule, with times and manner of monitoring, is included in this set of policies.

4. Board Process. These policies describe how the board is going to govern itself. They include the role of the president, committees, board job description and board internal dynamics. The board job products are linkage with the ownership, written governing policies, and assurance of executive performance. Optional products include fundraising and government relations or advocacy.

An important principle is that the board speaks with one voice and relates to one employee, the executive director. Board holism is fragmented by the use of traditional board committees, which normally concern themselves with some aspect of staff operations, and, therefore, accomplish little other than rubber stamping staff recommendations, or interfering with staff work. Under this model of governance, board committees are used to help the board do its job, not the staff's job.

If the board is to speak with one voice, it is not acceptable for individual board members to direct employees or the executive director to take action or produce reports, unless the whole board has spoken on the subject. This principle alone could save many organizations countless hours and substantial staff stress.

Conclusion

This approach to board governance defines the jobs of the board and executive director; gives boards leadership responsibilities to determine the mission and vision of the agency; keeps boards out of operations by focusing them on ends not means, other than to assure themselves that the means used are prudent and ethical. The executive director is an active participant in the discussions leading to the adoption of all of the policies.

The move to this model of board leadership takes time, and it takes letting go of old habits and processes. Boards will need outside assistance in making the transition. Board meetings will be different, and those board members who like dealing with administrative and program details might be somewhat uncomfortable. The major emphasis for selecting board members will be on people with vision who are connected to the broader ownership.

By implementing this model of board governance, the board and staff of nonprofit organizations will be united in a common vision and mission, will have delineated clear boundaries between the board and staff concerning staff methods and activities, will be in closer touch with their "community" and other parts of the external world, and, above all, will be producing worthwhile outcomes rather than inputs.

An important consequence of this model is that many organizations will need to be much more collaborative with others in order to fulfill their missions and attain their ends. A "drug-free community," or similar world-changing mission, is not possible without the involvement of many other groups and organizations.

Governance is not about managing an organization, but about creating a world. Governance is about dreaming.

Gerald Kaufman, the author of this essay, is a nonprofit organizational development consultant based in Philadelphia. He is headquartered at 126 W. Mt. Airy Avenue, Philadelphia, PA 19119 at can be telephoned at (215) 247-5070.

Chapter 7
Nonprofit Organization Ethics

> **Synopsis:** Nonprofit charities have a special obligation, both legal and moral, to uphold the highest standards of ethical practice, to be accountable to their boards and the public, to avoid conflicts of interest, and to treat their employees with dignity.

Introduction

Nonprofit organizations, especially those qualified under section 501(c)(3) of the Internal Revenue Code, occupy a special and unique place in American society. The uniqueness of the sector has many attributes.

All such organizations are supported by the nation's taxpayers: they are exempt from federal and state income taxes; contributors, for the most part, can deduct their contributions from their federal income tax (and from their state income taxes in most states, but not Pennsylvania); they are eligible to have their postage subsidized by the federal government; and many are exempt from state and local sales and property taxes.

In our highly competitive, individualistic society, the nonprofit sector provides a way to express our humanitarian values, to preserve our cultural heritage, to promote various causes, to educate, and to enlighten. It is often through coming together in nonprofit organizations that our citizens exercise their constitutional rights to petition their government, free speech, assembly, and freedom of religion. Nonprofits play a unique role as the intermediary between the citizens and their government.

Maybe most important of all, nonprofits formulate much of the moral agenda for society. One only has to think of the environmental movement, rape crisis and domestic violence centers, public subsidies of arts and humanities, public awareness of AIDS and support of AIDS programs, and countless other issues that people coming together in voluntary organizations were able to put on the nation's agenda.

Historically, the primary distinguishing characteristic of the nonprofit sector is that it is mission and value driven. Nonprofit organizations exist to accomplish some social good, however that may be defined. A set of values and assumptions underlies this view of the voluntary sector including altruism, cooperation, community, and diversity. The privileges granted to the sector and public expectations are grounded in this belief.

However, there is a trend away from this traditional source of values towards a for-profit value system that emphasizes competition, survival, market share, growth for growth's sake, and, above all, emphasis on the bottom line. This shift is fueled in part by increasing government contracting as nonprofits take on more responsibilities, scarce resources, the influence of board members from the corporate community, the demands of funders, and the increasing number of trained "managers" who come into the nonprofit sector without being imbued with its traditions and values.

Some economists view the nonprofit sector as a form of business that is the result of the failure of the market in the private and public sectors. These economists overlook the place of the independent sector in the civic life of our society.

The following are some issues relating to ethics that are appropriate for nonprofit boards and staff to consider:

1. Accountability

Accountability often is overlooked in discussions about ethics. Because of the unique status of 501(c)(3) organizations, they have a special obligation to the public to be accountable for results of their activities that justify their tax exemptions and other privileges. Organizations should continually challenge themselves by asking if the outcomes produced are worth the public investment.

Nonprofit boards of directors have a special obligation to govern with integrity. Governing with integrity means that the organization recognizes that it is accountable to the public, to the people it serves, and to its funders. Accountability includes the concept that nonprofit organizations exist only to produce worthwhile results in furtherance of their mission.

In addition, accountability encompasses a core system of values and beliefs regarding the treatment of staff, clients, colleagues, and community. Yet, organizational survival needs too often undercut core values. Although everyone in the organization is responsible, it is the board's ultimate responsibility to assure that its values are not compromised, and that the activities are conducted within acceptable limits.

A more subtle issue of accountability exists that is seldom discussed. Staff will sometimes pursue grants and contracts, or engage in direct solicitation campaigns, for the primary purpose of growing. Boards sometimes ask whether the executive director "grew the organization" as the primary criterion for measuring success. Boards have an obligation to ensure that all activities support the organization's mission.

2. Conflict of Interest

A potential conflict of interest occurs any time organizational resources are directed to the private interests of a person or persons who have an influence over the decision. Examples might include the leasing of property owned by a relative of the executive director or a board member, the board awarding itself a salary, the organization hiring a board member to provide legal representation, or the executive director hiring a relative or a board member's relative.

A conflict also can occur when the person or persons making a decision expects something in exchange from the person in whose favor the decision is made. One example of this is the case in which an executive director retains a direct mail firm, and the executive director's spouse is hired by that direct mail firm shortly thereafter.

In regard to board members, the cleanest approach is to adopt a policy that does not allow any board member to profit from the organization. It is the duty of every board member to exercise independent judgment solely on behalf of the organization. For example, suppose a board member who owns a public relations business successfully argues that the nonprofit needs a public relations campaign and then is hired for the campaign. The board member's self interest in arguing for the campaign will always be subject to question.

Suppose in the above example the board member offers to do the campaign at cost and it is the lowest bid. It may be that even at cost, the board member's firm benefits because the campaign will pay part of the salary of some staff members or cover other overhead. It may be perfectly appropriate to accept the board member's offer, even though it is a conflict of interest. However, it is absolutely essential that the board have a procedure in place to deal with these issues.

Some organizations permit financial arrangements with board members, provided that the member did not vote on that decision. Given the good fellowship and personal relationships that often exist within nonprofit boards, such a rule can be more for show and without substance.

A similar problem can cause a conflict in the awarding of contracts to non-insiders. There may be personal reasons for one or more members of the board or the executive director to award contracts to particular persons, such as enhancing their personal or professional relationship with that person.

There are instances when it is appropriate to have a contract with an insider, such as when a board member offers to sell equipment to the organization at cost, or agrees to sell other goods or services well below market value. Here, too, the organization should assure itself that these same goods or services are not available as donations.

It is essential for the board to confront and grapple with these issues and adopt a written policy to govern conflict of interest in order to avoid the trap of self-dealing, or its appearances.

3. Disclosures

There are many ethical issues and much disagreement within the nonprofit sector regarding how much disclosure is required to those who donate to charitable nonprofits. The first obligation of every organization is to obey the laws and regulations governing disclosure. Nonprofits have a legal and ethical obligation to report fundraising costs accurately on their IRS Form 990, to obey the requirement regarding what portion of the cost of attending a fundraising event is deductible, and to comply with Pennsylvania's charitable registration laws and regulations (see Chapter 14).

Nonprofits face a more difficult ethical issue when deciding how much disclosure to make that is not required by law, particularly if the organization believes that some may not contribute if those disclosures are made.

In the for-profit corporate world, the Securities and Exchange Commission demands full, written disclosure of pertinent information, no matter how negative, when companies are offering stock to the public. There is no comparable agency that regulates charitable solicitations by nonprofits. Nonprofits must be very careful to disclose voluntarily all relevant information and to avoid the kind of hyperbole that misrepresents the agency.

Another difficult issue is whether fundraising costs should be disclosed at point of solicitation. The costs of telemarketing campaigns or of maintaining development offices are sometimes 80%, or even higher, of every dollar collected. Some argue that people wouldn't give if costs were disclosed. Others argue that if the soliciting organization cannot justify these costs to the public, and in many cases they are not justifiable, then they are not deserving of support.

There are recognized ethical standards regarding public charitable solicitations promulgated by the following:

National Charities Information Bureau
19 Union Square West
New York, NY 10003-3395
(212) 929-6300
http://www.give.org/index.cfm

Council of Better Business Bureaus
4200 Wilson Blvd.
Suite 800
Arlington, VA 22203
(703) 276-0100
http://www.bbb.org

A different set of ethical issues exists around disclosures to foundation and corporate funders. For instance, what is the obligation of disclosing changed circumstances after the proposal is submitted and before it is acted upon, such as when key staff have announced plans to leave? If the organization knows that the changed circumstance might affect the decision, is it unethical not to disclose it?

4. Other Issues

Accumulation of Surplus

If funds of a charitable nonprofit are to be used for charitable purposes, what is a reasonable amount of surplus to accumulate? The National Charities Information Bureau suggests a ceiling of twice the current year's expenses or the next year's budget, whichever is greater.

Organizations should consider the circumstances under which it is appropriate to disclose to prospective donors the amount expected to be used to accumulate a surplus. Clearly, if a major purpose of the solicitation is to build a surplus, that should be disclosed.

Outside Remuneration

Executive directors and other staff often are offered honoraria or consulting fees for speeches, teaching, providing technical assistance or other work. The ethical issue is whether the staff person should turn the fees over to the nonprofit employer or be able to retain them. Potential conflicts can be avoided if the policy is based on the principle that all reasonably related outside income belonged to the organization. Thus, an executive director's honorarium for speaking to a national conference would revert to the employer, but his fee for playing in a rock band on weekends would be his or hers to keep.

An argument against this principle is that the employees' usage of their spare time should be of no concern to the employer. The argument on the other side is that the line between employer's and personal time is not so easy to draw. Is it ethical for an employee to exploit the knowledge and experience gained on the job for personal gain? Are we buying only time from our employees or do we expect that we are getting the undivided professional attention from that person?

If the board or executive director is silent on this issue, the assumption is that earning outside income is a private matter. It makes sense to have a clear policy on outside income before an employee is hired.

Salaries, Benefits and Perquisites

Determining an appropriate salary structure is perhaps the most difficult ethical issue in the nonprofit sector. Ethical considerations arise at both the high and low ends of the salary spectrum.

If an organization is funded by grants from foundations and corporations or by government contracts, the funders can and do provide some restraint on excessive salaries. However, if the nonprofit is funded primarily by individual donations or fees for service, such constraints (other than, perhaps, those relating to the intermediate sanctions regulations of the Internal Revenue Service—see pages 261-263) are absent.

Boards fall into an ethical trap if they reward executive directors based on the amount of income received, rather than on how well the mission is accomplished. A board can consider many criteria when setting the salary of the executive director. These include the size and complexity of the organization, what others in similar agencies are earning, and whether the salary is defensible to the public. Some nonprofits include proportionality in their salary structure by limiting the highest paid to a factor of the lowest paid (e.g. the highest can be no more than three times the lowest).

As a result of enactment of the *Taxpayers Bill of Rights 2*, there are now *legal* as well as ethical restrictions about paying excessive compensation (see pages 261-263). Ethical treatment of employees requires that each person be treated with dignity and respect, provided a salary that can provide a decent standard of living, and a basic level of benefits, including health coverage. A potential, critical conflict arises when a charitable organization working to spread its social values treats its staff in a way that conflicts with its organizational values.

Conclusion

There are many other ethical issues that nonprofit organizations will confront on a regular basis, such as: personal use of office supplies and equipment; personal use of frequent flier mileage; the extent of staff and board diversity; and the use of private discriminatory clubs for fundraisers, board meetings or other events. The list is endless.

There are many excellent publications on the subject of ethics, and a few of them are:

1. A series of articles by David E. Mason in *Nonprofit World*, published by the Society for Nonprofit Organizations.

The Society For Nonprofit Organizations
6314 Odana Road; STE 1
Madison, WI 53719-1141
(608) 274-9777

2. *Making Ethical Decisions (34 pages, $6.95 plus $3.25 shipping and handling).*

Josephson Institute of Ethics
4640 Admiralty Way
Suite 1001
Marina del Rey, CA 90292
(310) 306-1868

3. *Ethics and the Nation's Voluntary and Philanthropic Community.*

Independent Sector
1828 L Street NW
Washington, DC 20036
(202) 223-8100

What is important is that nonprofit organizations consciously engage in discussions about ethics and values on a regular basis, recognizing that the charitable nonprofit sector has a special obligation to uphold the very highest standards. Boards of directors of charitable nonprofits have an important role in this regard. Boards cannot play a more important role than assuring that nonprofits are accountable, and that they operate as mission- and value-driven organizations.

Many who choose to work in the nonprofit sector do so because the stated values of the sector and their personal values are in harmony. It is critical that such people be vigilant against the erosion of those very principles that attracted them to the work.

Only in this way can the public be assured that the charitable nonprofit sector remains worthy of its privileges and that the sector continues to occupy its special and unique place in our society.

Tips:

- **Challenge yourself and your organization to hold yourself up to the highest ethical standards, avoiding even gray areas of conflicts of interest and appearances of conflicts of interest.**

- **When in doubt, ask yourself, "How would I feel if my family and friends read about this on the front page of the daily newspaper?"**

- **Obtain salary surveys published annually by the Pennsylvania Society of Association Executives (PaSAE) and determine whether anyone in the organization has an unreasonable salary.**

- **Demand that all business relationships with the organization be "arm's-length" and obtain at least three bids on any work that costs at least $1,000, even if a board member claims that he/she will provide the product/service at cost.**

Chapter 8
Section 501(c)(3) Tax Exempt Status

Synopsis: Federal 501(c)(3) tax-exempt status is valuable not only because of the tax advantages to the nonprofit corporation, but for the organization's contributors. Corporations with this status may not substantially engage in lobbying or engage in partisan political activities.

Achieving 501(c)(3) status should be the principal objective after filing the Articles of Incorporation for virtually all nonprofits organized and operated for religious, charitable, scientific, literary, or educational purposes, testing for public safety, fostering national or international amateur sports competitions, and the prevention of cruelty to children or animals.

The federal regulation implementing Section 501(c)(3) tax-exempt status states (Reg. §1.501(c)(3)-1(d)):

> "(d) Exempt purposes. (1) In general.
> "(i) An organization may be exempt as an organization described in section 501(c)(3) if it is organized and operated exclusively for one or more of the following purposes:
>> (a) Religious,
>> (b) Charitable,
>> (c) Scientific,
>> (d) Testing for Public Safety,
>> (e) Literary,
>> (f) Educational, or
>> (g) Prevention of cruelty to children or animals.
>
> "(ii) An organization is not organized or operated exclusively for one or more of the purposes specified in subdivision (i) of this subparagraph unless it serves a public rather than a private interest. Thus, to meet the requirement of this subdivision, it is necessary for an organization to establish that it is not organized or operated for the benefit of private interests such as designated individuals, the creator or his family, shareholders of the organization, or persons controlled, directly or indirectly, by such private interests..."

For nonprofits whose activities are eligible, designation by the Internal Revenue Service for 501(c)(3) tax-exempt status is a major objective to be achieved as quickly as possible. This status confers several substantial benefits to the organization:

1. The nonprofit will be exempt from federal income taxes other than unrelated business income taxes (UBIT). The current rate of federal corporate income tax is 15% on the first $50,000 in taxable income, 25% on the next $25,000, 34% on the next $25,000, 39% on the next $235,000, and 34% on the rest up to $10 million. While many nonprofits will not generate large amounts of net revenue, particularly in their early years,

it is a major advantage to have the option to capture this net revenue for future expansion, venture capital, and to cover future operating deficits.

2.   Persons contributing to the nonprofit can take a deduction on their own income taxes for their contributions. Since the incremental tax rate for middle and upper income persons on adjusted gross income for the tax year 1998 is 28% (on income of $25,350-$61,400 for singles, $42,350-$102,300 for married filing jointly), 31% ($61,400-$128,100 for singles, $102,300-$155,950 married filing jointly), 36% ($128,100-$278,450 for singles, $155,950-$278,450 married filing jointly), and 39.6% (higher than $155,950 for singles and $278,450 married filing jointly), this represents an attractive incentive for persons to leverage their own contributions with the "tax expenditure" contributed by government.

3.   Many major donors (such as United Ways and certain foundations) will not make contributions to organizations that do not have 501(c)(3) status.

4.   The designation of 501(c)(3) status indicates a minimal level of accountability, policed by the Internal Revenue Service, which is a useful governmental stamp of approval of the charitable activities of the organization.

5.   Qualifying 501(c)(3) organizations may elect to self-insure for purposes of complying with Pennsylvania unemployment compensation laws (See Chapter 11).

There are several disadvantages:

1.   A 501(c)(3) may not engage in partisan political activity on behalf of political candidates.

2.   Such organizations may not substantially engage in lobbying or engage in propaganda.

3.   Such organizations have a higher level of accountability, and must, as all 501(c) exempt organizations, make their 990 tax returns available in their offices for public inspection upon request.

4.   There is a substantial application fee ($500 in most cases), and this fee is not refunded if tax-exempt status is denied.

Although not always the case, most incorporators of nonprofits have some altruistic motive for incorporating. In every state, including Pennsylvania, incidental profits of a nonprofit "shall be applied to the maintenance and operation or the furtherance of the lawful activities of the corporation, and in no case shall such monies be divided or distributed in any manner whatsoever among the members of the corporation." (excerpt from 15 Pa. C.S.A. §7309). Section 5551 of Title 15 further provides that "A nonprofit corporation shall not pay dividends or distribute any part of its income or profits to its members, directors, or officers." Thus the motives of the incorporators cannot be for personal gain. As one might expect, the motives are usually of an "eleemosynary" nature, i.e. for the betterment of society.

Many nonprofit corporations are formed because a person or group of persons is frustrated with the lack of government action to solve a problem that, in that person's view, should be solved by government. Congress historically has recognized that government cannot do everything for everybody even when the cause is just. Instead, Congress provides an opportunity for citizens to form organizations to do the activities themselves. They are rewarded by having certain privileges, such as the tax-exemption, provided that the activity falls within a statutorily enumerated list of activities.

Section 501(c) of the Internal Revenue Code lists more than 20 classes of activities that can qualify a nonprofit corporation for tax-exempt status. A list of these classes is provided in this chapter. Only one of these classes, 501(c)(3), permits a tax deduction for contributions made to organizations in that class, and requires that such organizations not engage in substantial lobbying or propaganda activities, or in political activities that advance the cause of candidates.

501(c)(3) status is not granted pro forma. There are stringent requirements for approval. Because of this, 501(c)(3) status is prized, and is viewed by many in the public as a stamp of approval by the federal government. The fact is that 501(c)(3) status does not necessarily imply government's endorsement of the organization's activities. In 1997, the federal government granted 47,015 501(c)(3) applications, denied 226, and took "other" action on 17,761, many of which were eventually approved after additional information was provided.

How To Apply for 501(c)(3) Status

To make application, an organization needs the following forms and booklets from the Internal Revenue Service:

- Form 8718—*User Fee for Exempt Organization Determination Letter Request*

- Form SS-4—*Application for Employer Identification Number*

- Form 5768—*Election by an Eligible Organization to Make Expenditures to Influence Legislation*

- Package 1023—*Forms and instruction booklets for applying for 501(c)(3) tax-exempt status*

- Publication 557—*Tax-Exempt Status for Your Organization*

The above forms and booklets can be obtained at any local IRS office (see Appendix C for addresses). They can also be ordered by calling a toll-free number (1-800-829-3676).

According to the IRS, it takes about eight-and-a-half hours to complete the basic form and several more hours to complete supplemental schedules. It also takes several hours learning how to complete the forms. It is advisable to be as careful as possible in completing the forms, since the wrong phrase can result in denial. Legal advice in applying for tax-exempt status is recommended, particularly from those with experience in what the IRS reviewers will be considering.

Some organizations are exempt from having to file the 1023. Among them are:

1. Those that will have gross receipts less than $5000 annually.

2. Bona fide religious institutions.

3. Certain groups affiliated with a parent organization that already has tax-exempt status, and that will send a letter extending its exemption to them.

Federal law expects that an application for 501(c)(3) status will be filed within 15 months after the end of the month in which the Articles of Incorporation are filed. If the organization files on time and the application is approved, 501(c)(3) status will be retroactive to the date of the Articles of Incorporation. There is a form to file if the 15-month deadline is not met. For more information about this option, see IRS Publication 557.

Fees

There is a $500 application fee to file the form 8718, *User Fee for Exempt Organization Request,* which must be submitted with the 1023. New organizations expecting gross receipts of not more than $10,000 for each of the first four years, or existing organizations that have not had gross receipts of that amount in each of the last four years, can qualify for a reduced fee of $150. The fee must be paid by check, but a corporate check is not required.

Several commercial publications offer step-by-step advice on filling out applications for 501(c)(3) tax-exempt status. Among the best is *How to Form your Own Non-Profit Corporation* by Anthony Mancusco (Nolo Press, 950 Parker Street, Berkeley, CA 94710).

A Short History of Tax-Exempt Status

In ancient times, government, whether secular or non-secular, recognized that certain activities assisted the role of government and were deserving of tax exemptions. Several thousand years ago, some of the best land in the Nile Valley was set aside tax-free by the Egyptian pharaoh for the priests of Osiris.

Modern tax-exemption law has its roots in England, with the passage of the Statute of Charitable Uses in 1601. According to *Unfair Competition? The Challenge to Charitable Tax Exemption* by Harrison Wellford and Janne Gallagher, current U.S. tax-exemption law draws its roots from an 1891 court case in Britain *(Commissioners of Income Tax v. Pemsel)* that provided a judicial definition of charity strikingly similar to the American legal standard.

The modern federal tax-exemption can be traced to 1863, when the income of charities was exempted from a corporate tax enacted to finance the Civil War. The 1894 Income Tax Act was eventually declared unconstitutional. Yet it served as the precedent for exempting organizations that were for "charitable, religious, or educational purposes." Such exempt organizations were recognized only if they relieved poverty and were not permitted to generate outside income.

A 1924 Supreme Court case, *Trinidad v. Sagrada*, decided that for purposes of tax-exempt status, the destination of the funds, rather than the source, was the key determinant. This case involved a religious order that sold food, wine, and other goods to support its school, mission, church, and other operations. Thus tax-exempt organizations were permitted to run profit-making enterprises provided that the net profits were funneled to tax-exempt purposes. This policy was revised by Congressional enactment of an "unrelated business income tax" (UBIT). From 1909 to the present, many other categories of tax-exempt status were added by federal statute (see below).

Tax-Exempt Status Other than 501(c)(3)

The Internal Revenue Code provides more than 20 other categories of tax-exempt status besides 501(c)(3). Those who wish to file for tax exempt status under section 501(c) for other than 501(c)(3) need to request Package 1024 from the IRS.

Among the other categories are:

501(c)(4)—civic leagues, social welfare organizations
501(c)(5)—labor, agricultural or horticultural organizations
501(c)(6)—business leagues, chambers of commerce, trade associations
501(c)(7)—social clubs
501(c)(8)—fraternal beneficiary societies
501(c)(9)—voluntary employee beneficiary associations
501(c)(10)—domestic fraternal societies and orders that do not provide life, sick, health benefits
501(c)(11)—teacher retirement fund associations
501(c)(12)—benevolent life insurance associations and other mutual businesses
501(c)(13)—cemeteries and crematoria
501(c)(14)—credit unions
501(c)(15)—mutual insurance companies
501(c)(16)—farmers' co-ops

501(c)(17)—unemployment compensation benefit trusts
501(c)(20)—prepaid group legal services organizations
501(c)(25)—title holding corporations or trusts

With limited exceptions, these organizations have the same federal tax benefits as a 501(c)(3). One major difference is that with few exceptions, contributors cannot deduct the amount of their contribution from their personal income tax payments. For many of these organizations, there is no limitation against lobbying activities, and most are permitted to engage in partisan political activity (although there may be a substantial federal excise tax associated with political expenditures).

Chapter 9
Insurance and Liability

> **Synopsis:** All nonprofit corporations must have worker's compensation insurance and participate in the unemployment compensation program. It is advisable for nonprofit corporations to purchase general business insurance. State and federal laws have lowered the liability threshold for directors and volunteers of certain nonprofit corporations.

General Liability Concerns of Nonprofit Corporations

Murphy's Law has many variations and corollaries. In its simplest form, it states that "If something can go wrong, it will." No one can foresee catastrophic events, and even if one could, it is virtually impossible to protect a corporation against all possible eventualities.

A nonprofit corporation, like a business corporation, should do everything in its power to mitigate the effect of claims against the corporation. The corporation, like any other business, could suffer personal injury or property damage claims caused by floods, fire, theft, earthquake, wind damage, building collapse, and slips and falls, just to name a few possibilities. Legal claims against corporations tend to be of the low-incidence, high risk variety. These claims do not happen very often, but when they do, the results can be disastrous.

Nonprofits are exposed to legal risks in many other areas. They engage in typical business transactions on a routine basis. They arrange for conventions, seminars and other meetings. They publish newsletters. They also are employers with the attendant risk that hiring, advancement, or firing decisions may be challenged based on contract rights, discrimination, or fraud. A nonprofit corporation could be exposed to the antitrust laws if its membership has a competitive advantage. Such nonprofit corporations could conduct various kinds of programs that permit their members to self-regulate, such as by business or professional codes, product standards and certification, or professional or academic credentialing, to use but a few examples.

As this chapter will indicate, nonprofit corporations should consider basic general liability insurance to cover personal injury and property damage claims. Consideration also should be given to purchasing directors and officers (D&O) insurance to protect their volunteer leadership from personal legal claims. Finally, a similar but broader type of insurance policy dealing with general professional liability protects not only officers and directors, but all association volunteers and staff as well.

General Business Insurance

Employee lawsuits, floods, fire, theft, earthquake (Pennsylvania records several measurable earthquakes annually), wind damage, building collapse, loss of business income, pollution, riot, lightning, war, landslides, nuclear contamination, power failures, falls, electrocution...the possibilities are endless for natural disasters, accidents, and crime. Fortunately, generic business insurance policies will protect a corporation from all of these, plus scores of other potential but unlikely occurrences. If the organization is willing to accept a reasonable deductible (an amount of damages the corporation pays before benefits are provided on the remaining amount of damages), a policy may cost as little as a few hundred dollars. It is a worthwhile investment to make, if only for peace of mind. Most policies include defending corporate leaders in the event they are sued for whatever reason relating to business activity. Prices for basic insurance are competitive. Be sure the corporation has liability and medical expenses coverage of at least $500,000, and that the policy will cover the legal costs of defending and settling suits against the corporation and its staff.

Workers' Compensation Insurance

Every state, including Pennsylvania, has a worker's compensation law. Pennsylvania's worker's compensation law was enacted in 1915, and was one of the first pieces of employer reform legislation enacted during a time when employers generally held all of the cards and thousands of workers were exploited and at the mercy of employers.

The purpose of worker's compensation is to provide income to workers injured on the job and to pay their medical bills. In exchange, the employee gives up the right to sue the employer. The income disabled workers receive is generally two-thirds of their basic salary, with a maximum payment equal to the state's average weekly wage. For 1999, the state average has been determined to be $588 per week. This is a "no fault" system, designed to avoid costly and time-consuming litigation while stream-lining the ability to provide benefits to eligible workers.

All Pennsylvania corporations, including nonprofits, are required to participate in Pennsylvania's worker's compensation program. Corporations typically purchase worker's compensation insurance from a commercial insurance carrier. Because there is a standard rate for each class of employee set by the Pennsylvania Insurance Department, the insurance premiums are theoretically the same from company to company. It is possible that future rates will be headed downward as a result of reform legislation signed into law by Governor Tom Ridge on June 24, 1996.

Several publications published by the Pennsylvania Department of Labor and Industry explain the state's worker's compensation program. All publications are available from the State Book Store for a modest charge. A pre-addressed postcard for obtaining most of the required forms and instruction booklets is included in the back of this book.

Unemployment Compensation Insurance

The unemployment compensation program in Pennsylvania is a job insurance program. Its purpose is to provide some limited protection against loss of income for workers who lose their jobs through no fault of their own. Virtually all nonprofit corporations in Pennsylvania are required to participate in the program, which is financed principally by a payroll tax on employers of from 1.5705% to 13.296% of the first $8,000 in wages for each employee annually. The rate is set based on each corporation's history of employment. In the past, there also has been a requirement that workers contribute to the program by means of a payroll deduction. For calendar year 1999, there is no such requirement.

The maximum weekly benefit under this program is two-thirds of the average weekly wage in the Commonwealth. For 1999, this maximum payment is $392 per week. There is an $8 weekly supplemental payment for those with two or more dependents.

Registration

All nonprofits that hire employees must register with the Pennsylvania Department of Labor and Industry's Office of Employment Security. After registering (by filing a PA-100 form available from the Bureau's Employer Tax Operations Field Services offices), corporations automatically receive a quarterly UC-3 form (see Chapter 11).

A pre-addressed postcard for obtaining these forms and related information is included in the back of this book.

Section 501(c)(3) Organization Reimbursement Election

State law permits, but does not require, 501(c)(3) tax-exempt organizations to elect the "Reimbursable Method" for complying with the unemployment compensation law. Under this method, the nonprofit 501(c)(3) is required to reimburse the Unemployment Compensation Fund for all regular unemployment compensation benefits that are expended. The federal government pays 50% of extended unemployment benefits to qualified workers, which accounts for the disparity. Congress often will extend the regular program during times of economic recession. The last time the period was extended was in November of 1993.

Organizations that select the reimbursable method will receive a Form UC-150, Notice of Amount Due for Compensation Paid, which is a bill. This bill must be paid within 30 days, even if a protest is filed within the 30-day period permitted.

The Bureau of Employer Tax Operations publishes several booklets explaining the details of the program. These booklets may be obtained by writing to:

Office of Employment Security
Bureau of Employer Tax Operations
Labor and Industry Building
Seventh and Forster Streets
P.O. Box 60849
Harrisburg, PA 17106-0849
(717) 787-7613

Among the most helpful booklets are:

Pennsylvania Unemployment Compensation Handbook (UCP-1)
Unemployment Compensation Information for Reimbursable Employers (UCP-16)—for Section 501(c)(3) organizations
Unemployment Compensation Information for Contributing Employers (UCP-3)

A pre-addressed postcard for obtaining these booklets is included in the back of this book.

Federal Unemployment Taxes

Nonprofit corporations other than those with 501(c)(3) status also are subject to Federal unemployment taxes (FUTA). The tax rate for 1999 is 6.2% of the first $7,000 paid to each employee. Businesses receive a credit on the amount of unemployment taxes paid to the state. The FUTA tax is paid by filing a 940 FUTA tax return. Quarterly deposits may be necessary depending on the amount owed. These deposits are made in the same manner as federal quarterly withholding deposits.

Liability of Officers, Directors, and Other Volunteers

Nonprofit corporation volunteers may suffer from the same potential liability for actions in performance of their duties as individuals involved with business corporations. Furthermore, as managerial people, volunteer officers and directors of nonprofit corporations are bound by the same basic principles governing their conduct as directors and officers of profit-making business corporations. They owe a fiduciary duty of reasonable care and the duty to act in the corporation's and its members' best interest. This involves a duty of loyalty or good faith in managing the affairs of the corporation.

Generally, this duty requires individuals to use due care in the performance of their duties for the corporation, to act in good faith in the best interest of the corporation as a whole and not for the interests of some but not all of the members, and a duty to avoid activity or transactions in which the individual has a personal interest. In short, in this litigious society, courts are tending more and more to impose responsibility on officers, directors, and volunteers of nonprofit corporations— including hospitals, charities, and educational institutions— for anti-trust problems, tort liability, and similar areas of liability exposure.

Volunteer Protection Act

Although few successful lawsuits have been brought against nonprofit corporation volunteers, the possibility that lawsuits can occur presents a "perception problem." At the federal level, the Volunteer Protection Act (VPA) was signed into law by President Clinton in July of 1997, with an effective date of September 16, 1997. The intent of the law is to provide limited legal immunity for the volunteers of charities who are involved in accidents that occur in connection with their charitable service. It would extend this immunity unless the person intentionally caused harm to others or showed flagrant indifference to the safety of those who were injured. The immunity does not extend to activities not authorized by the charity, nor to hate crimes or sexual offenses. It encourages states to grant liability immunity to nonprofit organization volunteers who are acting in good faith and within the scope of their official duties.

Good Samaritan Immunity Amendments

In Pennsylvania, the General Assembly has enacted Act 1988-179. This law adds a section to several related provisions dealing with Good Samaritan immunity (42 Pa. C.S.A. §8332.1 et seq.). The statute provides some protection for a "person who, without compensation and as a volunteer, renders public services" to a Section 501(c)(3) or (c)(4) organization. This act seeks to prevent successful lawsuits based on "simple negligence," and would permit a lawsuit only if "the conduct of such person (the volunteer) falls substantially below the standards generally practiced and accepted in like circumstances by similar persons rendering such services and unless it is shown that such person did an act or omitted the doing of an act which such person was under a recognized duty to another to do, knowing or having reason to know that such act or omission created a substantial risk of actual harm to the person or property of another."

Officers, Directors, Trustees Liability Statute

Act 1986-57, enacted by the PA General Assembly in 1986, provides limited liability protection for officers, directors, or trustees of certain nonprofit organizations in connection with negligence. This act provides protection to a "person who serves without compensation, other than reimbursement for actual expenses, as an officer, director or trustee" of a Section 501(c)(3) organization.

This act is broader than the Directors' Liability Act discussed below because it protects officers and trustees, in addition to directors. However, it is narrower in that it applies only to 501(c)(3) organizations.

Act 57 provides protection against "simple negligence," but would impose liability if "the conduct of the person falls substantially below the standards generally practiced and accepted in like circumstances by similar persons performing the same or similar duties, and unless it is shown that the person did an act or omitted the doing of an act which the person was under a recognized duty to another to do, knowing or having reason to know that the act or omission created a substantial risk of actual harm to the person or property of another."

Directors' Liability Act

The Directors' Liability Act, enacted by the PA General Assembly in 1986, provides a limit to liability for the directors of not only nonprofit corporations, but for-profit corporations as well. Act 1986-145 (42 Pa. C.S.A. §8362, et seq.) permits corporations to eliminate, subject to certain exceptions, the liability of directors for monetary damages for acts that do not constitute self-dealing, willful misconduct, or reckless-ness. It applies to all nonprofits, not just 501(c)(3)s, but does not deal with the liability of officers. Furthermore, the liability provisions of this law do not take effect automatically, but require each corporation to amend its bylaws for this purpose. This bylaw amendment must be voted on by the members of the nonprofit corporation (or, in the case of a business corporation, by the shareholders). Directors alone may not adopt this bylaw amendment.

Act 145 permits directors to rely in good faith on information, reports, and opinions, including financial data, prepared or presented by officers, employees, counsel, accountants, and other professional experts and committees of the board. They are entitled to give consideration to the effects of corporate actions on corporate constituencies in addition to members of the nonprofit corporation.

If a bylaw adopted by the members of the corporation so provides, the personal liability of a director for monetary damages is restricted to a situation in which the director fails to perform the duties of office in a way that constitutes self-dealing, willful misconduct, or recklessness. An exception to this general rule applies in the case of liability under a criminal statute or for the payment of taxes.

The Directors' Liability Act contains a statutory provision broadening the power of nonprofit corporations (and business corporations, as well) to indemnify and advance expenses to officers and directors who become involved in litigation or other proceedings. This change in the law permits corporations to indemnify officers and directors against whom lawsuits are brought, arising from their corporate conduct. The law provides that indemnification may be either by bylaw, agreement, or independent vote of members or directors even when direct indemnification was not previously thought possible. The corporation is permitted to create a fund to secure the payment of the indemnification.

The act simplifies and clarifies the authorization to advance reasonable and necessary expenses, with the proviso that repayment of the advanced amounts might ultimately occur if it is determined that the officer or director is not entitled to be indemnified. Of course, indemnification is no better protection than the total amount of money available to the nonprofit corporation. This may be one of the reasons insurance for directors' and officers' liability for nonprofit corporations costs more than for for-profit corporations.

Personal or Professional Individual Insurance Coverage

The foregoing statutory provisions provide some protection to individuals involved with nonprofit corporations. Nonetheless, many nonprofit corporations purchase either Directors and Officers (D & O) insurance to cover directors and officers, or a broader type of policy sometimes referred to as professional liability insurance, to protect not only officers and directors but all association volunteers and staff. Although premiums for this type of insurance continue to be high, it is expected that the decrease in exposure afforded by the recent statutes will result in lower claims, and, eventually, lower premiums.

Tip:

- **This chapter provides a general summary of the law with respect to liability. Seek legal counsel before making any corporate decisions with respect to liability suits and claims.**

Chapter 10
Fiscal Issues

Synopsis: All nonprofit corporations must keep certain financial records and provide a financial summary. There are three levels of financial verification—audit, review, and compilation. *Line-item* and *program* budgets are the two major forms of budgeting utilized by nonprofit corporations.

Bookkeeping

Both state and federal law require corporations to record all expenses and income in an organized format. This can be done using one of many popular computer programs or manually. Several basic decisions need to be made. First, the corporation must decide on the period for its fiscal year. Because federal law requires the 990 nonprofit tax return to be filed within four-and-a-half months (technically, by the 15th day after the fifth month after the end of the fiscal year) after the end of the fiscal year, that alone can determine when to begin the fiscal year. Other factors to consider are the fiscal years or the announcement date of grants of major funding sources, using a calendar year for simplicity, or beginning the fiscal year as soon as the first corporate income is received.

A second issue is deciding whether the bookkeeping system will be on a "cash" basis or "accrual" basis. Cash basis financial reporting is based upon when income was received and deposited and when expenditures were made. The "accrual" method factors in "accounts payable" and "accounts receivable" (i.e. when there is a legal obligation to pay someone in the future). Most novices find the cash basis easier and simpler. The accrual method, on the other hand, gives a more realistic picture of the actual financial situation of the organization, and thus complies with generally accepted accounting principles. This decision should be discussed with the organization's accountant, or whoever is likely to prepare the tax returns and annual financial report. This is the time when the foresight of placing a certified public accountant or two on the board of directors can pay dividends.

Some funding agencies may have other accounting and bookkeeping requirements that must be considered.

Audits/Fiscal Accountability

There are three levels of financial verification. In descending levels of scope, they are audits, reviews, and compilations. The level of financial verification required is often determined by the nature and source of funding for the organization. Many government grants explicitly require a minimum level of financial verification in their contracts. Such a contract may be a "pass-through" of funds from another source, and the original source may need to be tracked down to determine whether it has its own requirement. It is good advice to request this information, in writing, from any contracting agency that provides the organization with grant funds.

Each of the three financial verification levels requires that all organizational funds be kept segregated and all transactions be accounted for. Thus it is never good organization policy to sign over an incoming check payment to a third party. Instead, deposit the check into the organization's account and then write a new check to the third party. While ignoring this advice may save the time of making a deposit and writing a check, it will result in a loss of "paper trail" necessary to determine who paid what to whom, when, and for what.

In the absence of an overriding requirement in a contract, federal, state, and local governments require an audit report when the funds in the contract are $100,000 or more in any single year. State and local governments generally require a review if funding is between $25,000 and $100,000 annually. If funding is less than $25,000, a compilation report is usually acceptable.

Audit Report

The highest level, an audit, is a complete arm's-length verification of the accuracy and reliability of account statements and financial reports. Records are systematically examined and checked to determine how they adhere to generally accepted accounting principles, management policies, and other stated policies. The purpose of independent audits is to eliminate bias, self-interest, fraud, and unintentional errors. While an auditor can never obtain *absolute* proof of the representations made in a financial statement, the standard used is that of a "reasonable man" (or woman) who has "adequate technical training and proficiency as an auditor," according to the American Institute of Certified Public Accountants. Auditors have a professional code of ethics to insure their independence from the management of the corporation. Although they are paid a fee by the corporation, they are considered to be responsible to the public rather than to their corporate clients.

The American Institute of Certified Public Accountants has prepared a comprehensive publication entitled *Audit Guide* specifically to assist nonprofit corporations in preparing for their annual audits. This Guide can be purchased for $40.50 ($32.50 for members), plus $6 for postage and handling from:

American Institute of Certified Public Accountants
Harborside Financial Center
201 Plaza Three
Jersey City, NJ 07311-3881
1-800-862-4272 (for orders)
(201) 938-3000 (for general information)
http://www.aicpa.org

Many government agencies have audit requirements for recipients of their grants. So do many foundations and other umbrella fundraising organizations. The Department of State's Bureau of Charitable Organizations, for example, requires registered charitable organizations receiving contributions of more than $100,000 in the preceding year to have their financial reports audited by an independent public accountant. Those with contributions between $25,000 and $100,000 must have their financial reports reviewed (see next section) or audited by an independent public accountant. Those with contributions of $25,000 or less may submit a compilation. Legislation is likely to be introduced in the General Assembly, as has been done in previous sessions, to loosen these requirements for small charities.

Audits are often required by major umbrella fund-raising organizations, with exceptions when the revenues are relatively small.

The Financial Accounting Standards Board (FASB) has issued rules that affect the content of financial statements. These new rules took effect for most small nonprofits in 1996. Financial statements must include a statement of financial position (balance sheet); a statement of activities (revenue and expenses) that includes changes in net assets and any change in restricted and unrestricted net assets; and a statement of cash flow showing how money was obtained, spent, borrowed, repaid, and so on. Although these new rules do not have the force of law, they must be followed in order to have your financial statement certified as "prepared in accordance with generally accepted accounting principles." The board also issued rules changing the way multi-year contributions are recorded, and requires certain volunteer services to be recorded as revenue, particularly if those volunteer services would otherwise have had to be purchased.

Review

A second standard of financial verification, called a "review," is the application of analytical procedures by the accountant to the financial data supplied by the corporation. It is substantially narrower in scope than an audit. Much of the information supplied by the corporation is accepted at face value, although there may be a spot check to see if there are any glaring errors or any inconsistencies between expenses recorded and the checks that are written. The examination of internal control and the proper allocation of income and expenses is similar to that of an audit report. Unlike an audit, the review will not include a formal auditor's "opinion" as to the compliance with generally accepted accounting principles.

Compilation

The third level of financial reporting/verification, a "compilation," calls only for the proper classification of assets, liabilities, fund balances, income and expenses, from information supplied by management. Third party verification of assets and liabilities is not required, although internal supporting documents may be used in their place. "Spot checks" are employed only when the accountant is aware of inconsistencies in other areas of the examination. As in a review, the accountant will not render an "opinion" on the accuracy of the report.

In the absence of legal requirements, it is good policy for nonprofits that expend more than a few thousand dollars to have at least a review. Many nonprofits have certified public accountants on their boards who may be willing to arrange for a review of the corporation on a *pro bono* basis.

Budgeting

Some nonprofits can exist for years using volunteer labor, donations of stamps, in-kind printing and other services. and have no need to raise money or make any expenditures. Others are more likely to have some staff and pay office rent or, if not, still have expenditures for workshops, postage, printing, telephone, and other typical corporate expenditures. The annual budget document is the blue-print for both spending and income. A poorly conceived budget can lead to the corporation's demise. On the other hand, a well-conceived, realistic budget, can be the catalyst for program planning that will provide a corporate life for many fruitful, productive years.

There are two major types of budgeting used by nonprofit corporations. Both have their advantages and disadvantages.

Line-Item Budget

The line-item budget is as it says—a list of various categories and the amount the corporation expects to spend for each category. Corporations, from the largest to the smallest, have some of the same categories in a line-item budget. Among the most common are:

1. salaries
2. consulting services
3. professional services
4. taxes
5. benefits
6. telephone
7. postage
8. printing and photocopying
9. travel and entertainment
10. workshops and conferences
11. bank fees
12. dues
13. subscriptions and publications
14. data processing
15. equipment
16. equipment maintenance and repair

17. legal services
18. insurance
19. rent
20. miscellaneous
21. office supplies
22. maintenance and repairs
23. security services
24. utilities
25. bookkeeping and payroll services

As an expense is incurred, the amount of the check is entered in a journal prepared for this purpose, coded by the expense category. At the end of each month, the amounts of each category are aggregated on ledger sheets called a "monthly summary." The monthly totals should be compared to the budget in each category to determine whether spending patterns are consistent with the budget.

Program Budget

The second type of budgeting is called a program budget. The program budget also contains various line-items, but the difference is that *each* major program of the corporation is provided with a line-item budget. For example, if your corporation is having a conference, then the conference itself has a budget. Printing, postage, and telephone costs are attributed to the conference. Printing and postage costs may be associated with another program as well, such as a newsletter. Each program of a nonprofit, such as conferences, newsletter, membership, or publications, has its own budget. The advantage of the program budget is that one can determine quickly the incremental savings that will accrue if a particular program is eliminated. The disadvantage is it is not easy to allocate overhead costs (such as salaries and rent) to various programs.

It is not unusual for nonprofits to combine the two types of budgeting—to have a general line-item budget, but to allocate some spending in all categories to certain programs. For small nonprofits, line-item budgets are the easiest to prepare and follow, and program budgets provide better information.

Expense Reimbursement

Organizations incur expenses. Many of these can be conveniently paid by corporate check. Many others, should the organization desire, can be paid by corporate credit card, which is particularly useful for travel expenses. It is not atypical for newly-formed organizations to require two signatures on checks. This is not unreasonable for recurring expenses that can be processed well in advance, such as paychecks, federal withholding, rent, major equipment purchases, and taxes. It does present problems when making small, but reasonable, purchases on-the-spot. An expense reimbursement system should be designed to provide protection against one person making unilateral decisions on spending, but needs to be flexible enough to keep the organization from being hamstrung when trying to pay a $25 telephone bill.

One suggestion is to set up an "imprest account" to pay routine office expenses, requiring only one signature. The authorized person (such as the executive director) has a reasonable sum to disburse from this checking account, which is entirely separate from the "master" checking account. The imprest account is replenished from the master checking account using a check that requires the usual two signatures, only upon a review by the Chairperson or Treasurer (or both) of what was expended, including supporting documentation such as receipts. The account should provide an amount needed not only to pay reasonable expenses for the month, but enough to cover expenses for part of the following month, since several days or weeks may elapse during the processing of the expense report.

The organization leadership should provide general guidelines as to what types of expenses are acceptable for reimbursement, and what expenses should be absorbed by the staff. For example, hotel accommodations in any city can range from $30-$300. A dinner can be purchased for three dollars or $75. Many organizations refuse to make decisions concerning what is appropriate, and instead provide a per diem allowance. The staff member then must absorb costs that go beyond this amount.

Many other expense issues arise that require board policies. How much should be reimbursed for mileage? What if a spouse attends a conference with a staff member and shares a room, resulting in an incremental cost increase? How will expenses be reimbursed that cannot be directly documented with a receipt? All of these issues can be resolved on an ad hoc basis, but it is useful to think about the nature of expense reimbursement before it creates problems. Many organizations have failed because their budgets were depleted by discretionary spending in the absence of an expense policy.

Chapter 11
Personnel

> Synopsis: Nonprofit corporations with staff should have a written personnel policy. There are a number of state and federal laws that apply to nonprofit operations, and many standard forms that must be filed in order to comply with these laws.

Whether a nonprofit corporation has one salaried employee or hundreds, a written personnel policy can avoid disputes which, in some cases, can destroy an organization even before it gets off the ground. Obviously, a personnel policy for a small organization will be less complex than for a large one. It is advisable to review personnel policies of several organizations of similar scope and choose among the provisions that are sensitive to organizational needs. It is not necessary to reinvent the wheel, but *having* a wheel is important.

Qualified and trained personnel are an organization's most prized assets. Staff members need to feel that the organization is flexible enough to respond to their individual needs. Conversely, the organization must have the ability to operate efficiently, effectively, economically, and to treat all employees fairly and equally. A balance must be attained, and each organization can best determine for itself where the balance lies.

Before hiring the first employee, among the issues to consider and to develop policies for are:

- Should staff be paid employees of the corporation, or should the corporation hire a consultant? (Note: federal and state law permit persons to be hired as "independent contractors" rather than employees only if two conditions are met: the individual must be free from organizational control or direction over the performance of the services provided and must be customarily engaged in an independently established trade or business.)
- What should the job descriptions of staff contain?
- How much should each staff member be compensated? Should a staff person be paid on a salaried basis or by the hour?
- If an office is established, what should the office hours be, and where should the office be located?

It may be advisable for the organization to have a personnel committee. The role of this committee is to study the issues raised in this section, develop a personnel policy for ratification by the board, if appropriate, and to serve as the adjudicating body to resolve grievances by employees.

After a decision is made to hire employees, some of the issues to consider for inclusion in a personnel policy are the following:

1. **Hiring policies (see Chapter 12)**—How should job vacancies be advertised? Will there be affirmative action to recruit minorities? Should the search be national, statewide, regional, or local? Should current employees be given preference in hiring for vacant positions?

2. **Firing policies (see Chapter 12)**—What are the conditions that permit dismissal without appeal, such as "for cause"? Will there be severance pay? Will placement services be provided? Will notice be given of unsatisfactory job performance before dismissal?

3. **Probationary periods of employment**—Should there be a period of probation during which an employee can be terminated without access to any grievance procedure or will not be entitled to receive benefits, including leave?

4. **Sick leave, vacation, personal days**—How many days will be accumulated and how? Will a doctor's note verifying the sickness be required?

5. **Holidays**—Which holidays are paid holidays and which are optional? What is the policy with respect to the observance of religious holidays?

6. **Personal days**—How many personal days will be permitted, and how will they be accumulated? If not taken, will they be "cashed-in" upon retirement?

7. **Overtime policies**—Which classes of employees are eligible for overtime pay? Is overtime mandatory if requested by the corporation? Will overtime be compensated in salary or compensatory time?

8. **Compensatory ("Comp") time**—Should comp time be granted in lieu of overtime pay? Should it be required for routine doctor/dentist appointments?

9. **Full-time vs. part-time status**—How many hours per week qualify the employee for benefits?

10. **Health insurance**—Is there a group plan? Will gross salary be increased if an employee is covered by the health insurance policy of a spouse and desires not to be covered by the organization?

11. **Pension**—How long does it take for an employee to be vested? What is the employer and employee contribution required?

12. **Life insurance, and other benefits**—Is there a menu to choose from?

13. **Employee evaluation**—Who performs the evaluation? Under what conditions may employees exercise their legal rights under Pennsylvania law to examine their employee files? Who has access to personnel files?

14. **Merit salary increases; COLA increases**—What are the criteria used for salary increases, and how often and by whom are salaries reviewed?

15. **Continuing education benefits**—Who has authority to approve requests? What are the time and cost limitations? When do employees become eligible?

16. **Staff training/orientation**—Is a pre- or post-employment physical or other examination required? Is there a formal review for new employees concerning staff personnel policies?

17. **Maternity leave**—What documentation is required? What is the maximum leave the employee may take without losing the job?

18. **Bereavement leave**—How long will such leave be, and what relatives will be included in the policy?

19. **Family and medical leave**—For what purposes will this leave be granted, what documentation is required to accompany a leave request, will the leave be paid or unpaid, and what will the effect be on unused sick leave and vacation (see #17)?

20. **Pay for jury duty, military leave**—What is the organization's policy?

21. **Sabbatical leaves**—After how many years will employees qualify, how long, and will this be paid or unpaid leave?

22. **Expense reimbursement documentation**—How shall expenses be filed and what expenses are eligible? Is there a flat per diem for out-of-town travel or reimbursement? What amount will be reimbursed for mileage?

23. **Notice required for resignation**—What is the minimum notice required and what are the sanctions for not complying?

24. **System for resolution of employee grievances**—May employees appeal to the board of directors? Is there a committee for this purpose?

25. **Disciplinary sanctions for rule-breaking**—Is there provision for suspension with or without pay?

26. **Prohibition against secondary employment**—What types of outside earned income are prohibited or permitted?

27. **Telephone policy**—What is company policy with respect to personal calls at work, including long distance reimbursement?

28. **Payroll**—Will salary be provided weekly, every other week, or monthly?

While the issues may seem intimidating, a small organization may only have need for basic policies such as hours of operation, vacation and sick leave policy, benefits provided, and holidays. The rest can be determined on an ad hoc basis by the executive director, in consultation with the board's Chairperson and/or the personnel committee, if there is one.

Major Federal Laws Affecting Employers

Taxpayer Bill of Rights 2 (P. L. 104-168)

This law was enacted on July 30, 1996, but its provisions relating to excessive income are retroactive to September 1995. It includes "intermediate sanctions" provisions that authorize the Internal Revenue Service to levy excise taxes on excessive compensation paid out by 501(c)(3) and (c)(4) organizations, and to also penalize nonprofit managers who authorize such excessive compensation. The new law also provides for increased public disclosure of financial documents (see pages 81-82).

Fair Labor Standards Act of 1938 (52 Stat. 1060, 29 §201 et seq.)
Enacted in 1938, the law provides for a minimum wage, controls child labor, and requires premium pay for overtime.

Equal Pay Act of 1963 (P.L. 88-38, 29 § 206)
Requires that men and women performing equal work be paid equally.

Civil Rights Act of 1964 (P.L. 88-352, 28 §1447, 42 §1971, 1975a-1975-d, 2000 et seq.)
Prohibits discrimination, including employment discrimination, on the basis of race, color, religion, sex or national origin. Includes prohibition of certain questions being asked by prospective employers at job interviews.

Equal Employment Opportunity Act of 1972 (P.L. 92-2615 §5108, 5314-5316, 42 §2000e)
Amends the Civil Rights Act by expanding anti-discrimination protection.

Age Discrimination in Employment Act of 1967 (P.L. 90-202, 29 §621 et seq.)
Prohibits discrimination against persons age 40-70, as revised by the 1978 amendments.

Immigration Reform and Control Act of 1986 (P.L. 99-603, 7 §2025 and other references)
Requires employers to certify that their workers are not illegal aliens, and prevents discrimination on the basis of national origin.

Employee Retirement Income Security Act of 1974 (ERISA) (P.L. 93-406, 26 § 37 et seq., 29 §1001 et seq., and other references)
Requires accountability and reporting relating to employer pension plans.

National Labor Relations Act of 1935 (49 Stat 449, 29 §151 et seq.)
Authorizes workers to form unions and other collective bargaining units.

Pregnancy Discrimination Act of 1978 (P.L. 95-555, 42 §2000e(k))
Amends the Civil Rights Act (that prohibits discrimination on the basis of sex) to change the definition of "sex" to include "because of or on the basis of pregnancy, childbirth, or related medical conditions."

Drug-Free Workplace Act of 1988 (P.L. 100-690, 41 §701 et seq.)
Requires organizations receiving federal contracts valued at $25,000 or more to certify that they will provide a drug-free workplace, notify their employees of actions taken against those who violate drug laws, and establish a drug-free awareness program.

Americans With Disabilities Act of 1990 (P.L. 101-336, 29 §706, 42 §12101 et seq., 47 §152, 221, 225, 611)
Prohibits employers with 15 or more workers from discriminating on the basis of disability.

Family and Medical Leave Act (P.L. 103-3, 29§2601 et seq.)
Requires businesses with 50 or more employees to provide certain workers with up to 12 weeks annually of family or medical leave to care for a sick spouse, child, or parent, or to care for a new child.

State Laws Affecting Pennsylvania Nonprofit Employers

Solicitation of Funds for Charitable Purposes Act (10 §161.1 et seq.)
Provides for regulation and disclosure of organizations that raise funds from the public for charitable purposes.

Child Labor Law (43 §41 et seq.)
Prohibits the employment of persons under 16 with limited exceptions, and provides labor standards for the employment of persons 16-18.

Corporation Not-for-Profit Code (Nonprofit Corporation Law of 1972 and Nonprofit Corporation Law of 1988—15 Pa. C.S.A. §7101 et seq.; §7301 et seq.; and 15 Pa. C.S.A. §5101 et seq.)
Contains codified statutes that apply to all nonprofit corporations in Pennsylvania.

Directors' Liability Act (42 §8361 et seq.)
Reduces the liability for directors of nonprofit corporations.

Equal Pay Law (43 §336.1 et seq.)

Requires employers to provide fair wages for women and persons 16-21, and to keep records of hours worked and wages paid to their employees.

Pennsylvania Labor Relations Act (43 §211.1 et seq.)

Protects the right of employees to organize and bargain collectively.

Human Relations Act (43 §951 et seq.)

Prohibits discrimination because of race, color, religious creed, ancestry, age or national origin.

Employee Records Inspection Law (43 §1321)

Requires employers to make employee records with respect to qualifications for employment, promotion, additional compensation, termination, or disciplinary action available for inspection by the employee or his/her agent during business hours, and permits the employer to require that the inspection take place during the employee's or agent's free time.

Lobbying Registration and Regulation Act (Act 93 of 1998)

Requires persons receiving compensation to advocate the passage or defeat of legislation to register with the State Ethics Commission, and to disclose certain expenditures and contacts.

Minimum Wage Act (43 §333.101 et seq.)

Sets the Pennsylvania minimum wage.

Pennsylvania Workmen's Compensation Act (77 §1 et seq.)

Provides for a worker's compensation program (see Chapter 9).

Unemployment Compensation Law (43 §751 et seq.)

Provides for unemployment compensation to workers who lose their jobs through no fault of their own (see Chapter 9).

Standard Paperwork for Corporations with Employees

Federal Forms

1. Form SS-4, Application for Employer Identification Number—This is the first form to be filed when hiring an employee. Once this form is filed, the Internal Revenue Service will establish an account for the organization and assign a federal tax number (EIN). This number will be the organization's account for paying taxes and is requested by other government authorities for tax purposes. It is requested by most foundations and grant makers as well. This form should be filed at least a month before the number is needed. To obtain this form, call the IRS toll-free at 1-800-829-3676.

2. Form W-4—Employee's Withholding Allowance Certificate—Each employee must file with the employer a copy of form W-4, which documents the number of exemptions and additional federal withholding. The information in the W-4 enables the employer to calculate how much should be withheld from gross salary (not including state and local withholding).

3. Circular E—Employer's Tax Guide—Employers need to obtain a copy of this publication (order by calling toll-free 1-800-829-3676), in order to calculate the amount of federal income tax withholding, Social Security withholding (for calendar year 1999 set at 6.2% of gross wages up to $72,600), and Medicare withholding (for calendar year 1999 set at 1.45% of gross wages, without any ceiling). The amount of wages needed to earn a Social Security credit is $740 in 1999. Workers thus will need to earn $2,960 in 1999 to earn the maximum four credits for the year. Most workers need 40 credits to be eligible for retirement benefits.

4. Form 8109 Federal Tax Deposit Coupon Book—These are coupons the corporation sends with payment for the federal withholding described above and the required federal payroll taxes. The employer is required to match the employee's contribution to Social Security and Medicare. Thus, the check should be made out for the total of federal income tax withholding plus 15.3% of gross wages and salaries of all employees, consistent with the ceilings noted above on Social Security and Medicare. Form 8109 is also used for the payment of other taxes, including Unrelated Business Income Tax (UBIT), and Federal Unemployment Tax (FUTA). These tax payments are due by the end of the month following the month in which the payments are withheld. Most corporations file their tax deposits with a local bank, making the check payable to the bank. A bank that accepts federal tax deposits can provide information on the procedures for filing correctly.

5. Form 941—Employer's Quarterly Federal Tax Return—Each quarter, the IRS will send a form for reconciling federal tax payments that were deposited for the previous quarter. The final line will indicate if the corporation owes any payments to the IRS.

6. Form 940—Employer's Annual Federal Unemployment (FUTA) Tax Return—This form must be filed if more than $1,500 was paid in wages during any calendar quarter or if the organization had one or more employees at any time in each of 20 calendar weeks.

7. Form W-2—Wage and Tax Statement—This statement is given to all employees on or before January 31 and details their gross salary and amounts withheld in federal, state, and local taxes during the previous year.

8. Form W-3—Transmittal of Income and Tax Statement—This return looks like a Master W-2, and aggregates information for all employees. It is filed with the Social Security Administration accompanied by one copy of each employee's W-2.

9. Form 990—This is the tax-exempt nonprofit corporation's tax return.

10. Form 990-T—This is a supplement to the tax-exempt nonprofit corporation's 990 tax return that reports gross income of $1,000 or more from unrelated business income during the fiscal year.

11. Form I-9—This form is kept by the employer for each worker to certify that the workers are citizens, nationals, or aliens legally authorized to work in the United States. A pre-addressed postcard for obtaining this form is included in the back of this book. For more information, write to the Immigration and Naturalization Service office that serves Pennsylvania (INS, 1600 Callowhill Street, Philadelphia, PA 19130), or call the INS toll-free (1-800-755-0777) and follow the directions from the automated communications system.

12. Form 1099 MISC—This form must be filed if the organization pays more than $600 in the calendar year to those who are not direct employees. One copy is given to the individual on or before January 31. The other is sent with similar forms to the IRS on or before February 28, using **Form 1096** as a transmittal form.

State Forms

1. PA-100—Combined registration forms and instructions. Form to request a state Enterprise Account Number, sales tax license, and sales tax exemption—First issued in 1995, this form combines several forms previously required, consolidating 36 pages into a single 17-page form, and most of these pages are specialized applications that can be ignored. Organizations seeking a sales tax exemption, or a renewal of their exemption, must also file an **REV-72.** The information provided is shared with the Pennsylvania Department of Labor and Industry, although it does not replace any forms required by that department. Thus, organizations that file the PA-100 and neglect to file Labor and Industry forms are likely to receive a notice to that effect. A pre-addressed postcard for ordering this form is included in the back of this book. The department also publishes a 36-page booklet entitled *Retailers' Information,* revised in February 1998, which explains the responsibilities of the sales and use tax laws in great detail, and provides a list of the addresses of local Revenue Department district offices. To order this booklet, call toll-free 1-800-362-2050. Many of the department's forms can be obtained online at its web site: *http://www.revenue.state.pa.us*

2. PA-501/W3—Employer Quarterly Deposit Statement and Return of Withholding Tax—These coupons are comparable to the federal withholding coupons. One difference is that the coupons are mailed quarterly with the organization's check to the Pennsylvania Department of Revenue in envelopes provided by the department. The tax withholding rate in Pennsylvania for the 1999 calendar year is 2.8% of gross wages and salaries.

3. PA Form UC-2—Employer's Report for Unemployment Compensation—This is a quarterly return to report gross wages subject to unemployment compensation. The rate is printed on the forms provided, and applies only to the first $8,000 in gross wages for each employee for each calendar year.

4. DSCB:15-5110—Annual Report, Nonprofit Corporation—A 1982 state law (Act 46) requires all corporations to file an annual report with the Department of State if there are any changes in the names of its officers. The form must be filed on or before April 30 each year. There is no fee for filing the form. A pre-addressed postcard for obtaining this form is included in the back of this book. The form can be filed in person or by mailing it to:

Department of State
Corporation Bureau
308 North Office Building
Harrisburg, PA 17120-0029

The form may also be obtained from the Bureau's web site at:
http://www.dos.state.pa.us/corp/forms.htm

5. PA-3R—State Sales Tax Coupons—This is a booklet provided by the Department of Revenue to those who have sales tax licenses. A license is required for organizations that sell products and services, unless the sale is an isolated transaction. The booklet contains four quarterly Sales, Use and Hotel Occupancy Tax Returns, which are due three weeks after the end of each quarter. The **PA-3** is the pre-printed version of this form.

6. REV-1967—State Transmittal of Income and Tax Statement—This form is mailed to the State along with copies of W-2s for each employee, on or before January 31.

Local Forms

Local taxing authorities have individual forms for the forwarding of local payroll withholding. Check with all local communities of the organization's employees for procedures and forms.

Chapter 12
Hiring and Firing

Synopsis: Nonprofits have options for staffing their agencies. A planning process is necessary when hiring and firing employees, and there are legal requirements for doing so. There is a continuum for disciplining employees short of termination.

Few can argue with the view that a nonprofit's human capital is its most important resource. The executive director influences the direction, morale, image, and financial stability of an organization. Yet even the least senior employee can have a significant impact, negative or positive, on the organization. Employees can be creative, nurturing, versatile, ingenious, inspiring, and team building. And they can be disruptive, destructive, infecting morale and creating scandal that can ruin the reputation of a charity that took decades to foster.

The recent episode involving a national United Way executive is just one example of how a single individual can stain an entire sector. The shock waves from the New Era Philanthropy scandal are continuing to be felt. As our society becomes more litigious, poor performance by an employee can have disastrous consequences. Many human services nonprofits who work closely with the aged, children, and the disabled have experience with defending the actions of their employees in court, and are at risk for damage suits in the millions of dollars. In some cases, this may be a matter of life and death for at-risk clients. The responsibility for choosing staff in a nonprofit should not be taken lightly.

Each hired employee is an investment by a nonprofit not only in the salary paid to him or her. The chemistry of an organization is changed by the new hire, and bad hiring decisions can haunt a nonprofit for many years or destroy it completely.

In recent years, nonprofits have lost the stereotype of having certain characteristics compared to their for-profit counterparts. That stereotype often viewed nonprofits as—

- less hierarchically structured
- less willing or able to fire non-productive employees
- more informally managed
- paying less and providing fewer benefits for longer hours
- more altruistically managed, with less emphasis on bottom line
- more interested in their employees' personal satisfaction

There is plenty of evidence that this stereotype is no longer valid, or is at least becoming frayed at the edges. Nonprofits today face the same competitive and financial pressures to succeed as their for-profit counterparts. Nonprofits are becoming more comfortable hiring MBAs and those with for-profit business experience to manage their enterprises, where once social work degrees were the educational pedigree of choice.

Many of the jobs available in the nonprofit sector are equally available in the for-profit sector. For example, both often require a CEO, accountants, legal staff, supervisors, receptionists, government relations personnel, public relations officers, and administrative assistants and secretaries. For many of these jobs, the actual tasks performed by nonprofit employees are indistinguishable from those performed by for-profit employees.

Regardless, it is important to recognize that those who apply for jobs offered by nonprofits may retain the stereotypical image. It is useful to consider whether a prospective employee may have an unreasonable expectation of working for a nonprofit. This can be assessed during the job interview.

Hiring requires a positive attitude, which is often missing on the part of the hirer. First, if the hiring is being done to replace a fired employee, or resigned employee, the hirer often is distracted by having the disruption caused by the separation. The hirer often is in a position of having to perform a task that is not pleasant—putting aside current responsibilities to perform the job search and interview. Few, if any, managers enjoy this process.

Before embarking on hiring a new employee, it is useful to do some planning that considers:

1. What are the tasks and duties the new employee will perform?
2. Are these tasks absolutely necessary?
3. Could someone already in the organization perform these tasks? Do these tasks require special education, professional credentials and/or experience that are currently lacking?
4. Can we obtain these services through means other than hiring an employee? (see below)
5. How long will it take to hire a new employee, and will these duties still be required?
6. How will these tasks change over time?
7. What can we expect as far as productivity of this new hire?
8. What support services will this person require? For example, will we also have to hire a secretary or administrative assistant?

Options—Advantages, Disadvantages, Legal Considerations

Hired Staff—the Sunday paper classifieds are usually filled with hundreds of job openings from nonprofit organizations who have decided to hire full-time staff.

advantages: Employees have the most stake in the organization; they tend to be loyal, may work additional hours and be flexible in doing tasks not in the job description when necessary.

disadvantages: Employees must be paid even when work is not required, require payroll taxes and expensive benefits, are paid for vacations and when sick, possibly disrupting work flow.

Paid Contractor—private for-profit companies and individuals market their services to nonprofits to perform tasks that are intended to obviate the need for hiring full-time workers.

> **advantages:** The nonprofit does not have to withhold income, Social Security, Medicare, state and local taxes, pay unemployment and Social Security taxes. Contractors can be hired for short-term or long-term projects and can be terminated easily, do not require year-round benefits (although the equivalent is often built into the contract price), and do not obligate payment by the nonprofit unless the job is completed successfully. The contractor may have skills and resources that the nonprofit would not otherwise be able to afford except on a temporary basis.

> **disadvantages:** It may be legal only under certain limited circumstances. The Internal Revenue Service publication 15-A *(Employer's Supplemental Tax Guide)* provides details on the 20 factors that indicate whether an individual is considered an employee or an independent contractor. Independent contractors sometimes charge steeply in that they must cover overhead and marketing, and make a profit.

Volunteers—unsalaried workers, some who may be there not solely because they are altruistic and want to help, but because they may be fulfilling educational requirements, or disciplinary requirements ordered by a court (see chapter 13).

> **advantages:** They do not require a salary, and they are there not for a paycheck but, with rare exceptions, because they want to be.

> **disadvantages:** They do not have the paycheck as motivation, they generally work fewer hours than employees, and may leave the organization on short notice.

Temporary Hires— hiring people for short-term employment without a promise that the employment will continue beyond a certain date.

> **advantages:** They permit the organization to respond to seasonal fluctuations in workload.

> **disadvantages:** The recruitment and administrative burden of temp workers can be substantial.

Outsourcing to another organization—either contracting with an employment service for temporary workers, or contracting with an outside organization to perform the functions, for example, a payroll and accounting service, which could otherwise be performed by an employee bookkeeper.

> **advantages**—The organization can avoid the expense and administrative hassles of hiring employees.

disadvantages—This is often more expensive on an hourly basis than would be paid if a person is hired temporarily.

Process in Hiring

Search Process. Many nonprofits, through their personnel committees, develop a procedure to hire new employees. Search committees are often authorized by the board to develop job descriptions, prepare job notices, cull through résumés to identify several candidates to interview, and recommend a candidate to the board. Others entirely delegate the process to the executive director (unless, of course, it is a search for an executive director). In either case, the basic steps remain the same:

1. **Prepare a job description.** The job description is a useful planning document for the organization, and it also allows prospective employees to decide if they are interested in, and capable of, performing the duties expected of them.

2. **Prepare a job notice.** The job notice provides standard information such as job title, description of the job, education and/or work experience required, salary range, deadline for application, and the person to contact. Decide whether the notice will request applicants to send résumés, or file applications provided by the organization.

3. **Advertise the job.** Jobs may be advertised in daily newspapers, trade journals and publications, the newsletter of your state association, through the State Job Service, with educational institutions, on-line through the Internet, and, most importantly, internally.

4. **Review the applications.** Develop a process for reviewing and ranking for the purpose of deciding who gets invited for interviews. Remember to send a letter to those not interviewed, informing them that they were not successful.

5. **Interview candidates.** The interview should be a dialogue, not a monologue by the interviewer. Let the candidate talk, so that the interviewer can make judgments about how articulate the candidate is. It is useful to be friendly, ask a few softball questions first, and perhaps make a comment about something interesting on the résumé, such as a hobby, professional association membership, or award. Ask about any years that appear to be missing on the résumé.

There are questions that should be asked by the interviewers, and questions that by law cannot be asked. Among questions that may be asked are:

- What background and experience makes you feel you would be suitable for this particular position?

- What is your educational background, and how has that prepared you for this position?

- What has attracted you to apply for a position with this organization?

- What experience, education, or background prepares you for this position that would separate you from the other applicants?

- What former employers or teachers may be consulted concerning your abilities?

- What are your long-term professional goals?

- What are the two or three things that are most important to you in a new professional setting?

- What motivates you to perform? How do you motivate those who work with you or for you?

- What are some of your most important accomplishments in your previous position, and what did you do that was special to achieve them?

- Describe a situation in that you had a conflict with another individual, and what you did to resolve it.

- Are you more comfortable working with a team on a group assignment, or by yourself?

- What are your significant strengths and weaknesses?
- Why are you shifting direction in employment?

- Where do you see yourself professionally in five years?

- How do you feel about your current/previous employer(s)?

Among questions that cannot be asked are:

- questions relating to an applicant's race, sex, sexual orientation, national origin, religion, or age

- questions relating to physical and mental condition that are unrelated to performing the job

- questions that provide an indication of the above, such as the number of children, the applicant's maiden name, child care arrangements, height/ weight, whether the applicant is pregnant or planning to have children, the date the applicant graduated from high school, and whether the applicant is a Sabbath observer

- whether the applicant has ever been arrested or convicted of a crime, without proof of business necessity for asking.

The Pennsylvania Human Relations Commission publishes a booklet on this issue, entitled *Pre-employment Inquiries: What May I Ask? What Must I Answer?* This 8-page booklet provides details on exceptions to the above prohibitions, the justification for these prohibitions and exceptions, and related issues raised by compliance with the *Pennsylvania Human Relations Act* and the *Americans With Disabilities Act.* You may request copies from the Commission at:

> PA Human Relations Commission
> Suite 300
> 101 S. Second Street
> Harrisburg, PA 17101
> (717) 787-4410

6. **Select the best qualified candidate.** This is different than selecting the best candidate. The best candidate within the pool of applicants may be identified easily, but if that person is not quite up to the task, it is a mistake to hire him or her. It is better to begin the search again, or try to find another way to have those duties performed without taking a chance that a bad hiring decision will harm the organization, perhaps irreparably.

7. **Verify information from the résumé and interviews; investigate references.** Under Pennsylvania law, you cannot refuse to hire an employee based on a prior criminal conviction, unless that conviction specifically relates to the prospective employee's suitability for employment. Even in that case, the applicant must be informed in writing of a decision based on that, in whole or in part. For some nonprofit jobs, particularly those involving children, state law requires a State Police background check. It is not unusual for job candidates desperate to make their résumés stand out to embellish their educational or professional qualifications. A few telephone calls can ferret out many of these. This is a wise investment; someone who is dishonest enough to fudge qualifications on a résumé is likely to be just as dishonest when it comes to other professional issues. Investigating references can often turn up reasons for not hiring someone. It is good practice to request permission from the applicant to check references, and to contact previous employers. While a candidate may refuse for personal reasons to permit contact with a previous employer, it is sometimes, but not always, an indication of a flawed relationship.

Among the questions that are appropriate for prior employers are:

- How long did the applicant work for you?

- How was the quality of work of this applicant?

- What level of responsibility was the applicant given?

- How did the applicant get along with coworkers?

- Did the applicant show initiative and creativity? In what ways?

- Was the applicant a self-starter, or did he/she require constant supervision and direction?

- Was the applicant punctual?

- Is there anything you can tell me that would be relevant to my decision to hire or not hire the applicant?

8. Make an offer to the candidate and negotiate salary, benefits, and other terms of the offer.

9. Put the offer in writing once the offer is successful. Use a contract, if necessary or desirable. Once the contract is signed or the offer is otherwise accepted, notify other candidates that they were not successful, and arrange to orient the successful candidate.

Firing

The loss of one's job is often the most stressful and traumatic event in a worker's life, with the exceptions of the death of a close family member or divorce. For most managers, having to fire someone is unpleasant at best, and often traumatic. In many cases, it represents a failure not just by the affected worker but by the organization.

Managers must be careful how the firing is done; employee lawsuits over firings are becoming more common. When a nonprofit is unionized, even firings for the most egregious offenses may be challenged. It is also important to make sure that there is authority to fire. For example, the board chairperson may not fire the executive director without authority from the board, unless the bylaws provide for that. The executive director may not fire the communications director, for example, unless the organization bylaws and/or job description of the executive director makes it clear that he/she has this authority.

Planning Issues

Before firing an employee, it is important to do some advance planning. Among the issues to consider are how to deal with the workload performed by the fired employee, the effective date of the termination, what to tell coworkers about the action, how to assure that the employee will not take away sensitive files and other materials, what to tell the employee about health and life insurance continuity and pension benefits, how to deal with separating personal property and organization property, how and when to terminate e-mail addresses and passwords, how much severance pay and other benefits to offer, and whether any letter of recommendation will be provided.

When to Fire

It is usually appropriate to summarily (without warning) fire an employee for gross misconduct that threatens the organization. Examples of this are drinking on the job, the conviction of a serious criminal offense, the willful destruction of agency property, stealing from the agency, or causing harm to others (such as clients or other employees). Most unacceptable behaviors that eventually result in dismissal are not as abrupt, and it is only after the manager has attempted a series of mitigation efforts that have failed that the employee is told to leave. Among these behaviors are unexplained absences, chronic tardiness, insubordination, laziness, and general poor job performance. Many nonprofit managers are close to their employees and shy away from taking appropriate discipline. They need to realize that the health of the organization requires discipline, and that they are getting paid to assure that the organization functions. Problem employees inhibit otherwise productive coworkers.

Discipline Short of Firing

Poor performance on the job may be the result of many factors. These might include personal problems of the employee, miscommunication by the manager, or skills required to perform the task that, for whatever reason, the employee does not have. Each of these has a remedy and, if the manager is flexible, dismissal can be avoided. For example, the birth of a child or serious illness of a spouse or other close family member can leave a valued employee unable to function. Some time off, flextime, counseling, or temporarily decreasing duties can all help. Continuing education can improve job skills. Improving communication from the manager, either "coaching" on how to do the job better, or at least providing some feedback on what is going wrong, can avoid nasty firing episodes. Most employees want to do well, and many believe they are doing well but are never told that their professional work is actually considered poor by those who evaluate and manage them. For some employees, however, discipline is required.

Discipline Continuum

1. **Verbal communication.** Short of the gross misconduct referred to in the beginning of this section, this should always take the form of informal communication by the manager. It should be verbal, and one-on-one—definitely not in front of coworkers. The manager should explain the problem and seek an explanation from the employee of what the manager can do to help improve the worker's ability to perform. In many cases, this will be enough. Make a notation in your records when this communication was provided and what was said, and whether the employee acknowledged the problem and agreed to improve his or her performance.

2. **Written warning.** If there is no appropriate response to the verbal communication (e.g. the employee continues to show up to work late or misses reasonable deadlines), a written memo outlining the problem should be shared with the employee. It should not be accusatory, but should state that the employee is engaging in behavior that is unacceptable, needs to be changed, and that this memo follows up on a verbal communication.

3. **Written formal warning.** This involves a formal memo to the employee from his or her immediate supervisor, similar to the written warning, but notes that this new memo will become a part of the employee's permanent personnel file. The memo

should make it clear that the person's job may be in jeopardy unless there is significant progress measured by a certain date, and that this progress will be evaluated on or shortly after that date.

4. Suspension without pay. Some employees just won't comprehend the seriousness of being late or being disruptive unless there is a real financial penalty attached. A one-day suspension, without pay, makes it clear that the manager has authority to take action, and that permanent suspension (i.e. firing) is possible.

5. Firing. This is the last resort. In the larger nonprofit, this may actually have a beneficial effect on other employees if they feel that this troublemaker is hurting the organization. In the smaller organization, firing is rarely beneficial in the short term; a poor employee is often much more productive than no employee at all. In the nonprofit organization, firing should always be for cause. It is not appropriate to fire your administrative assistant who has been faithful, loyal and productive for 10 years just because the daughter of your college professor moved to town and needs a job, even if the administrative assistant has a contract that provides for employment "at will." Even if there is no avenue for the fired employee to appeal, a nonprofit manager should be convinced that the firing is called for, and could be defended in a court of law if necessary. Some may have to defend the firing in court, or before a grievance panel of some kind, such as a human relations commission. In recent years, courts have considered "wrongful discharge" suits and have awarded damages to fired employees who were dismissed unfairly. If in doubt that the firing is both legal and appropriate, consult an attorney.

How to Fire

1. It is common courtesy to make sure that the fired employee is the first to know, other than those up the chain of command who must know or be consulted first to obtain dismissal authority.

2. Fire the person in private, in a one-on-one situation.

3. Explain to the person why he or she is being fired, point out the previous attempts to reach accommodation, but don't turn the meeting into a debate or let the person plead for his or her job. That time is too late. Explain that the purpose of the meeting, in addition to letting the person know about the firing, is to share productive information about procedures and benefits.

4. Explain applicable company procedures and benefits, such as severance pay, outplacement services, the effective date of the firing, when to turn over keys and files, and COBRA benefits. COBRA (the Consolidated Omnibus Budget Reconciliation Act of 1985) permits employees who retire, are laid off, who quit, or who are fired for reasons other than gross misconduct to continue to qualify for group health coverage for up to 18 months after termination, provided they pay the premiums. The manager may make suggestions about other jobs.

5. If appropriate, arrange for an exit interview, permitting the employee the opportunity to share information about the organization, job description, coworkers, job function, and so on. While this exit interview may not always be pleasant, the information provided may be invaluable.

Chapter 13
Volunteers

> Synopsis: Volunteers are a crucial strength for nonprofits. They can be highly motivated, and can save organizational resources. There are significant disadvantages as well. Effective strategies for volunteer recruitment, training, and retention are presented.

Introduction

Nonprofit organizations rely on volunteer assistance to perform organization functions from receptionist to board chairperson. Indeed, the term "voluntary sector" is a working synonym for "nonprofit charities."

Nonprofit organization budgets rarely permit salaries for all needed employees. During times of economic uncertainty, nonprofit organizations are particularly vulnerable to budget cutbacks, ironically at the very same time that the demand for their services increases. Using volunteers is an effective way to stretch limited organizational resources, build community support, improve communications, and tap hard-to-get skills.

The changing demographics of the '90s—more single-parent households, more two-parent working families, more women in the work-force, an increasing incentive to continue working to maintain income rather than retiring—demand that volunteer recruitment, training, support, and recognition change to meet new realities.

National statistics provided by Independent Sector validate the view that citizens are volunteering more and more. According to statistics compiled by that organization, 48.8% of adults in this country provided volunteer service in 1995. This compares to 45.3% in 1987. The monetary value of this service was $201.5 billion in 1995, based on 20.3 billion hours of volunteer work. The average volunteer donates 4.2 hours/week. A 1995 survey commissioned by Independent Sector indicates that the plurality of volunteer work assignments are with churches, synagogues, and other religious organizations (17.2%). The second leading category of beneficiary agencies is "informal" (13.5%), followed by education (11.6%), youth (10.2%), health (8.8%), human services (8.4%), work-related (5.2%), recreation (4.9%), environmental (4.7%), public/societal benefit (4.5%), arts (4.1%), and political (2.5%). All other categories comprise 3.4%.

Volunteerism is alive and well in Pennsylvania. New public-private sector initiatives are strengthening the institutions that promote volunteerism. Partnerships are developing in schools, colleges, religious institutions, and the private sector. Successful volunteer programs tap "non-traditional" sources of volunteer strength. More and more, these partnerships are being directly encouraged by government.

Federal legislation signed on September 21, 1993, the *National and Community Service Trust Act* (P.L.103-82), provides additional incentives to promote volunteerism among the young and not-so-young, and pay them living and educational stipends as well. Pennsylvania nonprofit organizations are encouraged to apply for funding under the many grant programs established by this law. The federal budget for this program was $472 million. On February 1, 1999, President Clinton proposed increasing this amount to $585 million for the fiscal year beginning October 1, 1999. This amount would fund 69,000 AmeriCorps slots, with the expectation that the number would increase to 100,000 by 2002. In the past four years, more than 100,000 citizens have served in these positions. The total proposed budget for the Corporation for National Service for FY 1999-2000 is $848 million. This funds three programs—AmeriCorps, Learn and Serve America, and the National Senior Service Corps. Interested organizations should monitor local newspapers, the *Federal Register* and *Pennsylvania Bulletin* for RFP announcements, regulations, and briefings.

Pennsylvania has its own initiative called PennSERVE, headquartered in the Department of Labor and Industry. PennSERVE is the conduit for state and federal funds to promote volunteer programs in Pennsylvania, and currently is responsible for the 670 AmeriCorps slots allotted to the commonwealth. While no funding for new programs is available during 1999, there will be a competition for additional AmeriCorps and Learn and Serve America programs early in 2000. PennSERVE staff recommend that interested organizations call and get on the PennSERVE mailing list to receive notification about new funding availability. For more information, contact:

PennSERVE
Governor's Office of Citizen Service
1304 Labor and Industry Building
Harrisburg, PA 17120
(717) 787-1971

Benefits and Considerations of Volunteers

Among the benefits of using volunteers are:

1. They do not require salaries or fringe benefits. While this is the most obvious advantage, there may be other financial savings as well.

2. They are often highly motivated. Volunteers are there because they want to be, not because it is their livelihood. If it was "just a job," volunteers might be somewhere else.

3. They can speak their minds without fear of loss of a livelihood. Volunteers can often be a useful sounding board. They are often less shy about speaking out than a paid employee might be.

4. They may bring skills to the organization that it may not otherwise be able to find or afford.

5. They may have a network of community contacts who may be a source of contributions, expertise, prospective staff, or additional volunteers.

Among other considerations are:

1. Just because volunteers are not on the payroll does not mean that the organization incurs no costs. Volunteers need telephones, workspace, equipment, supplies, desks, and virtually everything else besides a paycheck. Training and orientation costs are just as high as for salaried workers.

2. Volunteer retention is often a problem. Paid employment elsewhere may replace volunteering. Family commitments or other duties may intervene. A volunteer can be easily captured by competing interests.

3. Volunteers, just as paid staff, dislike dull, repetitive, uninteresting work, and are more likely to quickly do something about it.

4. Volunteers are generally available for fewer hours per day and have a higher turnover than salaried employees. Many, such as students, volunteer for specific time periods and for short terms. They often require more hours of training and supervision per hour of productive work performed than employees.

Nonprofit Organization Volunteer Policy

To maximize the effectiveness of volunteer help, a carefully planned strategy is recommended.

Volunteer Job Description

Individuals are more likely to volunteer to assist an organization if they have specific information about the tasks that they are being asked to perform. Before requesting volunteer assistance, develop a detailed job description that includes at least the following information:

1. Examples of duties to be performed.
2. Specific skills or training needed.
3. The location where the duties will be performed.
4. The hours per week required.
5. The time period (e.g. weeks, months) the duties will be performed.
6. The supervision or assistance that will be provided.
7. The training that will be provided.

Volunteer Recruiting

Active recruiting is required to maintain a dedicated volunteer pool. The following are some ideas for generating volunteers:

1. Pass around a sign-up sheet at community speaking engagements where potential volunteers can indicate their interest. Be sure to provide space for addresses and telephone numbers, as well as space to indicate specific skills or interests.

2. Include information about volunteer opportunities in any public relations brochures, media stories, newsletters, and public service announcements. Many local newspapers have a regular column devoted to nonprofit organization volunteer opportunities.

3. Ask users of the organization's services if they would like to volunteer, if this is appropriate.

4. Target solicitation of potential volunteers to groups in the community that are likely to have time to share. The retired, school children, and church groups are excellent sources for volunteers.

5. Post volunteer opportunities on your Web site and on general sites that permit the posting of volunteer opportunities, such as IdeaList (see page 120).

Interview potential volunteers as you would potential employees. Be sure that their interests are compatible with the organization's. Find out what their motivation is for volunteering. Is it to perform a service or advance a cause? Is it to develop marketable job skills and make contacts? Is it to have a place to "hang out" and have access to a telephone? A volunteer can have the same organizational impact, negative or positive, as a paid staff member. The fact that a person is willing to work for free does not automatically make him or her the best candidate for the "job." The organization should not lower its standards in any way. Make sure that expectations are clear and performance is reviewed.

Tell potential volunteers about the organization, and obtain basic information about them, such as their skills, training, and interests. Ask about their time availability. Once satisfied that the right volunteer is matched with the right job, review the volunteer job descriptions with them and ask them if they are ready to volunteer for specific assignments.

Orientation

Make certain every volunteer receives a complete orientation before starting to work. In some instances, a group of volunteers may participate in a formal volunteer orientation program. In other situations, a one-on-one orientation at the work site is appropriate. Make sure to include the following:

1. Overview of the organization's mission.
2. Description of the specific task to be performed.
3. Confirmation of the hours required.
4. Statement of whom to contact if help is needed.
5. Individual to contact if an assignment will not be completed as scheduled.

Rewards

While volunteers don't receive a paycheck for their services, they should receive other types of payment. Remember to thank them for the work they perform. Both informal thanks and periodic formal award ceremonies to thank volunteers are appropriate. Encourage volunteers to attend training programs to update their skills. Include them in agency social events. Remember that extra "payments" to volunteers will pay off in effective service to the organization.

Virtual Volunteering

A growing number of organizations are harnessing a new source of volunteers—those unable or unwilling to work on site, but who are eager to participate in volunteering for their favorite cause by working from their home or work computer. Virtual volunteering has obvious advantages for those who are elderly, disabled, caretakers, or who otherwise are restricted in their mobility or willingness to travel to a volunteer site. And for many others who are too busy or otherwise unable to commit to a specific time and place for their volunteering, this non-traditional method opens up opportunities.

Virtual volunteers are being used to design and update web sites, prepare newsletters, respond to requests for information, research reports, and prepare advocacy materials. Virtual volunteering has appeal to those who are too busy to make a commitment, but have the ability to fit in volunteer work from home on an ad hoc basis—provided they have a computer and a modem. While there are some limitations involved in virtual volunteering (such as no hands-on supervision or the lack of face-to-face interaction), advances in technology are providing opportunities for people who otherwise would not make a volunteer commitment to volunteer. An eye-opening feature on virtual volunteering appeared in the April 17, 1997, issue of *The Chronicle of Philanthropy,* and I expect that it won't be too long until this nontraditional strategy becomes traditional.

Impact Online, an organization founded in 1994, administers a Virtual Volunteering Project. You can find information about how to begin, and even find volunteers at this site, which can be found at: *http://www.impactonline.org/*

World Wide Web Resources (see additional resources in Chapter 20)

IdeaList

http://www.idealist.org/

This site, sponsored by the New York-based Action Without Borders, is an excellent online resource for nonprofits, and boasts the participation of 16,000 organizations in 130 countries. Nonprofit organizations can join for free, although a donation is requested. Member organizations may post information about their address, mission, contact person, telephone number, web site URL and e-mail address. The organizations are categorized by 40 types to facilitate searches by the public. Organizations post information about volunteer opportunities available, a job description, what skills are requested, and the dates that the volunteer is needed. Organizations may also post information about events and materials, such as newsletters, annual reports, and other publications. Although not required, there is an application form for posting organizations that is used to verify the information. Go to *http://www.idealist.org/penn.htm* for Pennsylvania organizations.

Support Center for Volunteer Management

http://www.genie.org

Click on "answers" and search for "volunteer management" from the pull-down menu and then click "open sesame" for the current FAQs relating to volunteer management. This site is an excellent resource.

Energize, Inc.

http://www.energizeinc.com/supervising.html

This is a "virtual appendix" to Energize's book *What We Learned (the Hard Way)— About Supervising Volunteers* by Jarene Frances Lee ($21.95). At the time of this review, six volunteer supervisors in a variety of settings posted practical advice. The page includes information on how to post your advice as well. There are other useful documents viewable at the site (see *Planning for a Volunteer Center* at *http://www.energizeinc.com/art/avolc.html*)

TIPS:

- **Interview all prospective volunteers.**

- **Make sure their duties are clearly defined, that expectations are clear, and that their performance is reviewed.**

- **Have a policy for volunteer termination or reassigning volunteers just as for paid employees.**

- **Consider having a formal awards ceremony for volunteers.**

- **Perform an "exit interview" with volunteers who leave or are terminated.**

Chapter 14
Charitable Registration

Synopsis: Pennsylvania law requires all charities receiving more than $25,000 in charitable contributions to register with the Commonwealth before soliciting funds, and it defines the term "charities" broadly. All institutions of purely public charity must register as well. There is an extensive list of information that must be disclosed. Every printed solicitation and confirmation must contain a state-approved disclaimer statement.

Introduction

Under Pennsylvania law (Act 1990-202), charities are required to register with the Department of State's Bureau of Charitable Organizations. This obligation dates at least to 1919. Act 248, enacted June 20, 1919, required charities to file disclosure statements with the Board of Public Charities and pay a $2 fee. Subsequent revisions to the law were enacted in 1925 (Act 347), 1963 (Act 337), 1972 (Act 246), 1974 (Act 297), 1975 (Act 50), and 1982 (Act 90). Regulation of charities was expanded as a result of the enactment of the *Charitable Organization Reform Act*. Act 1990-202 was amended in July 1992 (Act 1992-92) to respond to many unintended negative consequences of the law, and to permit small charities to be exempt from burdensome paperwork requirements.

Disclosure by charities was augmented by enactment of the *Institutions of Purely Public Charity Act* (Act 55), signed into law in November of 1997. By the end of 1998, the Bureau reported that nearly 6,000 charities were registered.

Institutions of Purely Public Charity Act Disclosure

Section 9 of the *Institutions of Purely Public Charity Act* requires all institutions of purely public charity to file an annual report with the Bureau of Charitable Organizations even if they are not required to do so by Act 202. The report must be filed within 135 days of the close of the institution's fiscal year. It must include a copy of the annual return filed with the IRS, the date the institution was organized, information about any revocation of tax-exempt status by the IRS, and information about its affiliates. Religious institutions and institutions that receive contributions of less than $25,000 per year and have program service revenue of less than $5 million are exempt from filing this report. An annual filing fee of $15 is required. Failure to file this report subjects the institution to an administrative penalty not to exceed $500.

General Charitable Solicitation Disclosure Law

In a manner not unlike the lobbying law, charitable solicitation law was fraught with loopholes and provided the most minimal public disclosure. The public was unable to determine which charities were not allocating the funds they raised for charitable purposes. Public confidence in charitable giving was shaken by several egregious examples of certain charities being in full compliance with Pennsylvania law, yet reserving little or no revenues for the purpose for which they were soliciting. Scores of professional fundraisers would agree to raise funds for bona fide charities, only to provide token percentages of the money raised to the organizations. The rest they applied to fundraising costs—in effect lining their own pockets at the expense of the public.

Calls for reform came from both the general public and mainstream charities themselves. As the United Way of Pennsylvania explained in a January 1991 newsletter—

> *"United Way of Pennsylvania testified in support of the legislation. United Ways and hundreds of other legitimate charities, which are 'squeaky clean,' are adversely affected and risk loss of public credibility and confidence as a result of a small but growing number of 'charitable' fundraising efforts which raise money solely or primarily for personal gain under the guise of charity."*

Act 1990-202

The end result of this call for reform was the *Solicitation of Funds for Charitable Purposes Act*, Act 1990-202. Many in the philanthropic sector welcomed true reform in charitable solicitation disclosure. But there was concern among charitable organizations that the reporting and disclosure requirements of this law were, in some cases, burdensome and costly, and placed a real hardship on them. The General Assembly responded in 1992 by enacting amendments that had the objective of applying common sense to charitable solicitation regulation.

The major provisions of this act (Act 1990-202), as amended by the 1992 amendments (Act 1992-92), are as follows:

1. Every "charitable organization" that solicits contributions from the public (including foundations and businesses) for charitable purposes must file a detailed charitable registration form with the Department of State. Charitable organizations that receive contributions of $25,000 or less annually are exempt from registration requirements, provided that they do not compensate persons to conduct solicitations.

The term "charitable organization" is broadly defined as—

> *"Any person granted tax exempt status under section 501(c)(3) of the Internal Revenue Code of 1986 (Public Law 99-514, 26 U.S.C. §501(c)(3)) or any person who holds himself out to be established for any charitable purpose or any person who in any manner employs a charitable appeal as the basis of any solicitation or an appeal which has a tendency to suggest there is a charitable purpose to any solicitation..."*

For certain organizations, there are exemptions and exclusions from requirements of the act, including some religious institutions, law enforcement and fire-fighting organizations, and certain veterans' organizations.

The term "charitable purpose" is also defined broadly in Act 1990-202 to be—

> *"Any benevolent, educational, philanthropic, humane, scientific, patriotic, social welfare or advocacy, public health, environmental conservation, civic or other eleemosynary objective, ..."*

The registration statement must be refiled within 135 days of the close of the organization's fiscal year, and must include—

- The organization's name, and names under which it solicits contributions

- Its principal address and telephone number.

- Names and addresses of organizations that share in the revenue raised.

- The names and addresses of the organization's officers, directors, trustees, and the principal salaried executives.

- A detailed financial report, including a balance sheet, statement of revenues, expenses, changes in fund balances, funds raised from solicitation, and a breakdown in expenses and, if the organization is not required to file a 990 with the IRS, a list of salaries and wages paid.

- A copy of the organization's 501(c)(3) determination letter, if it has one.

- A copy of its latest IRS Form 990 federal tax return and Schedule A.

- The date of the organization's fiscal year.

- Whether the organization is authorized by any governmental authority to solicit contributions.

- Whether the organization or any of its officers, directors, executives, or trustees have ever been enjoined from soliciting contributions in any jurisdiction or have been found to have engaged in unlawful practices with respect to solicitation or administration of charitable assets.

- A "clear description" of how the contributions will be used.

- The names and addresses of professional solicitors and related personnel who are acting on behalf of the organization.

- The names of those who are responsible for the contributions received and who are responsible for their distribution.

- Whether any of the organization's officers, directors, trustees, or employees are related to each other or to those who run or work for professional fundraisers under contract with the organization, or to any supplier or vendor providing goods or services to the organization, and the names and addresses of those related parties.

For the initial filing, the organization must provide a copy of its charter, Articles of Incorporation, bylaws, and related documents, and tax-exemption status (along with its letter of exemption, if any).

Exemptions: Hospitals regulated by the Department of Health, registered educational institutions, and certain veterans' organizations, volunteer firefighters, ambulance rescue squads and their auxiliaries, are generally exempted from the registration requirements. Senior citizen centers, charitable nonprofit nursing homes, and parent-teacher organizations are generally exempt as well. However, organizations that have a paid fundraiser are not exempt.

2. At the point of solicitation, the charity must disclose the name, address, and telephone number of a representative to whom inquiries can be addressed, a "full and fair" description of the charitable purposes, and, upon request, the source from which a copy of the organization's financial report can be obtained. Every printed fund solicitation or confirmation, or reminder of a contribution, including if the contribution was solicited and pledged orally, must include the following statement:

> **"The official registration and financial information of (insert legal name of charity as registered) may be obtained from the Pennsylvania Department of State by calling toll free, within Pennsylvania, 1(800) 732-0999. Registration does not imply endorsement."**

Exempt and excluded organizations are not required to print this disclaimer. Every oral solicitation by a professional solicitor must include a clear disclosure of the name of the professional solicitor, that the professional solicitor is being paid for his services, the name of the person acting on behalf of the professional solicitor, the name of the charitable organization, and a description of how the contribution will be used.

3. Professional fundraising solicitors (those who are paid to raise money for a charity) must file registration forms with the bureau and post $25,000 bonds.

4. Written contracts must be made between charitable organizations and their professional fundraising counsels (those who advise charities on fundraising plans for a fee) and between the charities and fundraising solicitors that disclose the fees and services that will be provided. These contracts must be filed with the Department of State.

5. The law requires filing fees of $15 for organizations with less than $25,000 in gross contributions or for those eligible for the short form (see below), $100 for contributions between $25,000 and $100,000, $150 for $100,000-$500,000, and $250 for more than $500,000. It requires a $250 filing fee for professional fundraising solicitors and fundraising counsels.

6. There are stringent criminal penalties and civil penalties for violations.

Form Requirements

The short form (BCO-400) may be filed by those organizations that solicit only to their memberships; those that accept contributions for the relief of any individual specified by name during the solicitation when all of the contributions are held in trust solely for that person; and organizations whose fundraising is carried out solely by volunteers, members, officers, or permanent employees that do not receive contributions in excess of $25,000 during the fiscal year.

The Bureau of Charitable Organizations is aggressively enforcing this act. In 1992, the bureau was handing out token $100 fines to those it discovered were violating the law, with the message that its leniency was only temporary, until charities become familiar with the law. In recent years, the bureau has added investigation and audit staff, and has been working closely with the Attorney General's Office to crack down on violators. According to the bureau, more than 1,000 charities have been encouraged to "come into compliance" as a result of education, registration, and enforcement. The bureau has also mounted a public education effort to raise awareness about fraudulent fundraising practices. While willing to work with charities that are making good faith efforts to overcome compliance difficulties, the commonwealth's enforcement efforts can be tough—the bureau's web site as of February 1999 listed 57 names for which Cease and Desist orders against charities, solicitors, and fundraising counsels are outstanding.

A packet that includes the long form, short form, excerpts of the law, and instructions for filling out the forms may be ordered from:

Commonwealth of Pennsylvania
Department of State
Bureau of Charitable Organizations
124 Pine Street —3rd Floor
Harrisburg, PA 17101
(717) 783-1720 or
(800)-732-0999

A pre-addressed postcard for ordering the forms described in this section is included in the back of this book.

Chapter 15
Fundraising

> Synopsis: The basic rule of fundraising is to ask—ask the right people at the right time in the right way. There are many conventional ways to raise funds for a nonprofit organization, and creative ways as well.

ASK.

The rest of what is needed to know about fundraising—the amount to ask, who to ask, when to ask—are technical details, which will be expanded upon in this chapter. However, the simple asking of funds for an organization is the major point of this chapter, since it is rare, but not unheard of, that funds are sent to an organization unsolicited.

Pennsylvania law requires organizations to register with the Department of State's Bureau of Charitable Organizations *before* they raise funds for charitable purposes. Before launching a formal fundraising campaign, refer to Chapter 14 to assure compliance with current Pennsylvania law.

How Much to Ask For

There are enormous differences in fundraising techniques if one is trying to raise $10 million for a new hospital wing or $633 to finance the costs of filing Articles of Incorporation, 501(c)(3) application, and a roll of stamps. There also are many similarities.

First, the organization must start with a reasonable budget plan. How much is needed to finance the organization's first year activities? Will it have paid staff? Staff salaries, benefits, and payroll taxes generally are the largest line-items in any budget. The next decision that determines the order of magnitude in an organization's budget is having a separate office, which requires rent, telephone, furniture, equipment, and office supplies.

A good practice is to prepare three budgets:

1. A "low end" budget that assumes a minimum level to get the organization off the ground. The organization would cease to function if revenue did not cover expenses in this budget.

2. A "middle end" budget, which is as realistic as possible, and considers the likely availability of funds for the year, and

3. A "high end" budget that assumes there is a millionaire "angel" who loves the organization so much that he/she is willing to keep writing checks to keep it comfortable.

In asking for money, one should tailor the "pitch" to the demographics of the contributors. It helps to understand the motivation of the contributors as well. People give money for a reason. It may be because they share the organization's motivation for starting. It may be they feel guilty because otherwise they would not be doing anything to address a problem. It may be they desire power in the organization that they can get only by being a contributor. They also may be looking for ways to get a tax deduction, align themselves with a popular cause, or to become immortal (such as by contributing an endowed chair or building wing that would have their name on it). They may be contributing to an organization because they want a particular organizational leader to be their friend or to contribute to their own favorite cause.

The most successful fundraising is done by requesting contributions from people who have money to give away, who both know and respect the organization (or someone on its board or staff), and who are given reasons for contributing that are sensitive to their private motivations.

It is a good idea to select some board or advisory committee members based on their ability to tap funds from their friends and associates. Many of their well-heeled friends will write a check to virtually any cause solely because that influential board member picked up the telephone and asked them.

It is important to ask all board members to make a contribution to the organization. Many will be delighted to do so, recognizing that the organization, to be successful, does need some start-up funding, and it will make them look foolish if the organization is stillborn as a result of lack of seed money. It is not unusual for external funding sources to consider the extent to which board members participate in making contributions. Therefore, a participation percentage of board member contributions may be as important, or more so, than the dollar amount raised from board members.

Always suggest an amount when asking for a donation. Of course, the solicitor should consider the ability of the person to give that amount. The solicitor also should give examples of how that specific amount will be used to benefit the organization (e.g. "your $2,000 donation will purchase the computer system the office needs...").

IRS Substantiation Rules

The federal *Omnibus Budget Reconciliation Act* (OBRA), enacted in 1993, imposed new requirements on charities and donors with respect to substantiation of donations for contributions made beginning with the 1994 tax year. The law requires charities to provide a contemporaneous written acknowledgment of contributions of $250 or more when requested by a donor; the donor may not take a charitable tax deduction without having such a written acknowledgment. The practical effect is that charities are sending these statements routinely to their donors as a part of the "thank you" letter. The written acknowledgment must include the amount of cash paid or a description of property transferred by the donor, a statement of whether the donor received goods or services in exchange for the donation, and a good faith estimate of the value of such goods and services, if any.

The law requires charities that provide goods or services in exchange for the donation, if the donation is in excess of $75, to provide in writing a statement to the donor that the deductibility of the donation is limited to the excess of the amount donated over and above the value of the goods and services provided, and an estimate of the value of those goods and services that were provided by the charity. For example, if your 501(c)(3) organization holds a fundraising dinner and you estimate that your costs of catering and entertainment is $45 and you charge $100 per ticket, you must disclose to ticket holders that they can deduct the contribution of $55 per ticket purchased. IRS Revenue Ruling 67-246, 1967-2 C.B. 104 provides examples of fact situations that require this disclosure.

December 1996 final draft regulations issued by the IRS provide some guidance to charities on several issues. First, charities may ignore benefits provided to members that can be used "frequently" such as gift shop discounts, free or discounted parking, or free or discounted admission to the organization's facilities or events. Second, free admission to members-only events can also be ignored if the cost per person does not exceed $6.90. For those who pay more than $75 for a membership package that offers more benefits than a membership at $75 or less, then only the benefits offered to those with membership costs of $75 or less can be ignored when taking the charitable deduction. If an organization offers free admission to a fixed number of events in exchange for membership, then the IRS's interpretation is that the fair market value of the admissions must be deducted from the value of the contribution.

Charities must provide written substantiation of a donation to volunteers who wish to claim as a deduction the cost of unreimbursed expenses of $250 or more. The regulations also require that institutions such as colleges that raise money by offering their alumni the right to purchase hard-to-get athletic tickets must consider 20% of the payment for the tickets as the fair market value for the right to purchase the tickets, and may not be deducted.

There are many gray areas with respect to substantiation issues, and the IRS has not been totally clear in providing guidance to charities. It makes sense to consult an attorney familiar with this issue if there is any question about whether your organization is in compliance with IRS requirements.

Sources of Funding

Among other sources for funding are:

1. **Umbrella Fundraising Groups** (e.g. United Ways, Jewish Federations, Catholic Charities, Junior Leagues and similar service organizations)

In addition to providing an important source of funding, membership in a federated fundraising organization provides added visibility and community endorsement. This is especially important for those agencies that lack name recognition. While membership in a federated fundraising organization carries no iron-clad guarantee that funding levels will be sustained or increased (especially in a recessionary and highly competitive fundraising environment), member organizations fulfilling priority needs can count on relatively stable funding.

Although members sometimes chafe at accountability, program, and fundraising requirements imposed by umbrella organizations, few would trade their federated funding for total independence. While it sometimes appears that existing member agencies have a total lock on funding, the trend in recent years has been toward funding "cutting edge" programs that are highly responsive to critical community needs.

2. Foundations

Major foundations usually require written proposals, many of which can be time-consuming to prepare, and there is a time lag between application (and a response to questions from the foundation on issues that were not adequately covered by the application) and when the check is in the mail. Other foundations are run by benefactors who establish the foundations for tax purposes. The benefactor may write a check as soon as the request for funds is received. Most foundation proposals can be prepared by someone without special training or education. The trick is to research the kinds of organizations and activities of interest to the foundation and tailor the grant application to that information. It is also vitally important to tailor the submission to the application guidelines of the foundation, since many proposals are rejected on technical grounds even before they are judged on their substance. Many local libraries have sections devoted to foundation fundraising, including research materials with the names, addresses, and the types of funding provided by each foundation.

One excellent source of information is the *Directory of Pennsylvania Foundations* (4th Edition), which can be found in many libraries. This book provides extensive information about the funding history of all but the smallest foundations in the commonwealth. In addition, the Foundation Center provides a wide range of materials about foundations to seven specific libraries in the state (see Appendix D).

According to *The Art of Fund Raising* by Irving R. Warner, foundations are responsible for just five percent of philanthropy. However, the individual gift may be quite substantial, and the awarding of a major gift by a name foundation can have benefits beyond the financial reward. It can serve as a catalyst for other grants and give the beneficiary organization increased credibility.

3. Direct Mail

The key to direct mail fundraising is a mailing list of people who are likely to consider making a contribution. Professional services sell mailing lists categorized by various interests and demographics. Organizations may wish to send a few newsletters to such a list, and then follow up with a direct mail appeal. If an organization is a membership organization, its members are among the first who should receive an appeal for voluntary contributions. After all, they have already indicated their interest in the organization's activities and are most likely to know what the organization is doing and how its funds are being spent.

Others to include on solicitation lists are the following:

a. Persons who benefit from the service provided by the organization and families of such persons, provided this is appropriate.
b. Individuals who are in attendance at speaking engagements.
c. Persons who make contributions to similar organizations.

A fundraising letter should appeal to some basic instinct that will make the reader have an irresistible urge to run to his or her checkbook and write a check to the organization. Appeals that honestly portray the need of the organization and the importance of the services it provides are a basic component of direct mail letters. Among the most popular appeals are those that generate:

a. **Guilt**. Make people feel guilty that they are not participating in solving some urgent problem.

b. **Affiliation**. Appeal to the need to belong to an organization that is doing something worthwhile.

c. **Self-interest.** Find some way to show that by helping the organization, donors' own lives will be improved in some way.

d. **Ego**. Make prospective donors feel they are wonderful people only if they make a contribution.

e. **Idealism**. Appeal to the idea that the world or community will be a better place for everyone and only a chosen few selfless people will help this cause.

f. **Religious need to give to charity.** Religious organizations have relied on this for years, but many secular organizations find this line of appeal equally effective for certain target audiences.

4. Businesses

Many organizations receive operating funds and in-kind contributions of services, equipment, and supplies from businesses in their communities. Among these businesses may be:

a. Employers of board members.

b.   Suppliers of goods and services to the organization.

c.   Businesses that make contributions to other organizations in the community.

d.   Businesses that sell goods and services to board members, members, or clients.

e.   Major employers in the community.

Rather than visiting a business "cold," it is effective to involve representatives of businesses in the organization's program before asking them for funds. Among ways to do this are:

a.   Have business representation on the board.

b.   Establish a "business advisory committee" consisting of local business people.

c.   Invite business representatives to an "open house" to see the organization in action.

d.   Place business representatives on the organization's mailing list. Send them the newsletter and newspaper clippings about the organization's accomplishments.

e.   Invite business representatives to speak to the organization's board or membership about their products and services.

Many business corporations have established foundations that are staffed to consider funding applications from charities. The libraries listed in Appendix E will have information about these foundations.

5. Telephone Solicitation

Similar to direct mail, telephone solicitation is effective if done with the right list of names and correct telephone numbers. A college making calls to its alumni using student volunteers will certainly have a much better response than making calls at random. Similarly, an organization is well served if it can tailor calls to those with a likely interest in the purpose of the organization.

6. Government Grants

During the 1980s, federal government grants to nonprofits, particularly for social services, plummeted. Yet there are millions of dollars in federal and state grants to nonprofits that still go begging for takers. The trick is to identify the source of funds and determine eligibility. The *Catalog of Federal Domestic Assistance* is available in many libraries. It can also be found on the Internet, in searchable format, at *http:// www.gsa.gov/fdac/*. This document provides a summary of available federal grants and the qualifications and conditions for applying. While there is no comparable publication for grants at the state level, there are several sources of information. The *Pennsylvania Bulletin* is a weekly compilation of state regulations, and requests for proposals (RFPs) of state agencies are published therein. Subscriptions are $82/year and orders should be sent to:

> Fry Communications
> Pennsylvania Bulletin Subscriptions
> 800 W. Church Road
> Mechanicsburg, PA 17055
> (717) 766-0211

Note that the contractor and subscription price for the *Pennsylvania Bulletin* may change each July 1.

Another source of state government funding for nonprofit organizations in the past has been the "legislative initiatives" program (also known as WAMs—"Walking Around Money"). This was a program of the General Assembly that permitted state senators and representatives to sponsor government funding, with few strings attached, for their constituents. While adverse court decisions and increased public scrutiny have eliminated this program for the past few years, the Community Revitalization Program of the Department of Community and Economic Development has replaced it as a source of individualized grants to politically connected organizations—at least according to a leading watchdog group, Pennsylvania Common Cause. "There appears to have been linkage between voting with the Administration position and success in securing a grant," says that organization's executive director, Barry Kauffman, who suggests that other departments may also be participating in using budgeted funds to reward legislators.

For FY 1998-99, the amount available for this program in was approximately $35 million ($45 million appropriated by the General Assembly for the year) and the proposed budget submitted by the Governor includes $20 million for the fiscal year beginning July 1, 1999.

It may be a lucrative exercise for nonprofit organizations to make their needs known to their state legislators, and see if there are any opportunities for state funding. Even if your local legislators are pariahs to the Administration, state elected officials are often aware of programs within state government that may offer funds to nonprofit organizations, such as the Pennsylvania Council on the Arts, the Pennsylvania Humanities Council, and the Historical and Museum Commission.

Many grants to nonprofits are provided by county governments. Each county in Pennsylvania has a human service director. This person is a good contact to learn about government funding opportunities at all levels.

Other than WAMs, government grants usually are accompanied by lots of paperwork and operational requirements, some of which may be inconsistent with the manner in which an organization intends to operate. Some analysts view a 1991 U.S. Supreme Court decision (*Rust v. Sullivan*) as clearing the way for the federal government to impose even more restrictions on how government funds may be spent. If applying for government grants, learn about any additional requirements, in order to be in compliance with law.

7.   Revenue-Generation Other Than Voluntary Contributions

The following are strategies used by nonprofits to increase income:

- Newsletter subscriptions
- Newsletter advertising
- Annual fundraising dinner
- Reception for a famous person or someone well-known in the field of expertise of the organization/testimonial dinner
- Sale of publications
- Sale of services
- Sale or rental of mailing lists (make sure the buyer will use the list in a manner consistent with the organization's goals and will not resell the list to others)
- Small games of chance (carefully investigate Pennsylvania legal requirements, such as Act 1988-156 and the amendment made to it by Act 1990-195)
- Wills and bequests
- Social events (e.g. bus trips to sports events)
- Newspaper advertising to request contributions
- In-kind donations
- Card calling (using board and organizational members to do peer one-on-one solicitation)
- Fees from workshops and conferences
- Sale of exhibit space at workshops and conferences
- Special fundraising events such as bake sales, flea markets, and running races

Hiring a Consultant

There are hundreds of honest, hardworking, professional fundraising counsels who will, for a fee, provide an organization with fundraising advice or even handle all fundraising. There also are hundreds who are not reputable. The *Solicitation of Funds for Charitable Purposes Act* (Act 1990-202) was designed to make it more difficult for the latter to operate. The law (see Chapter 14) provides that professional fundraising counsels register with the Department of State, post bond, and provide disclosure. Before hiring one, Pennsylvania law provides an opportunity to check him or her out with the Pennsylvania Bureau of Charitable Organizations. It is also advisable to get plenty of references.

Tips:

- Review other organizations' solicitation materials and use effective presentations as a model for solicitation.

- Never hire a professional fundraising consultant/counsel who is not registered with the Department of State or before researching the registration information that person provided.

- Keep a file of newspaper clippings about benefactors in the community and others who would have a potential interest in the work of the organization. A few well-placed and well-timed telephone calls can be effective in reaching these influential people.

- When applying for grants, ask the funding source for grant application forms and instructions.

- Involve everyone in the organization in the fundraising effort—it is not prudent to isolate fundraising from the programs it funds.

- Always thank each donor, regardless of the amount received. A $2 check from an individual may have required as much personal sacrifice as a $1,000 check from a more wealthy contributor.

Chapter 16
Writing Effective Grant Proposals

Synopsis: Grant applicants should research the grantor before applying. They should not deviate from the format of the grant application except with express permission. There is a formula to follow for effective grant applications that, among other aspects, emphasizes the needs of the community rather than the needs of the applicant.

Introduction

Competition for government, corporate and foundation grants is increasing. At the same time that funding from government sources for human services is shrinking, the demand for human services is skyrocketing. Charities are becoming more sophisticated in how they seek alternative sources of funding. Many are hiring development staff with specialized training and experience in obtaining grants. Others without the resources to make such a major investment are forced to do what they can. The purpose of this chapter is to provide a framework for the preparation of proposals for those without substantial grantsmanship experience.

It is often useful for grant seekers to develop the attitude that the relationship between themselves and the grantors is collaborative. True, all of the wonderful plans you have in mind will never come to fruition without the funds. However, the grantor needs the creativity, dedication, staff resources, and vision provided by the grant recipient. A grant proposal that is seen as simple begging is not as likely to be as successful as one that encourages the grantor to become a partner in an effort that will have substantial benefits to the community and to society.

Before embarking on a costly and time-consuming search for grants, verify that the purpose of the grant is consistent with the mission of the agency. Some organizations apply for grants simply because the money is available and obtainable, and they have a scheme to win it. However, the successful grant application may result in the organization losing its focus if the grant is inconsistent with the direction of the organization. Even if the grant's purpose is consistent with the mission, consider whether the project is viewed as constructive by agency stakeholders, such as members of the board, clients, and staff. It may be useful to convene a focus group to gauge whether the grant would truly be beneficial to the agency and its clients.

In addition, organizations should consider cash-flow issues, grant eligibility, the politics of the grant, and the source of the grant. The check from the funder may arrive months after the agency has committed itself to hiring staff and paying other project costs. Is a source of funds available until the grant funds are received? Are there laws or other grant requirements that must be adhered to that, for any reason, you are unable or unwilling to honor? Have the grants being applied for been promised informally in advance to other organizations? Does the grantor have a reputation for making unreasonable demands on organizations it funds?

Researching the Grantor

Once you believe a funding source may have funds available, do not begin to write the grant application until you have tried to find out the answer to several questions from the funding source. Try to obtain an interview with a representative of the funder before beginning to write the funding application. Among the information you should have before beginning the proposal-writing stage is:

1. The application format

Why write a 30-page application when a three-page application would have been funded? Why write a three-page application and not get funded when a 10-page proposal would have been accepted? Many government agencies will send you a *Request for Proposal* (RFP) that will outline exactly what should be included in the application. Many larger foundations will provide specific instructions. If you are given written instructions by a funding source, do not deviate from these instructions without permission. One major reason why grants do not get funded is that the writer does not follow the instructions to the letter, and even minor deviations could make the proposal ineligible. If you believe a particular instruction does not apply to your situation, request written permission from the funder to make changes.

2. Motivation of the funding source

Many funding sources specialize in awarding grants for specific purposes. You will not receive a grant from such a funder unless the proposal clearly is responsive to the vision and mission of the funding agency. When applying for a government grant, for example, obtain and study the legislative history that led to a funding appropriation. When applying for foundation funds, be sure to obtain the donor's funding instructions. Many corporate and family foundations have a priority listing of the types of programs they fund and will be glad to share this information with you.

3. The amount of funds awarded by the grantor per award, and the amount of total funds awarded

This will be extremely helpful information if you can obtain it. In many instances, a government agency has a specific allocation of funds for a particular program. Large foundations set specific priority areas and make general allocations in the priority area. Foundation directories that provide this information are available in most public libraries. It just makes no sense to develop a grant application if the funds awarded by the source are too small.

4. Successful applications that were funded in previous funding cycles

Perhaps the best indicator of the types of funding applications that will be successful is a review of actual applications that have been funded. A strong argument can be made that government agencies have an obligation to provide you (as a taxpayer) with copies of funded applications. While you may have to review the applications at the agency's headquarters or pay for duplication, you should be able to review past grants.

Many foundations will provide a list of the previous year's grants and the total of each. You can contact the individual agency and ask for a copy of its funded application. While lists of past grants are often difficult to obtain from businesses, many annual reports and business newsletters include a list of grants that have been awarded and their source.

5. The names of individuals making the funding decisions and their backgrounds

When writing a grant application, it is important to know who will be reviewing it. If the reviewers have extensive expertise in your field, you will not have to define every term. In many instances, however, a foundation trustee or a business official on the allocations committee will not have any knowledge of your particular field. You will then have to carefully explain your services in layman's terms, spell out every abbreviation, and define each technical term you use.

6. The criteria used in making the grant selection

Knowing the selection criteria can be crucial in determining how to write a grant. Many grantor agencies have limited amounts of funds and will give preference to smaller grants. Others will make the selection based on non-cost factors and then negotiate the cost of the proposal. Knowing whether it will be helpful or harmful to have political officials contact the grantor agency is important information.

Sections of a Grant Application

1. Cover Letter

Many grant applications specifically request a cover letter and define what information should be included. If this is not specifically prohibited by the grant application format, write a short cover letter on agency stationery that:

- Is addressed to the individual at the grantor agency whose name, title, agency name, and address are absolutely correct

- Contains a one-sentence description of the proposal

- Provides the number of participants, jobs obtained, or other units to be funded by the grant

- Lists the total amount of funds requested

- Provides the name, address, and telephone number of the individual at the agency to contact to request additional information.

2. Executive Summary

Include in this section a succinct summary of the entire proposal.

3. Introduction

Provide important information that may not otherwise appear anywhere else in the grant application. Items you might include are the following:

- Your agency's mission
- How long you have been providing the type of service included in this program
- Brief history of your agency
- Major indicators that you are capable of operating programs efficiently and effectively
- If there are eligibility requirements in the proposal, state that you are eligible to receive the funds
- Statement of your I.R.S. Section 501 tax-exempt status
- Outline of letters of support from past clients, from representatives of cooperating agencies, and from legislative officials (The letters themselves should be included as appendices to the application.)
- Statement of how you will obtain funding for the program at the end of the grant period.

4. Need

For a grant to be funded, the agency must demonstrate the need of the individuals in the community for the service to be provided. What is the extent of the need and how is the need documented? The need described should be the need of the individuals in the community for the services, not the need of the agency. Rather than stating "we need a counselor because our agency doesn't have one" or "the funds for the one we had were cut back by the government," estimate the number of individuals who need counseling services. The need should be the need in your coverage area. While national or statewide figures might be given, if you serve a particular county, the estimate of need for that county should be provided. The need should be the need for the particular service you are providing. If you provide services for victims of domestic violence, for example, the estimated number of victims of domestic violence should be provided rather than unemployment figures or other available statistics. The need should be quantified. How many individuals do you believe are eligible for the particular service you provide in your coverage area?

Common sources of data are the following:

1. Census Data—Make certain you are using data from the 1990 and later censuses. In most cases, 1980 data is outdated. The "experts" on the census are at the Pennsylvania State Data Center, Penn State-Harrisburg, Middletown, PA 17057; (717) 948-6336.

2. County Planning Commissions—Call the office of your county commissioners to find the number for your county's planning commission.

3. State Agencies—The Departments of Education, Health, Labor and Industry, and Public Welfare are all excellent sources of data. The Department of Public

Welfare and the Department of Labor and Industry's Bureau of Employment Security have offices in each county.

4. Local Governments—Local police departments are excellent sources of crime data and local school districts can provide educational information.

5. Self-generated data—In many cases, you can provide the data from sources within your agency. Sources might be:

- Waiting lists
- Letters from potential clients requesting a service
- Letters complaining that a particular service is not in existence
- Testimony at public hearings
- Information obtained from questionnaires administered to present clients asking them to list other services they might like
- Community surveys

5. Objectives

Objectives are the proposed results of the project. Objectives should have the following characteristics:

- They are measurable. How many individuals do you estimate will participate in your program?

- They are time-based. How many individuals do you estimate will participate in your program in the next three months? In the next year?

- They are realistic.

The information to measure objectives can be obtained as part of your program. Do not list objectives in your proposal if the information to measure them would be impossible to obtain if the proposal is funded.

6. Project Description

Here is where you will outline your program. An easy way to remember what to include is to include the 6 W's of program writing:

1. Who? Who are the clients? How are they selected? What are the restrictions (e.g., age, income, geographical)? Who are the staff members?

If you are asking the funding source to pay for new staff members, include a job description and a qualifications statement that lists the educational, experience, and other job requirements. If you are applying for funds to continue existing staff, include a résumé and a biographical statement for each staff member.

2. What? What services will be provided? For educational programs, include a course outline. You may include relevant sections of an operations manual. For other programs, a narrative outlining the services would be appropriate. Still others might provide a "day in the life of a client." What outreach efforts will be made?

3. Where? Where will the services be provided? Give addresses of all main and field offices. If you will be obtaining new space with the program funds, what type of space are you seeking?

4. When? What are the hours that services will be provided? On which days during the year will services be provided? It is also useful to provide a timetable for project implementation.

5. With whom? What other agencies are participating with you in the provision of services? For example, include agencies referring clients to you for service. Outline the agencies to which you refer clients. It is important to obtain letters from the other agencies confirming any relationships you are describing.

6. Why? Why are you providing these services rather than other alternatives? Are you providing any unique approaches to the provision of services?

7. Budget

If it is not clear from the grant application forms, ask the funding source how much financial detail is required. Many businesses, for example, may only require the total amount you are going to spend. On the other hand, most government agencies require a line-item budget that includes a detailed estimate of all funds to be spent. Such a budget might be set up to include the following:

1. Personnel costs (salaries, fringe benefits, consultant and contract services)

2. Non-personnel costs (travel, space, equipment, consumable supplies, and other costs such as telephone, postage and indirect costs)

Some grantor agencies may require your agency to contribute a matching share. If you are permitted to include in-kind or non-cash expenditures, use the same budget categories as above. In the personnel category, for example, you would list the worth of the time volunteers are contributing to your program. In the non-personnel category, you would include the market value of the equipment donated to your program.

8. Evaluation

Inform the funding source that you will be conducting an evaluation of the services you are providing.

1. Detail who will participate in the evaluation process. Outline the participation of board members, staff members, clients, experts in the substantive field, and representatives of the community in the evaluation process. Some grantors require an independent evaluator.

2. Explain what will be evaluated. List some of the issues the evaluation team will consider. For example, the evaluators will review whether the need was reduced as a result of providing the services. Were the objectives met? Were the services provided as outlined in the Project Description section? Will the budget be audited by an outside firm and, if not, who will review the receipts and expenditures?

3. Specify what type of evaluation will be provided. Provide in as much detail as you can how the program will be evaluated. If formal classes are provided, include the pre- and post-test you will use to evaluate the classes. If a client questionnaire will be used, attach a copy to the application. Describe how the program data will be reviewed in the evaluation process. Include a description of the audit or the process you will use to review the budget items.

9. Conclusion

In no more than two or three paragraphs, summarize the proposal's main points and the reasons why the community will be improved as a result of successful completion of the project.

When you have finished writing your grant application, ask yourself the following questions before you send it to the funding source (in plenty of time to meet the application deadline):

- Is it free of the jargon of your field?
- Are all abbreviations spelled out the first time you use them?
- Have you followed all of the instructions in the Request for Proposal (RFP)?
- Are all words spelled correctly? Remember that your computer's spell-checker only tells you that the words you use are English, not that they are the correct words.
- Is it interesting to read?
- If you were the grantor agency, would you fund it?

Finally, get the application in the hands of the grantor before the deadline. The fundraising field is replete with horror stories about multi-million dollar proposals that were not even considered because someone put the application in the mail and it didn't arrive until well after the deadline. Make sure there is enough postage if the application is mailed. It is highly recommended that applications be either hand-delivered or sent by overnight courier, such as Federal Express or Airborne Express. Make several office copies before submitting the original, and be sure that you provide the number of copies requested by the grantor.

Chapter 17
Lobbying

> **Synopsis:** Those who attempt to influence state legislation or administrative actions must register with the State Ethics Commission and disclose certain expenses. There are effective strategies to communicate with legislators in person, by letter, or by telephone.

Lobbying is the time-honored tradition of communicating with elected or appointed officials for the purpose of influencing legislation and other public policy. The word itself derives from the outer room of the legislative chambers where paid professionals congregated, seeking to button-hole legislators before they cast their votes. In recent years, the term has developed a pejorative character as the public, justified or not, perceives special interest lobbyists as using their influence to work against the public interest.

Whether referred to as "advocacy," "government relations," or "lobbying," it is a right afforded by the first amendment to the U.S. Constitution and Article I of the Pennsylvania Constitution relating to freedom of speech, as well as the right to petition to redress grievances. Many of the public policy decisions made in Washington, Harrisburg, and by municipal government leaders have a direct effect on nonprofit organizations and the interests and clients they serve.

Many nonprofits are expressly created to advance one cause or another that is considered by a government body.

Organized lobbying is an effective way to communicate an organization's views on a pending issue, to promote a favorable climate for those served, and to directly influence the outcome of decision-making. In Harrisburg, many of the more than 800 registered lobbyists are employed by organizations who view themselves as working in the public interest—speaking for the poor and disenfranchised, improving the environment, establishing programs to serve the disabled, or expanding government support for vital human service and community needs.

Legal Requirements for Lobbying

On October 15, 1998, Governor Tom Ridge signed into law the *Lobbying Disclosure Act of 1998* (Act 93). This new law is a comprehensive registration and reporting law similar to that applicable in most states. Before this law was passed, Pennsylvania had, arguably, one of the weakest laws on the books, and there was only minimal enforcement. The new statute, which will take effect on August 1, 1999, will require lobbyists to register and make reports to the State Ethics Commission rather than the Clerk of the House and Senate. Lobbying is defined in the law as:

"Lobbying." An effort to influence legislative action or administrative action. The term includes:

(1) Providing any gift, entertainment, meal, transportation or lodging to a state official or employee for the purpose of advancing the interest of the lobbyist or the principal; and

(2) direct or indirect communication.

Legislation and legislative action are defined broadly:

"Legislation" is defined as:

Bills, resolutions, amendments and nominations pending or proposed in either the Senate or the House of Representatives. The term includes any other matter which may become the subject of action by either chamber of the General Assembly.

"Legislative action" is defined as:

An action taken by a state official or employee involving the preparation, research, drafting, introduction, consideration, modification, amendment, approval, passage, enactment, tabling, postponement, defeat or rejection of legislation, legislative motions, overriding or sustaining a veto by the Governor, or confirmation of appointments by the Governor or of appointments to public boards or commissions by a member of the General Assembly.

The State Ethics Commission is required to develop regulations to implement the new law, with appropriate opportunities for public comment, by April 13, 1999 and submit them to the Independent Regulatory Review Commission. The latest version of the regulations as of press time was published in the *Pennsylvania Bulletin* on January 30, 1999, and the text may be found at the commission's web site *(http:// www.ethics.state.pa.us/PA_Exec/Ethics/lobbyregs.pdf)*.

General Registration and Reporting Requirements

Lobbyists (defined as "any individual, firm, association, corporation, partnership, business trust or business entity that engages in lobbying on behalf of a principal for economic consideration. The term includes an attorney who engages in lobbying.") and Principals (defined as "Any individual, firm, association, corporation, partnership, business trust or business entity on whose behalf a lobbyist influences or attempts to influence an administrative action or a legislative action") are required to register as such with the State Ethics Commission within 10 days of acting in any capacity as a lobbyist or principal.

Lobbyists must disclose their names; permanent business addresses; daytime telephone numbers; the names, permanent business addresses and telephone numbers of their principals; and the registration numbers and acronyms of affiliated political action committees. Lobbyists are also required to provide a recent photo of themselves. Each lobbyist must file a separate registration statement for each principal represented.

Principals must disclose their names; permanent addresses; daytime telephone numbers; the name and nature of their businesses; the names, registration numbers and acronyms of affiliated political action committees; the names and permanent business addresses of their lobbyists and, if the organization is a principal, the number of dues-paying members in the past calendar year.

Changes to registration statements must be filed within 14 days after the change occurs.

General Reporting Requirements

Lobbyists and principals must file quarterly expense reports with the commission. The report must list the names of all lobbyists by whom the lobbying was conducted, the general subject matter or issue being lobbied, and aggregate, good faith estimates of the total amount spent for personnel and office expenses relating to lobbying, including salaries and other forms of compensation. It is sufficient to report prorated salaries for lobbying activity. The report must also include a single aggregate good faith estimate of the total amount spent for direct communication; the total costs for gifts, entertainment, meals, transportation, lodging and receptions, given to or provided to state officials or employees or their immediate families; a single aggregate good faith estimate of the total amount spent for indirect communication, and report each occurrence of a state official or employee receiving from a principal or lobbyist anything of value that would otherwise need to be reported. If an official or employee is named in an expense report, then he or she must be given written notice of that fact to permit disclosure under the ethics standards and financial disclosure section of the new law.

No registration or quarterly reports are required from those whose lobbying activity is limited to preparing testimony and testifying before a committee of the General Assembly or participating in an administrative proceeding of an agency. If an individual engages in lobbying on behalf of that individual's employer, and the activity represents less than the equivalent of $2,500 of that employee's time during any reporting period, then that employee is exempt. Also exempt are principals whose total expenses for lobbying during any reporting period do not exceed $2,500. There are additional exemptions in the law.

Fees

There is a biennial fee of $100 for lobbyists and principals, payable to the State Ethics Commission for purposes of expenses associated with administering the law.

Forms

The State Ethics Commission is in the process of developing forms to use for both registration and reporting. Neither will be available until the Independent

Regulatory Review Commission approves the final regulations of the commission. When it does so, these forms will likely be able to be accessed not only by mail (State Ethics Commission, 309 Finance Building, P.O. Box 11470, Harrisburg, PA 17108-1470) but through the commission's web site at: *http://www.ethics.state.pa.us/ PA_Exec/Ethics/*. For more information, contact the commission at (717) 783-1610.

Penalties

It is a second-degree misdemeanor to fail to register or report as required by law. If the violation is found to be intentional, the penalty is bumped up to a third degree misdemeanor. In addition, the commission has the authority to prohibit the violator from lobbying for up to five years.

Effective Strategies for Lobbying and Advocacy

- Know Your Legislators—Give them the information they need to help the nonprofit organization meet its objectives.

- Identify Key Contacts—Survey the organization's network to discover who has a personal or professional relationship with key public policy decision-makers, and who contributes to political campaigns.

- Target Decision-Makers—Pay special attention to legislative leadership, the majority and minority chairpersons of relevant committees, and their staffs.

- Use Local Resources—Identify constituents connected to the organization, and match them up with their legislators for advocacy contacts.

- Schedule Lobby Days—Many nonprofit organizations and other groups schedule a Capitol lobby day. Such events typically include a briefing on an important pending issue by an organization's executive director, a rally and/or press conference in the Capitol Rotunda, scheduled office visits to local legislators and legislative leadership, and a closing session to exchange information gleaned from those visited.

- Schedule Press Conferences—Non-governmental organizations can hold press conferences in the Capitol Rotunda or on the steps of the Capitol. This is done by scheduling the event with the public events bureau of the Department of General Services. The bureau's telephone number is (717) 783-9100. The bureau provides the sound system, and there is no fee. Organizations should post a notice in the Capitol News Room (E-524, Main Capitol) announcing the time, date, and purpose of the event. A day or two prior to the event, 40 copies of the news release should be delivered to the Capitol News Room manager. He or she will distribute them to the media outlets that routinely cover the Capitol.

- Circulate Petitions—While viewed as one of the least effective forms of lobbying, the presentation to a legislator or government official of a petition signed by thousands of persons is a worthy "photo opportunity" and may get some coverage.

- Present Awards—Many nonprofit organizations present a "Legislator of the Year" or similar award to recognize key legislators for their interest in the issues of concern to that nonprofit. These awards further cement a positive relationship and ensure continued access to that legislator.

- Arrange Speaking Engagements—Most legislators are delighted to receive invitations to address groups of their constituents. Such gatherings provide opportunities to educate the legislator on issues of interest to the organization.

- Provide Contributions—Money is still considered to be the mother's milk of politics. While corporations, by law, cannot make contributions themselves, individuals and corporation-affiliated Political Action Committees (PACs) may and do. Those that make contributions find that their access to public policy makers is vastly improved. As a general rule, the more an organization's activities are perceived to be in the public interest, the less need there is to rely on making political contributions to develop access and to deliver the organization's message.

- Request Public Hearings—Public hearings held by a legislative committee provide an opportunity for media coverage, a forum for an organization's point of view, and a way to galvanize support for an issue. Having an organization's clients fill a hearing room sends a clear message to the committee members and staff.

While it is true that the suggestion by a committee chairperson to hold hearings on an issue may be a strategy to delay or kill a bill, public hearings can nevertheless be utilized by the organization to focus attention on an issue. A hearing can generate public and media support. It can provide a forum for improving the proposal, thereby minimizing opposition to the legislation.

501(h) Election

The U.S. Congress in 1976 enacted a new law that expanded the rights of nonprofits to lobby. However, it was not until August 30, 1990, that the IRS and Treasury Department promulgated final regulations to implement this law. In the preceding 14 years, there was a pitched battle between nonprofits and the Congress. Nonprofits fought diligently to preserve their rights to lobby under the Constitution and the 1976 law. Some in the executive branch also sought to deny those rights. The principal issue is the definition of the term "substantial," since the law prohibits 501(c)(3) nonprofits from carrying on "substantial" lobbying activities.

The regulations permit electing organizations to spend on lobbying, on a sliding scale, up to 20% of their first $500,000 in expenditures, and up to 5% of expenditures over $1.5 million, with a $1 million ceiling in each year. Organizations can spend no more than a quarter of their lobbying expenses on grass roots lobbying (communications to the general public that attempt to influence legislation through changing public opinion).

These regulations exclude certain expenditures from lobbying, including—

1. Communications to members of an organization that brief them on provisions of legislation, but that do not urge that they take action to change those provisions.
2. Communications to legislators on issues that directly affect the organization's own existence, such as changes to tax-exempt status law, or lobbying law.

Of major importance to nonprofits, the organization is no longer subject to the "death penalty" (i.e. the total revoking of their tax-exempt status) for violations. Instead, a system of sanctions is used.

All 501(c)(3)s must report the amount they spend on lobbying on their 990 tax returns.

Lobbying Disclosure Act

President Clinton, on December 19, 1995, signed into law the *Lobbying Disclosure Act* (P.L. 104-62). This is the first major lobbying reform at the federal level in almost 50 years. The new law took effect on January 1, 1996.

The law now requires lobbyists who lobby the President, Vice President, members of Congress, and high-ranking members of the executive branch to register with the House and Senate within 45 days after a lobbying contact. A lobbyist is defined as a person employed or retained by a client whose lobbying activities include more than one contact, but not when the lobbying activities constitute less than 20% of the lobbyist's time over a six-month period. Registration is required only when the lobbying income is more than $5,000, or when total expenses are more than $20,000. Lobbyists required to register must also file six-month activity reports that detail who they represent, how much they are paid, who they have lobbied, and what issues they lobbied on. Section 15 of the law permits those tax-exempt charities required by the IRS to report lobbying expenses to make good faith estimates of their lobbying expenses. The bill also includes a provision (Section 18) that places restrictions on lobbying by nonprofit civic leagues and social welfare organizations, among others, that receive federal funds.

IRS Regulations on Lobbying

The August 1990 regulations of the Treasury Department with respect to lobbying are quite complicated. An excellent 1995 57-page publication, *Being a Player, A Guide to the IRS Lobbying Regulations for Advocacy Charities,* is available from The Alliance for Justice, 2000 P Street, Washington, D.C. 20036. The guide explains in clear and precise terms what is permitted under these regulations, and includes many sample forms and worksheets. The cost is $15. Obviously, the booklet will need to be updated to reflect the requirements of the *Lobbying Disclosure Act.*

Contacts With Legislators

1. Visiting a Legislator

- make an appointment, if at all possible

- arrive promptly, be warm and courteous, smile, speak for five minutes or less on a single issue

- don't threaten, or exaggerate your political influence (if you are really influential, the legislator will already know)

- listen carefully to the legislator's response and take notes; be polite, but keep the legislator on the subject

- leave the legislator with something in writing on the issue, if possible

- request that the legislator do something to respond to the organization's position—vote in a specific way, take action on a problem, or send a letter to legislative leadership requesting action

- follow up the meeting with a thank-you note, taking advantage of this second opportunity to reinforce the organization's views and remind the legislator of the action requested

- do not feel slighted if referred to a staff member—legislators often have last-minute important meetings or unscheduled votes. Staff members are valued advisors who, in some cases, have as much influence as the legislator (or more) in the process and may have more time to help

2. Writing to a Legislator

- restrict letters to one issue; be brief and concise

- clearly indicate the issue of concern, the organization's position on it, and the bill number, if known

- write the letter in a manner that will require a written response, and include a return address

- use facts to support positions, and explain how the issue affects the organization, its members, and the community

- use professional letterhead, if appropriate; type the letter, if possible, or write neatly and legibly

- try not to indicate that the letter may be a form letter sent to scores of other legislators

- make the letter positive—don't threaten the loss of votes or campaign contributions

- follow up after the vote on the issue to indicate to the legislator that the organization is following his or her actions with interest and that it appreciated or was disappointed by that vote

3. Telephoning a Legislator

- speak clearly and slowly

- make sure that callers identify themselves in a way that will permit the legislator to reach them or the organization by letter or telephone

- follow the guidelines listed above for writing and visiting, which are equally appropriate for telephoning

Tips:

- **Those who expect to spend a substantial amount of time in legislators' offices should register as lobbyists, even if they feel the law may not require them to do so. The judge of whether the person doing the advocacy is in compliance with lobbying laws will not be that advocate.**

- **Comply with all reporting requirements, keeping in mind that a violation of the state or federal lobbying laws may result in serious criminal penalties.**

- **If the nonprofit corporation is a human service provider, invite local legislators to tour the facility and observe the services being provided.**

- **If the corporation is a membership organization, invite local legislators to speak to the membership.**

- **Encourage members to make individual contributions. It is good advice not to get involved in partisan politics, particularly if the corporation has 501(c)(3) status. Those that do choose to participate in partisan politics should be scrupulous about separating personal political activities from the corporation and not using corporate resources for partisan political activities.**

Chapter 18
Political Activity by Nonprofits

Synopsis: Charities are proscribed by law from engaging in electioneering. However, many political activities, such as candidate forums, questionnaires, awards, and compiling voting records, are not only permissible but are important activities for charities and other nonprofit organizations.

Introduction

Volunteer leaders and executives of nonprofit organizations are, generally, key opinion makers and play an important role, both in their organizations and in their personal lives, in shaping public policy. Many elected officials got their first taste of community service by serving as a nonprofit board volunteer. Many elected officials continue to serve on nonprofit boards, and their expertise, and political influence, are often of great value.

Yet there has been an historic concern that nonprofits, particularly nonprofit charities, may be using taxpayer-financed subsidies to unduly influence the outcome of elections. This concern has been codified in federal and state law that, in general, prohibits 501(c)(3) organizations from engaging in political activity, and places severe restrictions on other tax-exempt organizations. Pennsylvania law mimics federal law, prohibiting corporations and unincorporated associations, other than Political Action Committees (PACs) and other organizations formed solely for political activity, from making contributions or expenditures in connection with the election of a candidate. Referenda issues are not covered by this law, however, and charities are free to actively support or oppose them.

A 501(c)(3) organization by federal law explicitly may "not participate in, or intervene in (including the publishing or distributing of statements), any political campaign on behalf, or in opposition to, of any candidate for public office." This means that 501(c)(3) organizations may not participate in political campaigns of candidates for federal, state or local office. Under state and federal law, no corporation, nonprofit or for-profit, may make campaign contributions. However, any expenditures by a charity, for or against a candidate, can result in the loss of the organization's tax exempt status, the assessment of a large excise tax, and potential fines against the charity's executives and volunteers. Charities may not endorse candidates or oppose candidates for public office. Generally, a person is considered to be a candidate for public office when he or she makes a public announcement to that effect, or files a statement with the elections commission of an intention to run. Expenditures made prior to that time or after the election are not considered to be political activities.

Dept. of Treasury regulation §*1.501(c)(4)-I(a)(2)(ii)*, as amended in 1990, expressly forbids 501(c)(4) organizations from engaging in direct or indirect participation in political campaigns on "behalf of, or in opposition to, any candidate for public office" as part of its definition of "social welfare." However, a subsequent IRS Ruling (Rev. Rul. 81-95, 1981-1 C. B. 332) has interpreted that this regulation does not impose a total ban on political activity by 501(c)(4)s. The level of political activity that is permitted by 501(c)(4)s without jeopardizing their tax exemptions is still unclear. What is clear is that the political activity by the organization must not be a substantial part of its activities, and the activity must be consistent with the organization's social welfare mission, according to the May 1992 *Harvard Law Review* (p. 1675), which provides substantial guidance and applicable case law on this complicated legal issue.

Among the types of expenditures that may be considered political activity are candidate travel expenses, fundraising expenses, polls, surveys, candidate position papers, advertising and publicity, and money paid to the candidate for speeches or other services. Expenses relating to non-partisan voter registration drives are not considered political expenses.

Individual Political Activities

Volunteers and agency staff of charities have the same First Amendment rights as anyone else. There is no prohibition against such persons making political contributions, volunteering to work on a campaign, signing letters of support (provided any reference to their charitable organization affiliation clearly indicates that the reference is for identification purposes only), and issuing statements on a candidate's behalf. However, the resources of the charity cannot be used for electioneering. Charitable organization leadership and staff should not write letters on a charity's stationery in support of a candidate. They should not turn the offices into a *de facto* campaign office for the candidate, using the telephone, copy machine, computer, and other resources, even during non-business hours.

Penalties

Beyond the sanctions of loss of tax exemption authorized by the 1954 Revenue Act, the Revenue Act of 1987 increased the sanctions available to the IRS in enforcing the prohibition against political activities. It also provided the IRS with the authority to seek an injunction to bring about an immediate cessation of violations that are deemed to be "flagrant." Most political campaign expenditures by 501(c)(3)s and 501(c)(4)s are now subject to a 10% excise tax applied to the organizations and a 2.5% excise tax (up to $5,000) applied to each of the managers of the organization who knew that a political expenditure was being made. This tax only applies if the expenditures were willful, flagrant, and not due to reasonable cause. If the illegal expenditure is not corrected, an additional 100% tax is imposed on the organization and 50% (up to an additional $10,000) on each manager who knew of the violation. Correcting the violation means that the managers tried to recover the contribution and took steps necessary to stop future violations.

While this area of law has a substantial gray area, there are several important general rules to be aware of in guiding an agency's quasi-political activity. Each case that has been decided by the IRS is fact-specific, and their rulings provide only general guidelines. The best advice for charitable organization leadership and staff is to provide a wide margin for error when contemplating engaging in political activities and not to engage in any activity that would even raise the specter of being improper, even if such an activity falls within the legal framework provided by current case-law.

Quasi-Political Activities

Among the most common issues raised by charities are the following examples of border-line, quasi-political activities:

1. Voting Records. There is nothing illegal about a charity annually publishing a compilation of voting records of the Congress or the General Assembly. Some guidelines to follow are that the compilation should not be released only before an election, it should list the voting records of all of the public officials or in a relevant region (rather than selecting out only those who are up for re-election, or who are targeted by the organization because they consistently vote for or against the organization's public policy positions), it should involve a wide range of subjects, it should not imply approval or disapproval of the public officials, and it should not be disseminated beyond the membership or mailing list of the organization, i.e. the general public.

2. Questionnaires. It is not only permissible but advisable for charities to communicate with candidates, informing them of the organization's positions on issues and requesting their views. When candidates run for office, it is a vulnerable time for the shaping of their public policy positions. Many regret the positions they have taken during the election in response to a seemingly innocuous questionnaire. However, the use of these responses by an organization can be troublesome.

The IRS has ruled (Rev. Ruling 78-248) that it is permissible for charities to send a questionnaire to candidates and publish the answers in a voter's guide. However, the charities should make an effort not to demonstrate obvious bias in the questions, or to favor one candidate over another by making editorial comment. Organizations with a narrow range of interest, such as a Pro-Life or Pro-Choice group, are more in jeopardy by publishing the results of a questionnaire than a group with a broader range of interests, such as the League of Women Voters. If it is viewed by the IRS as a back-door method to influence how your constituency votes, then it could place an organization's exemption in jeopardy.

3. Public Forums. Many 501(c)(3) organizations have a Candidates' Night to permit their volunteers and staffs to meet the candidates and question them about issues. This is not illegal, and is expressly permitted by the IRS, provided it ensures "fair and impartial" treatment of the candidates (Rev. Rul. 86-95). However, such programs should be conducted with common sense. The moderator should be someone who can be even-handed. All *bona fide* candidates should be invited, although it is not a prerequisite that they all accept the invitation for the event to be scheduled. Organizational leaders should refrain from making editorial comments about the positions of the candidates. Any account of the event in the organization's newsletter or other publication should be even-handed and should refrain from making editorial comment in favor of, or in opposition to, a candidate's views.

4. Mailing lists. The mailing list of a charity may be a valuable asset in the hands of a candidate. Many organizations get substantial revenue from selling, or renting, their mailing lists. There is no prohibition against selling a mailing list to a candidate for public office. However, giving the mailing list to a candidate is tantamount to making a political contribution. Also, all candidates must be given the same opportunity to purchase or rent the mailing list; no favoritism is permitted. As noted elsewhere in this publication, the sale or rental income from organizational mailing lists is potentially subject to federal unrelated business income tax, despite recent court rulings that decided they are not.

5. Awards. Many charities give "Legislator of the Year" or "Public Citizen of the Year" awards or similar citations to elected officials. However, making such an award just prior to an election in which the awardee is a candidate may be considered improper electioneering. From a practical viewpoint, even if this is done without any intention to help that candidate, a charitable organization's volunteers or contributors who may not like that particular candidate could view it as a disguised attempt at electioneering. It is a good policy to avoid providing awards to candidates during election periods.

Note: The above analysis is not intended to serve as legal advice about any particular set of facts, but only as a review of currently available reference materials on this issue. Consult a lawyer for a definitive answer to any particular legal problem.

Tips:

- If you as a nonprofit executive are a "political animal" who *must* get involved in partisan political activity, find another entity, such as a PAC or a political party committee, to channel those energies, and never use your organization's stationery for political purposes.

- Seek experienced and competent legal counsel before engaging in any political activity that falls into a gray area.

- Use permissible political activities to the advantage of the organization, such as candidate forums, candidate questionnaires, and awards to public officials.

Chapter 19
Communications

Synopsis: Organizations need to effectively communicate their objectives, activities and accomplishments to attract funding, participation, and public support. Publications, media contacts, and workshops are among the methods to communicate organizational interests.

Introduction

A well-planned public relations/communications strategy is important for two reasons. First, the organizational leadership has made a major investment in forming a nonprofit corporation, and a solid public relations effort will promote the organization's purposes. Second, few newly-formed nonprofits begin with a silver spoon in their mouths. The first few years often are a fight for survival financially.

There is a "Catch-22" at work here in many cases. New organizations must accomplish something useful quickly to obtain the credibility necessary to attract financial assistance. Yet the organizations often need this financial assistance to accomplish their missions.

Public relations thus serves an important internal function. It promotes the organization in a positive light and generates the essential public support needed to perpetuate the organization. An organization may be quietly successful in changing public opinion, advancing a legislative agenda, or providing vital services to worthy clients and its members. But if the right people—the board, funders, and potential funders and leadership—are unaware of the organization's successes, then its continued existence may be at risk.

Menu of Standard Nonprofit Communications Tools

An organization may be shy about tooting its own horn. But if it declines to do so—early and often—then its horn may be taken away. There are thousands of creative ways to get the name of an organization in front of the public in a positive context. Among the conventional techniques nonprofits use are the following:

1. Organization Brochure

Each nonprofit organization, from the largest to the smallest, should have an organizational brochure. The brochure should clearly include the name, address, and telephone number of the organization, e-mail address, Web site address, its mission, its purposes and principal interests, its affiliations (if any), its federal tax-exempt status and how to make contributions, the names of its board members, advisory committee, and key staff people, and its major accomplishments. The organization's logo should appear on the brochure (see page 194). If the organization is a membership organization, the brochure should provide information on dues and how to join.

The brochure should be distributed with all major fundraising solicitations. It should be a standard component of press packets, and be distributed at speaking engagements made on behalf of the organization. All board members should have a supply of brochures to distribute to their friends and colleagues who may be interested in joining, contributing, volunteering, or assisting in other ways.

2. Organizational Newsletter

The organization should, no less than quarterly, publish a newsletter for distribution free-of-charge to all board members, all dues-paying members, significant opinion leaders on the issue(s) of interest to the organization, political leadership (such as members of the General Assembly, local members of Congress, and local elected officials), the media, current and potential funders, and colleagues in the field.

Among the items the newsletter may contain are—

- Recent board meeting decisions.
- Legislative action in Washington, Harrisburg, and municipal government of interest to the membership and clients.
- Schedules of upcoming meetings, workshops, conferences, and training sessions.
- Messages from the executive director and/or board president.
- Articles contributed by experts on the board or from the membership about issues of interest to the readership.
- Articles about organization accomplishments such as grants received, advocacy accomplished, coalitions joined, and letters of commendation received.
- Profiles of people involved in the organization.
- General information about status of issues of interest to the organization.

The newsletter need not be fancy, but should be as current as possible. It is advisable to select a creative and descriptive name for the publication and establish a master layout, so that subsequent issues will have the continuity of similar design.

The newsletter is often the only contact hundreds of influential people will have with an organization. As such, it is vitally important to present a professional, accurate, and aesthetically pleasing format. The newsletter should be carefully proof-read and *all* typographical and grammar errors eliminated. Make sure articles on one page continue correctly on subsequent pages.

Headlines should help busy readers find their way through the newsletter. Tricky headlines can be annoying. Double check all headlines for appropriateness. Double check all names, telephone numbers and addresses included in the newsletter.

3. News Releases

The media in Pennsylvania annually provide millions of dollars in free publicity to nonprofit organizations. The typical mode of communicating with the media is through the mailing (or faxing) of a standard news release. The news release is a pre-written "news" article that includes the name, organization, and work telephone number of the key organizational contact person at the top. If the release is *really* important, include the home telephone number as well. The release should be dated, along with "For Immediate Release" or "Embargoed Until (insert date/time)" as appropriate.

Examples of topics for news releases can be the following:

    a.   An organization's official comment on a new law or legislative proposal, new regulation, or court decision affecting the organization's clients or members.

    b.   An accomplishment achieved by an organization.

    c.   The release of a study or survey commissioned by an organization.

    d.   The hiring or promotion of a staff member, or change of leadership within an organization.

    e.   Awards given by or to an organization.

News releases are distributed to those who are most likely to print or broadcast them. A news release to a TV or radio station should be no more than six or seven sentences, nor more than two double-spaced pages for the print media. Most news releases will be edited before final publication or broadcast, although many neighborhood newspapers will print news releases word-for-word.

If the organization is based in Harrisburg, news releases can be distributed to most media outlets that cover the Capitol, including the AP wire service, by leaving 40 copies at the press center in the Capitol (Room E-524).

The basic style of the body of a press release is the following:

    a.   Precede the text with a catchy, descriptive headline.

    b.   Put the most important sentence first.

    c.   Place subsequent facts in the descending order of importance.

    d.   Include suitable quotes of organizational leadership when appropriate. The quote should express a view/opinion, rather than providing a fact that could appear in the release narrative.

e. Ensure that the text answers the basic questions of "who," "what," "where," "why," "when," and "how."

4. Press Conferences

Organizations with a story of major interest to the public may want to consider holding a press conference. To do so, a media advisory is distributed in the same manner as a news release, telling the press where and when the press conference will be held, the subject, and speakers. It may be helpful to make follow-up calls to the news desk of the local newspapers and broadcast stations. At the press conference, written materials (a press packet consisting of a copy of a written statement, the organization's brochure, and materials relating to the topic of the press conference) should be distributed.

If the press conference is being held at the Capitol, special arrangements must be made in advance with the General Services Department' special events office (783-9100) for scheduling a site and providing a sound system. It is advisable to have the press conference at a site convenient to the press (i.e. the Capitol Rotunda or media center), but if the event is truly newsworthy, the press will attend.

Another good idea is to arrange for a black-and-white photo of the organizational representative speaking at the press conference. The photograph may be accompanied by a picture caption and sent to media outlets not covering the press conference. Don't forget to include a press packet, as well.

A banner with the organization's logo, draped in front of the podium, creates a photograph that is useful for future annual reports, newsletters, and related publicity. Take into account that 1-hour commercial photo developers may require several days to develop black-and-white film.

5. Public Service Announcements

Many TV and radio broadcasters regularly broadcast public service announcements (PSAs) for nonprofit organizations free-of-charge. PSAs are an excellent and cost-effective way to get an organization's message, and its name, to thousands of viewers and listeners. The last line of such an announcement can be "This message is brought to you by (the name of your organization) and this station as a public service." The rest of the announcement can be a 30-second sound bite of information of interest to people—how to obtain a free service, how to avoid health and safety risks, or even how to join or volunteer for your organization while accomplishing some vital objective in the public interest. Before preparing a PSA, check with a potential broadcaster for the technical specifications relating to the form and format of the announcement. Some stations may be willing to *produce* your announcement without charge, as well as broadcast it.

6. Conferences and Workshops

Well-planned conferences and workshops can serve a useful public relations function. A one-day conference can bring together interested lay leadership and professionals in a shared field of interest, introduce them to the organization, increase networking among the participants, and advance the organization's interests. The charge for the workshop can be set to cover all anticipated costs, or even to generate net revenue—provided it is planned well in advance and the plan is executed properly.

There are scores of major decisions to make in running a conference, such as choosing speakers who will generate attendance and excitement, preparing and distributing the conference brochure, selecting the site for the conference and arranging for exhibit space and advertising. There are hundreds more minor decisions that need to be made as well, such as choosing the type of name tag to use, deciding who staffs the registration table, and choosing the luncheon menu. There are many sources of advice on how to run a successful conference, and many of these can be borrowed from the local library.

7. Intra-Organizational Communication

Board and key contacts need to know what is happening beyond what they read in the organization's newsletter. Periodically, it is useful to send out "Action Alerts" or "Background Briefings" that describe the status of a problem and what they can do to participate in its resolution. Some organizations have a specially printed piece of stationery for these messages. A sample letter may be included if the organization is encouraging its constituency to write letters. However, the organization should urge writers to use their own words. The address or telephone number of the person they should contact should always be included.

8. Annual Report

By law, all nonprofits must prepare an annual financial report. Many nonprofits use this opportunity to supplement and embellish the financial information (provided they wish to make this public) with a report on the operations of the nonprofit during the fiscal year. The annual report can be professionally designed with fancy layout, fonts, charts, graphics, and color pictures, which imply progress and success in meeting organization goals and objectives. It can also be a typewritten report photocopied on plain paper. In either case, it is an opportunity to communicate what the organization has been doing on behalf of its Board and membership, clients, funders and the public, as well as its goals and plans.

9. Other Publications

Many nonprofits publish small booklets about various issues of concern, which are disseminated to their constituents and other interested parties. It is one more way to get the name of the organization in front of more people, and it is another effective way to communicate the organization's views to those whose opinions count. Subjects of such publications could be—

- The latest developments on issues of interest.
- How to contact government offices.
- How to lobby on behalf of the organization's issues.
- The General Assembly, and who serves on committees of interest to the organization.

These publications can also be considered the written equivalent of the public service announcement. Many institutions, such as hospitals, community centers, nursing homes, day care providers, and libraries, will distribute these public relations booklets free-of-charge to the organization's target audience.

10. Membership/Board Surveys

Membership and board surveys can be, but may not always be, a useful tool to obtain information and feedback. The target of the survey may feel a sense of connection to the organization, and the survey will provide useful input from the membership. Member surveys can be tailored to suit the needs of the organization. For example, many advocacy nonprofits periodically survey their boards and/or membership to determine who among the board and membership has influence or personal relationships with key public policy decision-makers. Surveys can be used to gauge the effectiveness of organization programs and activities.

Christine Finnegan, a Managing Editor of Morehouse Communications, adds this advice:

> *"Be sure your survey goes to the right people, asks the right questions, and is easy to complete and return. If you don't plan to believe, abide by, or use the results of the survey, don't waste your time."*

11. Speakers' Bureaus

Many groups, such as men's and women's clubs, fraternal organizations, educational organizations, membership organizations, churches and synagogues, have speakers at their regular meetings. Organization leaders may wish to proactively seek invitations to discuss the activities of their organizations with these groups. They may be the source of volunteers, donations, ideas, or simply good will and public support. Local newspapers (don't forget the "Shopper" newspapers) list many of these club meetings and their presidents. Addresses can be found in the telephone book, if not listed in the announcement. Members of the board can be deputized to speak on behalf of the organization. Many of them have associations with other organizations and clubs that would be delighted to host a speaker.

12. Newspaper Op-Ed Articles

Virtually all newspapers will print feature-length opinion articles on their Opinion/Editorial (Op-Ed) pages. Many will include a picture and a line of biographical material about the author. The Op-Ed page is usually the page most read by a newspaper's readership, along with the letters-to-the-editor page. It is an excellent forum to share an organization's ideas on an issue and bring attention to the organization. There are many cases in which a thoughtful Op-Ed article has resulted in legislation being enacted by Congress or the General Assembly to address the subject of the article.

13. Letters to the Editor

Letters-to-the Editor are an effective way to "talk back" to a newspaper when an article or editorial unfairly and erroneously shapes an issue. They can also be an effective medium to reinforce a position and permit the writer to expand on that position from the perspective of the organization. The general guidelines for writing letters-to-the-editor vary from paper to paper, but usually provide for writing on a single issue, being concise (no more than three paragraphs), using non-threatening language, and providing information that might not be available to the readers from any other source.

14. Developing a World Wide Web Home Page

Thousands of nonprofit organizations are establishing home pages on the World Wide Web (See Chapter 20). These pages communicate information about donations; volunteer opportunities; products, services, and publications; and general information about the agency. These pages can be prepared and maintained for very little cost and permit the general public to access information by computer modem from the privacy of their own homes and offices.

15. Forming a Coalition

There is strength in numbers. Two heads are better than one. Whatever the cliché, many organizations find a benefit in pooling their resources to accomplish an objective. One strategy is to form a coalition of other organizations to address an issue of critical importance. There are many advantages of doing this, and a fuller discussion of coalition-building is provided in Chapter 21.

Chapter 20
The Internet for Nonprofits

Synopsis: Nonprofits have an exciting, new resource in the Internet. Once connected, organizations can share information cheaply and quickly, and use search techniques to find information. Nonprofits can set up their own pages on the World Wide Web.

The recent explosion of useful resources for nonprofits on the Internet is perhaps the most exciting positive development for this sector in years. The 1995-96 edition of this book devoted just a single paragraph to the Internet. The 1997-98 edition had a 10-page chapter, which served as the foundation for an entire book published in 1998 by White Hat Communications titled *The Non-Profit Internet Handbook.* Thousands of nonprofit institutions whose leadership had barely heard of the Internet a few years ago are not only connected, but have their own World Wide Web (WWW) sites.

Nonprofit executives have taken advantage of this revolution in communications by using the Internet to troll for donors, lobby their members of Congress, advertise job openings, purchase office equipment and supplies, hold on-line meetings and information sessions, market their services, check references of prospective consultants, distribute board documents, reserve library books, generate grass roots advocacy letters to government officials, research new laws and regulations, and download the latest Supreme Court decisions, all without leaving their offices. Need a 990 tax return form? Download it from the IRS web site *(http://www.irs.ustreas.gov).* Need driving directions to your board meeting for your board members? Have a computer generate not only the directions but even a map, and e-mail them *(http:// www.mapblast.com).* Have a general question about how to deal with a sensitive organizational issue? Ask for advice on the soc.nonprofit.org mailing list (view the frequently asked questions file for this mailing list, including subscription information, at *http://www.nonprofits.org).*

In previous years, if you wanted to distribute a document to a board, you had to photocopy the document, collate it, stuff it in envelopes, put correct postage and mailing labels on the envelopes, and mail it. The recipient would receive it 2-5 days later. Time could be saved by faxing the document, or broadcast faxing it, to the list of recipients, but the cost of long distance charges could be substantial. Via the Internet, the same operation results in almost immediate delivery of the documents to every person on the list, for the price of a local telephone call. The Internet is revolutionizing the way all businesses operate, and the nonprofit sector is finding that the benefits to the for-profit world are just as applicable to the nonprofit sector.

Having Internet access is like having your own private library, entertainment center, news and clipping service, private club, and nightly gala soirée, with several important differences—the library is the largest ever created in the world by a factor of perhaps 10,000, and you have a private genie to conjure up at will who can virtually instantaneously find and bring you almost any piece of information you want.

Saving money, while of prime concern to nonprofits, is only one advantage of utilizing the Internet. Perhaps the most exciting aspect is that nonprofit executives can communicate cheaply and efficiently with like-minded counterparts who may be in an office next door or on another continent. The culture of the Internet has developed so that it is easy for people who have something in common and information to share to find each other and begin a one-on-one or one-on-ten-thousand dialogue without having to laboriously screen out the other 80-100 million people who also are participating.

Many nonprofit executives report that attending a national conference results in serendipitous contacts with previously unknown colleagues, which generate new ideas, new strategies for solving problems, interchanges that promote innovation, collaboration opportunities among people otherwise separated by geography and useful social contacts. The Internet has become all of this and more. The velocity of communication interaction among people has made a quantum leap as a result of the Internet. Nonprofits that don't take advantage of the new opportunities afforded by this emerging technology to save money, expand markets, and promote themselves may be left in the dust by competitors that do.

What is the Internet?

The Internet is a term that describes the connection among millions of computers all over the world that supports communication between them as a result of a standardized connection protocol called TCP/IP (Transmission Control Protocol/ Internet Protocol). For the typical Internet user, all of the technical details are totally transparent; communicating from an Atari computer or a mainframe on the Internet makes no difference, provided each computer is running the same protocol.

The Internet was developed in the early 1970s by the Department of Defense for the purpose of providing communication that was disaster-proof. Initially, it was used by technical folks and academicians. It was clunky at best, used an obscure communications language, and the information shared was, at best, esoteric. Only in the last seven years or so has the Internet become a part of the popular culture and available to the masses. New communications software, commercial providers that market to the general public, the emergence of the World Wide Web, advances in technology such as high speed modems, and competition in the industry have made Internet access popular. Millions without their own personal computers have access to the Internet through libraries, educational institutions, and the workplace.

Each resource on the Internet has an address to enable a user to find it and connect to it. That address is called a URL (uniform resource locator). The URL has a standardized format that is useful in identifying its source.

Equipment Needed to Connect to the Internet

To make a connection to the Internet, five components are required:

1. A computer and monitor. The computer stores the communications software, provides the mechanism to download and store data from the Internet, provides a convenient way to dial into the Internet, and takes advantage of many new technological wonders, such as using the Internet to have real time audio conversations. Although a printer is optional, you will find it useful to print out much of what you find on the Internet.

2. A telephone line. The Internet communicates by sending packets of data over the telephone line. A nonprofit may purchase a dedicated telephone line, which will be used only for computer communication. More typically, a nonprofit will either purchase a supplemental telephone line or, if on-line time is minimal, use an existing line. Many nonprofits go online using a separate line previously dedicated solely to the fax machine. Obviously, when on-line communication is occurring on the dedicated fax line, no faxes may be received or sent by the organization.

3. A modem. Most personal computers sold today have a built-in modem, typically 56k baud. The higher the baud rate, the more data can be transferred over the telephone line within a given time frame. A 2,400 baud modem is sufficient for the transfer of text, although large documents take proportionately longer. With the advent of the World Wide Web, which takes advantage of graphics, sounds, animations, videos, and other byte-intensive files, the modem speed becomes critical. The World Wide Web is almost unusable with a 2,400 baud modem. Many nonprofits find that even a 56k baud modem is not sufficiently fast, and there are technological breakthroughs that use special digital cable modems to provide data transfers several times faster than the conventional analog modems of most personal computers.

4. Communications software. A computer without communications software is like a car without an engine. It may look nice, but you aren't going to go far. Like cars, communications software can be a Volkswagen Beetle or a Mercedes. Fortunately, at least basic communications software is included in virtually every PC computer sold, in the form of the communications programs included in the Accessories folder of Microsoft Windows. There is an equivalent for MAC-based systems as well. Many PCs also include demonstration or full versions of communications software designed to connect to the Internet, provide e-mail management, a Web browser, FTP software, and a newsgroup reader. Among the most popular are: Internet Office!, The Instant Internet Kit, Internet Valet, Quarterdeck InternetSuite and Internet In a Box. Many of the programs included in these packages may be obtained in some version for free from various sources; these packages will not connect you to the Internet without a monthly fee to a service provider.

5. Service provider. While it is possible to set up as one's own service provider and make a direct connection to the Internet, doing so is expensive, time-consuming, and technically difficult. The choice for almost all nonprofits has become to purchase an account with a commercial or nonprofit Internet service provider. Among the national service providers are CompuServe (1-800-848-8199), America Online (1-800-827-6364), Prodigy (1-800-776-3449), and The Microsoft Network (1-800-386-5550). Hundreds of local Internet service providers have sprung up to compete, and many charge less than the national companies, but for the most part provide fewer services. Typical costs for a service are $10-20/month. For that, you get access to the Internet and other content offered by the provider for a limited number of hours each month, and an additional charge for each hour on-line above that threshold. Almost all providers also offer the option of unlimited access to the Internet for a set monthly fee.

Practical Applications of the Internet

Among the most popular services and applications of the Internet are e-mail, the World Wide Web, FTP, Telnet, chat, newsgroups, and mailing lists.

E-mail: Most of the data transmitted over the Internet is in the form of electronic mail. These are text communications that are sent from one person to another over the Internet. E-mail is a "store and forward" system that permits someone to send a message to someone else for later retrieval. Each Internet user is given an Internet address that is used to send and receive e-mail. E-mail messages also can have computer files attached to them. Experienced users refer to messages sent via the U.S. Postal Service as "snail mail." Letters are to e-mail what smoke signals are to long distance telephoning. E-mail avoids playing "telephone tag" and for a fraction of the cost of faxing.

Mailing Lists: Mailing lists are a form of e-mail. Users who subscribe to a particular list may send a message on a topic of interest to that list. The message is automatically distributed as e-mail to every subscriber on the list. Thus, if you subscribe to the nonprofit mailing list *soc.nonprofit.org*, you can send a message to the list that gives details about your upcoming national conference on drug and alcohol abuse, and every subscriber will see that message as e-mail. Some mailing lists generate hundreds of messages a day and others perhaps one each day. If you are paying a server for each message, or have limited storage space for e-mail messages, it may be important to you to limit the number of lists to which you subscribe.

To subscribe to a mailing list, the subscriber generally sends an e-mail message to an administrative address in a standard format that automatically processes the request. The administrative address is different from the address to which messages are sent that are intended for the entire distribution list.

Some popular nonprofit mailing lists are:

CFRNET (communication among foundations, institutions, and business)
command: SUBSCRIBE CFRNET
address to subscribe: listproc@ripken.oit.unc.edu

FUNDLIST (fundraising)
command: SUB FUNDLIST
address to subscribe: listproc@hcf.jhu.edu

FUNDSVCS (fundraising)
command: SUBSCRIBE FUNDSVCS
address to subscribe: majordomo@acpub.duke.edu

GIVING (fundraising)
command: SUBSCRIBE GIVING
address to subscribe: listproc@envirolink.org

USNONPROFIT-1 (general nonprofit issues)
command: SUBSCRIBE NONPROFIT
address to subscribe: nonprofit request@rain.org

GRANTS (grants and foundations)
command: SUBSCRIBE GRANTS
address to subscribe: listserv@philanthropy-review.com

The command to subscribe is usually: subscribe name of list firstname lastname where firstname and lastname are your own names. The command is e-mailed, without any other message, to the administrative address.

Newsgroups: A newsgroup is another form of Internet communication that provides for group discussion of a narrow topic. It is like a bulletin board in the supermarket, where you have to take action to see it and read messages posted there, with an opportunity to post a reply for others to see. Sending a message to a newsgroup results in each subscriber of the newsgroup having the capability of seeing the message without receiving it as e-mail. Typically, someone makes a comment on a newsgroup, another person responds to the comment, and so on until there is a string of related messages on a topic. Simultaneously, others on-line will start another string of messages. All of the messages are stored, often chronologically, and given a title, and viewers can pick and choose using a newsgroup reader (specialized software to facilitate reviewing newsgroups) to decide which messages to look at. One of the most popular newsgroups of interest to nonprofit organizations is: *soc.org.nonprofit.*

FTP: FTP, or file transfer protocol, is the tool used to connect to a computer and transfer files from one to the other. Using FTP, you can "upload" the file of your nonprofit's newsletter to the Foundation Center. Or you can "download" a list of the top 40 charities. For example, the Nonprofit Center may have a document called "Ethics of Fundraising." FTP connects your computer with the computer that has the file, so you can transfer it to your own hard drive or floppy disk and then print it out. As technology improves, more information providers are providing more user-friendly ways to upload and download files from their web sites, and it won't be long before knowledge about FTP will no longer be necessary to successfully transfer files on the Internet.

Telnet: Telnet is the protocol to connect with a computer in a remote location and interact with it in real time, as if you were directly operating that computer on site. Using Telnet, one can use software that is locally unavailable or play games or engage in simulations with others who also are logged in. Like FTP, Telnet is also becoming an anachronism with the advance of more user-friendly information transfer technologies.

Chat: Chat is the Internet equivalent of ham radio. Using chat software, one can have a "conversation" with someone by using the computer keyboard, all in real time. What you type and the response of the other participant(s) appears on your screen simultaneously. It is possible to have a nonprofit board meeting entirely by chat. Most commercial providers provide for privacy among those who participate. More popular, however, are informal chats among those who just happen to frequent a chat room. More and more, these chat rooms are becoming specialized, so participants have something in common. Many web sites, including those of nonprofit groups, use software, often provided free by commercial providers, that permits visitors to participate in chat. In return for the use of free chat rooms, the visitors often see advertising messages controlled by the software provider, not under the control of the organization that is sponsoring the individual chat room.

The World Wide Web

The World Wide Web (WWW) permits Internet users to link to resources on other computers, even if those computers are on the other side of the world. World Wide Web resources are reportedly expanding at the rate of 20% each month. The Web supports not only text, but graphics, photographs, full motion videos, and sounds. Web pages are often formatted to give the appearance of an on-screen magazine, but there is one major difference. World Wide Web pages are formatted using computerized codes, called HTML (hypertext markup language), that permit the user to use a mouse or other pointer device to click on one part of the screen and be connected to a totally different World Wide Web page, which may be generated from a server on the other side of the world. For example, a World Wide Web page relating to libraries can be coded with links to libraries in hundreds of places. By clicking on one of these links, the computer's browser transports the user to the World Wide Web page of that library. To see World Wide Web pages and navigate through these links, "browser" software is required.

The Web contains information made available by people and organizations. No one is in charge of maintaining or organizing the Web, so what you see is only what someone else saw fit to make available. Using the Web is free and, so far, most of the content on the Web is free, as well. But an increasing number of sites are charging for access, and it is not unusual for organizations to provide limited access to a site free to the public, and restrict access to certain pages to their members or those who pay a fee.

World Wide Web History

"The World Wide Web" is probably the term most commonly thrown around in discussions of the Internet. You might see it abbreviated "WWW" or "W3." The Web was "invented" by physicists at the European Laboratory for Particle Physics (CERN). Their basic problem was that they wanted to find an easy way to cross reference a document with its end notes and bibliography, which at that time, often required leaving the first document and searching for the second. The objective was to code the link to the second document at the same time one was viewing the first document. The Web you see now—with graphics that can be clicked on, flashy colors, and eye-catching animations and backgrounds—turned the WWW from what was a sterile,

1850s newspaper style to what looks more like a television or movie screen with an attitude.

The World Wide Web is exactly what its name suggests: a Web of interconnecting sites that span the world. Each "Web site" or "home page" belongs to, and is operated by (or abandoned by), some organization or person. Sometimes the terms "Web site" and "home page" are treated as synonymous, but there is a subtle difference. Web site refers to a collection of pages of a person or organization, while the home page is the main "gateway," "index," or table of contents to the rest of the Web site.

All Web pages contain only that information that the person or organization wants to make available to the larger Internet public. For individuals, it might be a self-description or a list of interests and links to their favorite Web sites. For an organization, it might be a description or advertisement of its services, or it could be information relating to its mission.

So imagine now, a global newsstand or television network in which each and every person has the ability to create his or her own "home page show." Some people use this ability to entertain, sell goods and services, share news, ideas, or stories. Some home page shows are good, and some are pretty awful. Some are self-serving only and some altruistically offer the world some useful information and communication contacts.

Anyone with a Web browser can view these home page shows. Just as any brand of television shows the same program on the same channels, browsers show the same web pages, even if the tint, contrast, and general layout may vary from browser to browser.

A key feature of the Web, with its millions of home pages, is the ability for each page to lead you to other pages. On almost any home page, you will see some text (or pictures) underlined (or outlined) and/or in colorful boldface. These are the "hypertext links" that, when clicked on with the mouse, trigger your browser to move along to another Web page. Note that sometimes one of the links will lead not to another Web site when clicked, but instead will link to an individual's e-mail address. A message form will appear, allowing you to write a message to the designated person. These are called "mailto" links.

The ability to create links is the magic of which the World Wide Web is formed, and is one way the Internet is different from television shows or newspapers. TV show producers generally want you to keep viewing their shows and not move elsewhere, and written publications are intended to be read in sequential order. The Internet is often referred to as "thinking in parallel," since it allows and encourages you to explore more in depth whatever diversionary routes you wish to take.

Deciphering a Web Address

A URL ("uniform resource locator") is the address for Web sites. Each Web page has a unique address. Typically, Webmasters organize the URLs of their pages in a manner similar to how directories and subdirectories are organized on a computer, by using forward slashes (rather than back slashes) to organize these pages. For example, a home page might have the URL:

http://www.organization.org/webpage.html

The home page might have a link to "press releases" with the URL:

http://www.organization.org/webpage/pressrel.html

The September 18, 1999, press release on the organization's Legislator of the Year award might have the URL:

http://www.organization.org/webpage/pressrel/091899.html

This is an important point to understand. Perhaps you are given the URL for a document and your browser gives you a "404" message (indicating that there is nothing available at that URL). Instead of giving up, you can try finding the page you are looking for by using the URL one directory higher, or two or three directories higher, as may be necessary. There are many times when you can find the information you are looking for even when you are given an incorrect URL.

Let's quickly deconstruct a Web address. The Web site address for White Hat Communications' The Online Nonprofit Information Center is:

http://www.socialworker.com/nonprofit/nphome.htm

The first thing you might notice is that there are no spaces. This is not a coincidence. No spaces are allowed in a URL, and this is why words are often separated by dots ("."), dashes ("-"), tildes ("~"), slashes ("/"), and underlines ("_").

Starting from the end, in the above address, the suffix, ".htm," indicates that the document is a Web page using HTML (hypertext markup language) codes. This is the code used to create Web pages, and these files usually end in "html" or "htm."

Next, each single slash mark ("/") lets you know that you are descending into further file directories in the person's server, just as you do in your own computer to find particular files or documents. This is useful to know, because there are times when you might know an address for a site that is likely to be in the ascending files. For example, suppose you wanted to find the main page for White Hat Communications. You could guess that the home page would be at *http://www.socialworker.com.* Entering this will, in fact, get you to the main page for White Hat Communications.

To "surf," "browse," or "navigate" the Web (these are all equivalent terms), you simply open your browser and type in the URL of a page, and from there explore various links. You can fully access the Internet's resources even if you hardly ever enter a URL by hand. Your browser will start you off at a default home page (usually the browser company's Web site), but you can set it to start at any site you wish—your own, a favorite organization's, or a favorite navigation launching point, such as the Yahoo! directory *(http://www.yahoo.com)*. One browser feature you will come to rely on is the "back" button. Suppose you start to jump from page to page during your navigation, and realize that you have gone well off-track. The back button will retrace your steps as far back as you wish before going forward in a new direction. For a quick return to the beginning, you can always click the "home" button and begin anew.

Most browsers have a "bookmark" function that automatically records a favorite link for future use. Thus, in order to return to that page at a future time, you need only to click on the stored reference in the bookmark list, rather than having to type in the entire address.

Frames

A popular Web page development is the use of frames, a device that allows more than one HTML document to be displayed on your monitor at the same time. Usually, one frame will contain a "Table of Contents" consisting of links. When you click on one of the links, the referenced document appears in another frame, while the first frame remains on the screen. In essence, you are then viewing two Web pages in one. The page that is displayed in the second frame may be another page in the same Web site as the first, or it may be a page from another site.

A significant disadvantage of using frames is that not every Web browser is compatible with them. If you are using a browser that is not, and you try to access a page with frames, you will typically get an error message such as, "Your browser does not support frames. You cannot access this site." Some of these messages may have a link to a site that permits you to download, at no charge, a browser that supports frames. Your only recourse at this point is to download (or buy) a browser that supports frames. Some sites have a frames and a non-frames version, and we recommend that you provide both if you plan to build a site using frames, so you will not alienate (or lose as visitors) those who do not have a frames-compatible browser.

How to Find Resources on the World Wide Web

One of the complaints about the Internet in its early years was that you could find a plethora of fascinating data bases, files, and information, but it was almost impossible to find something you were actually seeking to find in advance. Commercial companies offered services to assist researchers in finding Internet resources, and often charged handsomely. Recently, that has changed dramatically with the development of powerful search tools, all of which can be accessed free of charge. Among the more popular search engines are Yahoo *(http://www.yahoo.com)*, Lycos *(http://www.lycos.com)*, Excite *(http://www.excite.com)*, and Alta Vista *(http:// altavista.digital.com)*. Users access the search engine by connecting to its address, and then fill out an on-line form with the term or terms to search. For example, typing the term "nonprofit" in the Yahoo search engine generates within a second or two more than 500 responses in the form of links. Clicking on any one of these links transports you to the referenced page.

The search engine administrators usually provide a procedure for registering a new World Wide Web page with them so that it will appear in searches. Nonprofits that develop their own World Wide Web pages should register their pages with as many search engines as they identify.

Directories

A directory is analogous to a library card catalogue. It organizes information on the Internet by pre-selected categories. You may find directories useful when looking for a specific Internet site if you know the site exists. For example, if you are looking for the site of Penn State University, using a search engine will likely provide a response of thousands of related possibilities, few of which will take you to the home page of that institution. However, using the Yahoo Directory *(http://www.yahoo.com)*, you can find the main category *Education* and work your way down through categories to find exactly the page you want (i.e. by clicking serially on the following: *Universities, United States, Public by State,* and *Pennsylvania* until you reach *Penn State University@).*

Web Rings

Web rings are linked groups of independent Web sites on a related topic. When you go to a site that is associated with a Web ring, you will find an area, usually at the bottom of the site's page, where you can click to go to the next site in the ring, the previous site, a random site in the ring, or a list of all sites on the ring. If you are hoping to find a number of related sites on a particular topic, you might check to see if there is a Web ring. You can search for Web rings by keyword at: *http://www.webring.org.* Other sites helpful for finding Web rings are Looplink *(http://www.looplink.com)* and The Rail *(http://www.therail.com).* Some find that it is easier to find information about a particular topic through a Web ring search than through a conventional search engine. As of February 1999, there were more than 60,000 Web rings with more than 1 million sites. Among the Web rings you can find of interest to nonprofit organizations are those on domestic violence, AIDS, homelessness, disabilities, cancer, and premature babies.

Obtaining a Domain Name

A domain name is the part of the Internet address after the "@" sign. For example, my personal e-mail address is: gary.grobman@paonline.com. Paonline is my Internet Service Provider (ISP), and "com" indicates that it is a commercial provider. However, I could, for a fee, have this changed to: gary.grobman@whitehat.org without changing my ISP.

The uniform resource locator (URL) provided by an ISP is often quite long, and is not as elegant as an individualized URL that contains the organization's name. Most ISPs will, for a fee, provide an organization with its own domain name, or you can do it yourself by registering with the Internet Network Information Center (InterNIC). In either case, there is an initial $70 fee for the first two years, and an annual fee of $35 after that. This is in addition to any fees charged by your provider.

Applications must be submitted electronically, by filling out a template on the World Wide Web site of InterNIC *(http://www.rs.internic.net)* or by FTP to the text version *(ftp.rs.internic.net).* If you do the latter, log on as *anonymous* and use *guest* as the password. You will need your name and address, the domain name you want to use (e.g. yourname.org) and the primary and secondary server Internet protocol number, which you can obtain from your ISP. Names are assigned on a first-come, first-served basis and are checked for prior use and for whether they are in some way objectionable.

Developing Your Own World Wide Web Page

There are thousands of commercial services all offering to design and administer World Wide Web pages for a fee. With a minimum of technical background, you can do it yourself. Software is available for free that works with popular word processing programs to convert documents into HTML language. The latest versions of most popular word processing programs can save documents as HTML files suitable for posting on your Web site.

Once one knows the HTML codes to insert, one can even prepare a World Wide Web page entirely in Windows Notepad or other programs that create ASCII files, the most simple files that consist entirely of text characters. Among the types of information that can be found on typical World Wide Web pages of nonprofits are:

> newsletter, annual report, press releases, brochure, how to contribute or volunteer, financial data, action alerts, job openings, information about board and staff members, publications, upcoming conferences and seminars, product catalogs and order forms, a way to e-mail the organization, and links to other organizations' and government-based home pages related to the mission and purpose of the organization.

Internet Etiquette (a.k.a. Netiquette)

The culture of the Internet has developed over a short period of time and has changed as millions of new users have joined. Most servers have written rules about proper use of their service. There are general written and unwritten rules regarding the Internet. Among some of the more useful are:

- Don't type entirely in capital letters. This is considered the computer keyboard equivalent of "shouting," and can result in being flamed (being sent a threatening or denigrating unsolicited message).

- Don't put a message on a newsgroup, mailing list, or even personal e-mail that you would be embarrassed to have circulated to 1,000s of people. It just might happen.

- Don't send copyrighted material to a newsgroup or mailing list without permission from the copyright holder.

- Spend time "lurking" (the equivalent of listening quietly) on a newsgroup or mailing list before diving in by posting messages. Many groups and lists have a file associated with them called an FAQ (Frequently Asked Questions). Read it before posting your first message.

- Don't post clearly commercial messages on a newsgroup or mailing list. Announcements about new products are fine; sales pitches are strictly verboten and usually result in flame messages.

Problems With the Internet

The Internet is not without its problems. Consumer fraud exists, just as it does in the non-virtual world. Although newly developed software has improved the security of communications (particularly important since financial information, including credit card numbers, is routinely sent through e-mail), it is not fool-proof. In general, all data is transferred through the Internet using ASCII files, which are virus-proof. However, viruses can be transmitted through attached files that are converted by coding software to binary files.

Copyright issues relating to electronic communication still are unresolved. Finally, the Internet has opened up an entire new world for exploration, and studies indicate that for some people, it may be psychologically addicting.

Numerous books, magazines, and media articles have been written exploring the costs and benefits of the cyberspace revolution.

Useful Internet Resources for Nonprofits

Thousands of charities and other nonprofits have their own World Wide Web sites. There are scores of interesting and handy gateways to them, and other sites that have substantial resources of interest to nonprofit organizations. Perhaps the best thing about accessing these Web sites is they are free-of-charge to visit (other than the fee to your service provider for Internet access). Among them are:

1. The Internet Nonprofit Center
http://www.nonprofits.org

This site, first put online in 1994, is now under new sponsorship, the Evergreen State Society of Seattle, Washington. The site features a nonprofit locator, permitting users to search by name, key word, or zip code for all 501(c)(3) and (c)(4)s in the United States. The site's library includes publications and data about nonprofits and the nonprofit sector compiled by third parties, and also includes files of ethical standards published by the National Charities Information Bureau and the New York Philanthropic Advisory Services organization. The site includes files of current and back issues of *Nonprofit Online News,* and plenty of links to other sites of interest.

2. The Foundation Center
http://fdncenter.org/

The Foundation Center is an independent nonprofit information clearinghouse established in 1956. The Center operates five libraries, and provides materials to hundreds of public libraries (see Appendix E). The mission of the organization is to foster public understanding of the foundation field by collecting, organizing, analyzing, and disseminating information on foundations, corporate giving, and related subjects. Included at the Center's Web site is a weekly electronic newsletter called *Philanthropy News Digest*, published every Wednesday online, but which can be subscribed to by e-mail to arrive on Tuesday evenings. The site has a searchable archives, an excellent reference on how to prepare grant applications *(A Proposal Writing Short Course)* and standardized grant application forms. There is access to an online librarian who will answer your questions about where to find resources and basic information of interest to nonprofits. Just fill out the online form with your question.

3. Libertynet
http://libertynet.org

LibertyNet is a nonprofit organization that provides free or low-cost Internet services to the Philadelphia area's government and nonprofit institutions. It acts as an Internet Service Provider (ISP), providing e-mail, access to the Internet, communications-related technical assistance, as well as educational programs and a schedule of events. LibertyNet was founded by the local public TV/radio station (WHYY), University Science Center, and the Franklin Technology Partnership. The home page provides links to scores of Philadelphia-area institution home pages, and has links to local and state politicians. As of February 1999, LibertyNet was the host to 600 nonprofit and commercial web sites, and provided Internet access to almost 1,000 nonprofit members.

4. The Pennsylvania State Government Home Page
http://www.state.pa.us

This is the gateway for state government information—here you can find links to departments and agencies; executive orders, press releases, state budget proposals, financial reports, and speeches of the governor; tourist information, including calendars of events and maps; state lottery results; and links to federal, state, and local government offices. Department of Revenue forms, information about charitable organization disclosure, and a history of Pennsylvania are just a click away. The site is searchable, and is available in both frames and text formats.

5. Electronic Billroom
http://www.legis.state.pa.us/WU01/LI/BI/billroom.htm

This site became operational at the end of 1998. You can search the database by subject and obtain the full text of bills introduced during the General Assembly from 1993 to the present. The bills are available in PDF format as well, so you can print them out just as they look from the Capitol document room. To find out what is happening in the House or Senate, visit *http://www.legis.state.pa.us* to access the homepage.

6. GuideStar
http://www.guidestar.org

GuideStar, administered by the Williamsburg, VA-based Philanthropic Research, Inc., publishes comprehensive reports about individual American charities. Its purpose is "to bring the actors in the philanthropic and nonprofit communities closer together through the use of information and communication technologies. GuideStar collects and analyzes operating and financial data from the IRS Form 990 and from voluntary submissions from the charities themselves." The database consists of more than 650,000 reports on individual charities, and the site is colorful, accessible, and well-designed. The database can be searched, at no charge, by any number of parameters, such as name, location, or type of charity. This is simply the best site on the 'Net for finding financial information about charities. Charities can provide their reports and update them on-line at no charge. The site also includes links of interest to charities, and essays about philanthropy via the "GuideStar Forum" button. There is a page for nonprofits to post information, classified ads, online newsletters, and press releases. The News Spotlight has information about the voluntary sector, conferences, and links. The Resource Exchange matches donors, volunteers, and nonprofits who need them, and the Learning Center has files on how to be an informed donor, become a more effective nonprofit staff person, and more.

7. Nonprofit Managers' Library
http://www.mapnp.org/library/index.html

While much of this site is targeted to the needs of Minnesota nonprofits (such as local grant information), it is an excellent resource for all. There is a Nonprofit Job Board and a Nonprofit's Yellow Pages. The site boasts updated files on ethics, fundraising, communications skills, marketing, organizational change, risk management, strategic planning, and much more. There are numerous and useful links to outside organizations that make this site an excellent resource for those interested in grants, foundations, government information, and general information useful to nonprofits.

8. Philanthropy Journal Online
http://www.pj.org

This is the online version of a newspaper, based in North Carolina, that posts breaking news stories of interest to the nonprofit community. You can subscribe to the e-mail version for free.

9. The Nonprofit GENIE
http://www.genie.org

This site is a project of the Southern California Center for Nonprofit Management. Here you can find book reviews of nonprofit management books, plus 110 entries in a comprehensive Frequently Asked Questions (FAQ) for nonprofit managers, organized in nine general categories, such as insurance and strategic planning. There are plenty of interesting links to nonprofit resources as well.

10. The Chronicle of Philanthropy
http://www.philanthropy.com

The site provides highlights from this publication, which is the trade journal for America's charitable community. The tabloid format biweekly is the number one source for charity leaders, fundraisers and grant makers, and the Web site provides more than just a taste of what its subscribers receive in snail mail every two weeks. The site is updated every other week at 9 a.m. on the Monday before the issue date, and job announcements are updated on the Monday following that. The principal categories of this site are gifts and grants, fundraising, managing nonprofit groups, and technology. Each of these headings is further divided by a news summary, workshops and seminars, and deadlines. Also on the site are front page news stories, a news summary, conferences, Internet resources, products and services, and jobs. Most of the articles consist of one-sentence summaries but are still useful, particularly if you don't have the $69 in your budget to subscribe to the publication for a year. The "Jobs" button transports you to a searchable database of hundreds of positions available. In some respects, this searchability makes the Internet version of the *Chronicle* more useful than the conventional version. There is also a handy directory of "Products and Services."

11. The Nonprofit Times
http://www.nptimes.com

This is the online version of the monthly tabloid newspaper, and has full-text articles from the latest issue, as well as classified advertisements.

12. Independent Sector
http://www.indepsec.org

This site is the first place to go for definitive statistics of interest about the nonprofit sector (click on *Facts and Figures*). It also has files on the Y2K problem, ethics, accountability and leadership issues (*Accountability and Effectiveness*), and even advice on how your organization can use the new philanthropy stamp in promotion campaigns. There is current information about new laws and regulations affecting charities, and public policy advocacy updates.

13. HandsNet
http://www.handsnet.org

Founded in 1987, HandsNet links more than 5,000 public interest and human services organizations using the Internet to promote collaboration, advocacy, and information-sharing by the sector. The public pages are updated daily, and the members-only pages are considered to be the most valuable around for nonprofits that engage in advocacy. The site's Action Alerts provide lots of government links, state-of-the-art information on current issues (most of which is provided by member organizations whose niche includes that particular public policy issue), capsule summaries, sources to find more information about the issue, sample advocacy letters, and information about new legislation. The Weekly Digest includes samples from hundreds of policy, program, and resource articles posted by members.

14. Nonprofit Gateway
http://www.nonprofit.gov

This site's strength lies in its convenient and user-friendly links to federal departments and agencies—executive, legislative, and judicial—and an easy-to-use guide to access publications of importance to nonprofits, such as the Federal Register, the Catalog of Federal Domestic Assistance, and access to the General Services Administration. It appears not to have been updated for at least two years. It has a grid of federal agencies that permits easy access to each agency's home page, page on grants, and its search page—a convenient feature.

15. The Contact Center's IdeaList
http://www.idealist.org/tools/tools.htm

This site is a great resource. It contains a searchable database of 10,000 nonprofit organizations (you can click on a form to add your organization to the database), a page on "Computing and the Internet" with links to free and low cost servers, publications on Web site development, HTML tutorials, and a list of organizations that offer free products and services to charities. The "Tools for Nonprofits" button transports you to the Computing and the Internet page, Employment and Internship Opportunities, and Fundraising. The fund-raising page includes application forms for several grants and a "Proposal Writing Short Course." There are plenty of links to other organizations, although they are not attractively organized. The directory is organized geographically and by the organizations' areas of focus. Nonprofits that ask to be included in the directory are requested to make a $25 voluntary contribution, but otherwise the site is free.

16. Pennsylvania Department of State Corporation Bureau
http://www.dos.state.pa.us/corp/corp.htm

Here you can find definitive general information about record searches, name availability, name reservations, how to obtain copies of documents and get them in a hurry if you need them, filing and registration guidelines, fee schedules, and, perhaps most important, getting copies of forms you need online. There is a useful FAQ (Example: Q: Can corporate seals and corporate kits be obtained from the Corporation Bureau? A: No. They may be obtained from a local stationery store or any office supply store). There is also a link here to the Bureau of Charitable Organizations (see below).

17. Dept. of State's Bureau of Charitable Organizations
http://www.dos.state.pa.us/charity/index.htm

This site has information about whether you need to register with the bureau, and what forms you need to file, whether you work for a charity, represent an "institution of purely public charity" that must register as a result of Act 55 (see pages 222-224), a fundraising counsel, or a fundraising solicitor. There are files of facts and statistics about charities in Pennsylvania, a complaints hotline, consumer information about charitable giving, a searchable database of charities registered with the bureau, information about charities against whom the Attorney General's Office has issued cease and desist orders, and the full text of the charitable solicitation registration law, Act 202.

18. Impact Online
http://www.impactonline.org

This site provides a posting area for nonprofits to advertise volunteer opportunities that can be performed online, and has excellent resources relating to "virtual volunteering." From the home page, click on "Virtual Volunteering" for cutting-edge information about harnessing the power of those who are homebound, those who are unable to commit to a specific time and place for volunteering, or those who are simply too busy— but who have valuable skills they are willing to share. The "Volunteer Match" may help you find suitable volunteers for your organization who can transcend the limitations of geographical inaccessibility, as well as general volunteering resources.

Chapter 21
Forming and Running A Coalition

> Synopsis: Many nonprofit organizations form and participate in coalitions to accomplish objectives that would be difficult to achieve by themselves. There are significant advantages and considerations to forming a coalition, but the fact that they flourish is indicative of their value. This chapter discusses the pros and cons of creating and/or participating in coalitions.

Introduction

The tapestry of advocacy efforts at the international, national, state, and local levels is replete with collaborative initiatives that bring together diverse interests to accomplish a common goal. As a nonprofit organization seeks to accomplish its mission, its leadership often finds the value of creating formal and informal partnerships among like-minded organizations. As in any endeavor, there are traps and pitfalls in creating and running a coalition.

While it is often said that "two heads are better than one," it is equally rejoined that "too many cooks spoil the broth." Both of these clichés often are equally valid when applied to a coalition, and it is important for an organization leader to be able to assess which one applies predominantly before embarking on coalition-forming.

The Coalition

A coalition is a group of diverse organizations that join together to accomplish a specific objective that is likely to be achieved faster or better than if the organizations acted independently. There are many types of coalitions, and the structure is often dictated by political as well as financial considerations. The prototypical coalition involving state government issues consists of a convener coalition partner who has identified an issue, usually of direct importance to the convener's organizational membership.

The convener then "rounds up the usual suspects" by soliciting membership in the coalition to constituencies that will participate in the coalition. He or she schedules periodic meetings of the coalition at which members share information about the issue and develop a strategy to accomplish a specific goal of the coalition that, as is often the case, is the passage of legislation to solve the problem. It is not unusual for the coalition to continue even after the legislation it focused upon is enacted into law.

Structures of coalitions

• *formal organization.* Some coalitions structure formally, creating a distinct nonprofit corporate structure, such as a 501(c)(3), which will permit the coalition to hire staff, seek tax-deductible contributions from the public, rent office space, and have a system of governance that parallels, in many respects, the constituent organizations that comprise the coalition. Obviously, one would not seek to create such a complex legal entity if the objective of the coalition was to be achieved in the short term. It is not atypical for a new 501(c)(3) coalition staff to spend much of its efforts raising funds to keep it in business rather than focusing on the actual mission of the coalition. Even if funding is stable, many formal coalitions spend an inordinate amount of time on intra-organizational issues, compared to achieving their stated purposes.

Examples of formal coalitions in Pennsylvania are the Pennsylvania Alliance, a coalition that incorporated in 1994 for the purpose of monitoring the activities of the so-called "religious right;" the REACH Alliance, which was formed to coordinate advocacy relating to private school tuition vouchers; and Independent Sector, which was formed to advocate for the interests of the philanthropic sector.

• *semi-formal coalition.* These coalitions consist of organizations that have some financial resources themselves, and are able to fund the activities of the coalition. While not incorporated as separate legal entities, these coalitions nevertheless may have office space and staff. The office space may be provided as an in-kind contribution from one of the coalition members, and the staff may or may not be an employee of one of the membership. The Nonprofit Advocacy Network (NPAN) is an example of such an informal coalition structure. At one time in its history, NPAN was an unincorporated association that employed an administrative consultant. NPAN published the first two editions of the *Pennsylvania Nonprofit Handbook,* held a conference, and paid for legal services that financed amicus briefs in certain tax exemption cases (see Chapter 24). The level of activities required a more formal structure than that described below, but there was no interest among most NPAN members in creating a separate corporation. Another example of this type of coalition is the Pennsylvania Coalition to Abolish the Penalty of Death.

• *informal coalition.* Most coalitions are informal, consisting of a convener organization leader, but with no dedicated organizational staff or budget, or separate bank account. The convener organization convenes the coalition, sends out meeting notices, holds the meeting in the convener's office, and staffs the coalition as a part of its routine organizational duties. Costs can be shared among coalition members, and the convener duty can be rotated among members. In general, member organizations are not bound by the positions taken by the coalition. Examples include the Pennsylvania Coalition for Human Services and the Public Education Coalition to Oppose Tuition Vouchers.

• *group networks.* A group network is a type of informal coalition that has been formed to serve an information sharing function with less emphasis on coordinated action. These networks have no staff, no budget, take no positions, and are useful in raising the consciousness of participants about a particular issue or set of issues. These networks also are valuable in bringing people together to "network," and to build trust among organizational leadership. While efforts to coordinate action on an issue are often the result of a network-based coalition, the network itself often does not take a formal role in the coordination; rather the discussions among the participants in and after the meeting result in the synergistic effects of the network. Among examples of these coalitions in Pennsylvania are informal efforts to ban corporal punishment, expand the school breakfast program, provide third party reimbursement of clinical social workers for mental health services, and support an increase in the minimum wage.

Advantages of Forming a Coalition

- coalitions focus attention among the media, opinion leaders, and those with advocacy resources on a specific issue. Any organization, no matter how large and powerful, has a limited ability to get its message across to the public, government officials, and the media. Building a coalition is an effective strategy to call attention to an issue, as messages that are not perceived to be important from one organization may be considered important when heard from another organization.

- coalitions bring together experts on a particular issue. A convener of a coalition often has a burning desire to solve a particular public policy problem and has well-developed organizational skills, but may lack the technical expertise to develop the solution. Creating a coalition is a strategy to bring together experts in the field who collegially can participate in developing a solution.

- coalitions provide a forum to resolve turf issues and to limit destructive competition. Very few important public policy issues are so narrow that a single organization is the only one with a direct interest in a resolution. Virtually any public policy issue, particularly those that influence human services, affects a broad range of advocacy organizations whether it impinges on children, schools, the environment, business, the disabled, or the aged. Trying to solve a problem without the "buying in" of key decision-makers is a recipe for disaster. Coalitions provide the framework for obtaining the cooperation of opinion makers who otherwise would be threatened by any effort to change public policy that violates their political turf.

- coalitions provide credibility to an issue and the convener organization. One obvious application of this principle is the effort, often unsuccessful, of various extremist organizations that are not accepted in society, such as the KKK, to try to form or participate in coalitions that have a goal that is consistent with a community consensus. Another principle is that organizational messages that are viewed as self-interest are viewed negatively. When coalitions include organizations that are viewed to be acting in the public interest (such as those affiliated with the religious community or the League of Women Voters), an organization is better off having the message delivered by a coalition.

- coalitions permit resources to be shared. Coalitions benefit by the resources of their membership, be it money, volunteers, staff, office equipment, or meeting space. It is more cost-effective for an organization to form a coalition to permit resources to be shared, rather than having to pay the entire bill oneself.

- coalitions provide a path to inform new constituencies about an emerging issue. For example, the religious-based advocacy community's constituency may not have access to detailed information about a specific state budget problem, other than seeing an occasional newspaper article. It is one thing for welfare recipients to write to their legislators requesting a grant increase, and another for middle class taxpayers to write advocating for an increase based on economic justice, not self-interest. Coalitions provide a framework for expanding constituencies beyond those of the convener.

- coalitions result in positive public relations for a convener coalition-builder. New organizations build respect by forming and running a successful coalition. While the "credit" for a success achieved single-handedly can be savored, achieving that success is often much more difficult than with help from a coalition. By bringing other organizations together and working for a common goal, those organizations learn to work with the convener, to build trust, to get visibility for the new organization, and to make it more likely that the convening organization will be invited to participate in other coalitions.

Disadvantages of Coalitions

- it is often difficult for members of a coalition to focus on an issue that is usually not the priority issue for any member of the coalition other than the convener.

- coalition members who are not the convener often have an agenda different from that of the convener, and may seek to exploit the coalition for their own goals in a manner that may be inconsistent with the purpose for which the coalition was formed.

- coalitions usually reach agreement on issues by consensus, which is sometimes difficult to achieve. When it is achieved, the result is often the lowest common denominator and dilutes the aggressiveness that might have been necessary to solve a problem.

- coalitions require an order of magnitude more time to make decisions than would be required by the convener acting alone. Many coalition members require major decisions to be discussed by their own boards. There is a lag time between when a decision is requested and when a decision can be made by a coalition compared to an individual organization. Even scheduling a coalition meeting to discuss when a coalition consensus can be developed can be extremely difficult at times.

- many important coalition partners have organizational difficulties that make them used to working independently rather than in coalition.

- coalitions require organizational work (such as preparing agendas, mailing materials, and coordinating meeting times) that can be substantial.

To Form a Coalition or Not

There are many questions that should be answered, and an honest assessment made, in determining whether forming a coalition to solve a problem is constructive. Among them are:

1. What is the outcome I wish to achieve with this coalition? Is it realistic to achieve it by myself? Are the chances for success improved with a coalition?

2. Whose turf am I treading on by trying to solve this issue alone? Is there a more appropriate organization to form this coalition?

3. Are there constituencies in my own organization that will react negatively if I form this coalition?

4. How much will a coalition cost me in terms of money, time, focus?

5. Who should be invited to participate; who should not be invited?

6. Who are the experts out there that I do not have access to unless I form a coalition?

7. Will my prospective coalition participants get along?

8. How will the coalition dissolve after my goals are achieved?

9. What kind of commitment do I need from participants, and is it realistic to expect to receive these commitments?

How to Form a Coalition

- Make sure that there are no irreconcilable major differences between coalition participants, either as a result of ideology or personal enmities.

- Identify all organizations that have a direct or indirect interest in the issue.

- Invite, if appropriate, organizations that would increase the credibility of the coalition.

- Make sure that the effort is not perceived to be partisan.

- Invite outside experts to either serve on the coalition or speak to it.

- Consider business, labor, education, religious advocacy, good government citizen groups, health, local government, state government, federal government, beneficiaries of success of the coalition's objective, provider associations, lobbyists, experts on the issue, community leaders, foundation and other grant maker representatives, charities, and religious leaders as coalition members.

Tips:

- **Remember that if the objective of the coalition were the most central focus of all members of the coalition, they would have formed it first.**

- **Respect the fact that your coalition is perhaps one of many, and keep meetings short with the agenda focused. Encourage all in attendance to participate, but don't dominate the discussion yourself or let any other participant dominate. Reach consensus as quickly as possible and then move on.**

- **Delegate the work of the coalition to participants (such as by forming committees when necessary to develop a consensus).**

- **Make the meeting pleasant by being hospitable (such as providing soft drinks or lunch).**

Chapter 22
Miscellaneous Administrative Issues

> Synopsis: The offices of nonprofit corporations require computers, filing systems, and office equipment that are sensitive to organizational needs. The Postal Service offers discount postage rates to organizations that prepare bulk mailings in a manner consistent with its format and regulations.

Office Equipment

Many small nonprofit corporations are headquartered in the residences of their incorporators. There are obvious limitations to that, particularly if the corporation needs to expand its "shoe box" existence. For those who rent or own office space, some basic equipment items to consider (and budget for), are:

1. File cabinets (legal or letter size).
2. Postage meter, postage scales.
3. Typewriter, word processor.
4. Copy machine.
5. Fax machine.
6. Telephone system.
7. Telephone answering machine.
8. Computer, including CPU and keyboard, printer, monitor, and peripherals, such as modem, scanner, mouse, and Zip™ drive.
9. Electronic printing calculators.
10. Office furniture (including desks, bookcases, supply shelves, cabinets, chairs, lamps, end tables, coat racks, umbrella stand).

Staffing Patterns

Thousands of registered nonprofits operate effectively with no paid staff, while others, such as colleges and hospitals, have staff in the thousands. Salaries are by far the largest budget expenditure for organizations with paid staff. A typical "one man band" staff configuration has an executive director or director who performs all of the operations of the corporation. There may be the need for some part-time assistance to do bookkeeping or help with a special project on occasion, but it is not impossible for one versatile person to run a highly successful corporation. More typical is a two-person office—an executive/administrator and a secretary/clerk who performs the routine office management functions.

Nonprofits that can afford additional staff may have an assistant director, who may be responsible for publications, membership, or development (a euphemism for fundraising). Other typical generic staff positions of nonprofits are government relations representative, program director, publications specialist/newsletter editor, administrative assistant, public relations/community relations specialist, librarian, office manager, Web master, and data processor. Many nonprofits provide specific services. Hospitals will hire doctors, nurses, social workers, and lab technicians. Colleges will hire professors, deans, admissions officers, and custodians. The organization's mission may determine the types of specialists hired (see Chapter 11).

Many nonprofits choose to start small—hiring one staff member—and then expand with experience and fundraising, so there is a reasonable expectation that the budget can be supported in the long run. If a nonprofit is too ambitious at first, the staff may end up spending most of its time raising funds to support salaries rather than accomplishing the mission of the agency.

Stationery/Logo

Every nonprofit corporation needs to have stationery in order to provide a professional first impression. This stationery need not be fancy or expensive, although it is generally a good practice to print stationery on bond paper with some cotton content, which is heavier than the 20-pound stock used in the copy machine. Most corporate stationery has a graphic (also known as a "logo") that is descriptive of the corporation. This graphic can also be used on the masthead of a corporate newsletter, on the Web site, on mailing labels, brochures, press packets, and other promotional literature. Paying an artist to draw a distinctive and creative logo is usually a good investment, although it is often possible to make one by using some of the popular "clip art" or graphics software programs. If you do not have a scanner, a computer store may be willing to scan logo art work, so it can be printed out in various sizes or "imported" into computer-generated publications as needed.

Filing Systems

The filing systems of nonprofit corporations usually evolve over several years, and are as individual as each corporation. Several factors should be considered in setting up a filing system.

Keep files of the corporation's internal operations separate from other files. For example, keep the files relating to tax-exempt status, corporation budget, office leases, insurance, taxes, Articles of Incorporation, membership, mailing lists, lobbying and charitable registration in a different place from files about general political and public policy issues. A corporation should have correspondence files—one for "outgoing" and another for "incoming." One nonprofit always makes three copies of all out-going correspondence—one for the "outgoing" file, one for the "incoming file" stapled to the incoming letter that generated the outgoing letter, and one for the subject file that relates to the issue of the letter. "External" files can be subject matter relating to the mission of the corporation. However, "internal" files will be similar from nonprofit to nonprofit. Among typical internal files are:

> allocations, annual report, Articles of Incorporation, bank statements, board meeting agendas, board minutes, board meeting packets, bookkeeping, brochure, budget, bylaws, computer, dues structure, expenses, financial reports, grass roots alerts, insurance, mailing lists, newsletters, office equipment,

office leases, payroll, personnel, photographs, planning, postal service, press mailing list, press clippings, press releases, printing, grants, publications, speeches and testimony, special projects, tax-exempt status, taxes, and Web site. Some of these files will have sub-categories (e.g. newsletter—previous, newsletter—current), and others will be categorized by year.

Computer

Perhaps there remain a handful of nonprofit executives who are quite satisfied replying to correspondence the old-fashioned way—either writing replies using pen and paper, or banging out an answer on the same trusty Remington typewriter they used when they were in college. Many of them are satisfied with what they have—and don't begin to question this primordial existence until they are faced with having to bang out 3,000 "personal" letters asking for funds to save their jobs or tire of personally addressing 6,000 newsletters each month. The computer is, with good reason, a fixture in the modern nonprofit office.

The good news is that in the hands of a knowledgeable operator, a computer can do a variety of tasks and save thousands of expensive staff hours. The bad news is that they can be expensive, can be complicated to learn, and can "crash" at the most inopportune times.

Hardware and Software

This handbook provides only the most cursory review of basic decisions. It is geared to the small nonprofit interested in the advantages and disadvantages of purchasing a personal computer and the basic options.

Among many issues to consider when purchasing a computer system are:

1. Who will be using the system, and will they be sufficiently trained?

2. Is software available that is compatible with your hardware, and will this software be capable of providing the output you need?

3. Are you paying for features or capacity you are unlikely to ever need?

4. Is there sufficient follow-up support to answer questions, troubleshoot problems, and provide maintenance?

5. Is the system Y2K compliant?

Basic Hardware Decision: Apple or IBM-Compatible

In the old days, these two types of computers were as incompatible as Beta format and VHS for VCRs. What once were uncrossable boundaries between these two hardware systems are now being crossed and integrated. Basically, the Apple-based MacIntosh ("Mac") computers are considered to be more "user friendly," and employ a pointing device ("mouse") to choose among various options on a monitor. The operating system is usually a "graphical user interface" (GUI) that doesn't require the user to memorize all sorts of esoteric commands. On the other hand, IBM and IBM "clones" are generally less expensive and have more programs that are compatible, but require more knowledge on the part of the user. IBM and its imitators have developed software that imitates the user friendliness of the Mac. Increasingly, the Mac-based hardware is permitting the use of files created using IBM-compatible software. Each system has those who swear by it and swear at it. The state-of-the-art is advancing so swiftly that this decision may become moot in the near future.

Microsoft Windows v. DOS (Disk Operating System)

Most IBM-compatible personal computers use one of two operating systems, which control how software and files are managed. Windows uses a "graphical user interface" system that utilizes a mouse to choose among various options— a "point and click" system. Windows supports "multi-tasking," allowing several programs to run at the same time, thereby increasing productivity. The latest version is Windows 98 and most general business software is Windows-compatible.

DOS uses keyboard commands for most operations, and is quickly becoming obsolete.

Typical Software for Nonprofit Personal Computers

There are thousands of programs available that are being used by various nonprofits. In general, there are several families of programs that are useful in a typical computer-based nonprofit office. Among them are:

1. Word Processing—WordPerfect, Lotus Write, and Microsoft Word are among the most popular word processing packages. An advantage of word processing programs is that an entire document does not have to be retyped in order to make corrections or to make multiple copies. This is a major productivity enhancement if an organization desires to send a "personal" letter to 50,000 potential contributors. With a word processing program, an entire letter need not be retyped because of one error.

2. Spreadsheet—Lotus 1-2-3, Quattro Pro, and Microsoft Excel are among the most popular spreadsheet programs. In simple terms, the objective of a spreadsheet is to perform operations and calculations on numbers and automatically adjust a total when one number in a sum is changed. Spreadsheets are indispensable for bookkeeping, budgeting, and similar documents. Many spreadsheets contain graphics capability that permits numerical data to be displayed in pleasing and informative formats.

3. Database—D-Base, Q&A, Filemaker, Paradox, Access, and Label Pro are among the most popular database programs. The objective of a database

is to sort data into various fields, which can then be used to generate mailing lists, store information that can be sorted, and perform other similar tasks.

4.   Desktop Publishing (DTP)—Adobe PageMaker, Microsoft Publisher, Quark Express, First Publisher, and Publish-It are among the most popular DTP or page layout programs. These programs "import" graphics and output from word processing programs and can manipulate the result on screen in an eye-catching format. Text can be printed out in a variety of type faces and sizes, giving documents the appearance of having been professionally designed and typeset.

There are several software "suite" packages that provide the above types of programs all in one and are designed to work with each other. Before purchasing any software (which can be obtained for free from computer bulletin boards or cost thousands of dollars), it is best to seek advice from those who are knowledgeable about the advantages and disadvantages of each program.

Nonprofits affiliating with a state or national association should check with the staff of that organization to ascertain what software packages are used. Often, these organizations share data among their affiliates in only one format. While software is available to make conversions between formats and hardware configurations, substantial time, energy, and money can be saved by having compatible computer systems.

Computer Communications/Internet (see Chapter 20)

Computers that have modems provide a gateway to communications with millions of other computers and their databases and bulletin boards, and permit you to send letters, computer files, and simple messages (i.e. e-mail) through the telephone wires. Commercial on-line services such as Microsoft Network, CompuServe, and America OnLine, provide news, weather, and other information valuable to nonprofits, bulletin boards that permit the sharing of experiences and problem-solving by those with similar interests and access to the Internet. The Internet is a network of computer networks. As many as 80 million people and organizations, including most governments, libraries and institutions of higher learning, have connections to the Internet, affording virtually instantaneous communications among those connected. Using a commercial service permits communications between your personal computer and a computer on the other side of the world for the cost of a local telephone call. "Conversations" and "meetings" can be held in "real time" with each participant typing questions and responses into the keyboard.

Computer-assisted communication will revolutionize how business is conducted by nonprofits, and staff should be prepared to harness advances in technology to their advantage.

Credit Card Sales

Nonprofit organizations are businesses, and have many aspects in common with for-profit businesses. They sell products and services, such as memberships, publications, counseling, and tickets to events. They also solicit donations from the public, and it is not unusual for many to be comfortable making these donations by credit card, either through secure forms on the Internet or, more conventionally, through the mail. Inexorably, we are becoming a cashless society, and the public increasingly relies on credit cards for their financial transactions. Nonprofit organizations should consider whether having "merchant status" is advantageous.

Qualifying for merchant status for popular credit cards such as Visa, MasterCard, American Express, and Discover is routine for some nonprofit organizations. Organizations typically approach their bank to set up an account. You can find hundreds, if not thousands, of financial institutions willing to establish merchant accounts on the World Wide Web. One way to find them is to search under the term "credit cards."

Startup fees, account maintenance fees, per transaction fees, and the bank's percentage of sales commission for processing each transaction varies by financial institution, and may be negotiable. You will also need a system for transmitting the information about the transaction to the financial institution for processing, typically a terminal sold or leased by the financial institution, or computer software. The financial institution, within a few business days, credits your account for the amount of the sale after deducting transaction charges. You have to enter the card information and sales information into the terminal or software, and verify that the card is bona fide and the purchaser has not exceeded his or her credit limit. As you might expect, there is some paperwork involved, and inconvenience when a purchaser challenges a sale. On the other hand, entrepreneurial nonprofit organizations may lose out on revenue opportunities unless they satisfy the expectations of their customers.

Postal Service Issues

Nonprofit corporations typically generate a large volume of mail in the course of sending out annual reports, newsletters, program brochures, fundraising solicitations, surveys, grass roots action alerts, and meeting notices. Mass mailings, as a result of U.S. Postal Service advances in technology, have become more complicated. Because of recent reforms that substantially change the way both organizations who qualify for nonprofit mailing status and others must prepare bulk mail, the U.S.P.S. has expanded its outreach by providing educational programs.

The Postal Service offers free training on how to process bulk mailings. Call the U.S. Postal Service's regional bulk mail center to get information on the next scheduled workshop.

General Postage Rates

The U.S. Postal Service publishes the *Postal Bulletin,* which details the latest rates, fees, and changes in regulations. Subscriptions to this bi-weekly are available for $108/year and single copies are $7. A more comprehensive publication, *Domestic Mail Manual,* is published twice annually, and is available for $30. Copies of the latest edition are available from main post offices. For subscriptions, contact:

Superintendent of Documents
P.O. Box 371954
Pittsburgh, PA 15250-7954
(202) 512-1800
(202) 512-2250 (fax)

Postage Meters

Postage meters permit organizations to affix exact postage to letters and packages without the inconvenience of purchasing stamps of varying denominations. The postage is printed by the meter, and the organization pays in advance for the postage used. Most new postage meter systems permit postage accounts in the machine to be replenished by telephone/modem, although for older systems, this is done typically at the local post office. Postage machines are not sold but, in accordance with federal law, are rented by commercial companies. A license is required from the Postal Service, but the paperwork is handled by the vendor. Pitney Bowes is the firm that developed the system and is the leader in the field. Competing companies can be found in the Yellow Pages under "Mailing Machines and Equipment." The cost of renting a machine is $24.75 per month and up, including a postage scale, depending on the system's sophistication.

Bulk Mail Permit Procedures

Organizations that desire to participate in the bulk mailing program must first obtain an imprint authorization from the Postal Service. The one-time only imprint fee of $100 is good for both first and standard class (formerly known as "third class") mailing. Mailing permits must be renewed annually, and there is a $100 fee for first class and $100 for standard class. The form to file is different for organizations seeking nonprofit mailing status. These organizations file a form 3601 with the Postal Service, while other organizations file Form 3624. The Postal Service automatically forwards the correct form when it is time to renew the permits.

A pre-addressed postcard for ordering these forms is included in the back of this book.

Having such an imprint entitles the organization to pay the postage in advance without having to affix postage to each individual piece of mail. The permit also provides a discount, provided that there is a minimum of 200 pieces or 50 pounds in the bulk mailing and the mailing is sorted and processed in accordance with post office regulations. Each piece must be correctly Zip-coded or it will not be accepted.

Once in receipt of the imprint permit, the organization can affix the imprint to mail pieces using a rubber stamp, or they can print it directly on the piece.

The bulk mail discount can be large. The rate for a first class letter rose to 33 cents per ounce and 22 cents for each additional ounce effective January 10, 1999. A comparable piece of mail sent standard class bulk rate can be sent for a little more than half of that amount, depending on how it was prepared. There are substantial discounts to encourage bar-coding of bulk mailings.

501(c)(3)s (or organizations that have the characteristics of such organizations) may qualify for the U.S. Postal Service's Special Bulk Rate. The basic rate for letters under 3.2 ounces is 16.9 cents. However, this rate can be reduced further, depending on the nature of the pre-sort and the destination.

Automation

Bulk mail postage rates are substantially lower for mail that can be handled by automated equipment. For example, the rate per piece for a 5-digit bar-coded first class letter, up to 1 ounce, is 24.3 cents, compared to 30.5 cents for non-automated pre-sorted. Computer software is available at reasonable cost that will automatically place a U.S. Postal Service-compatible bar code on each label generated by your computer. Even if you do not have bar-coding capability, providing enough space for the Postal Service's equipment to optically read the address on each label and place its own bar code, while not reducing your postage rate, will qualify you for time-saving reductions in bulk mail preparation. Consult the U.S.P.S. for more information about this "upgradable mail."

The entire system for pre-sorting to comply with Postal Service regulations is too complicated to be described briefly. A thumbnail sketch of this system is provided below.

Size of Standard Class Letter Mail

The dimensions of letter size bulk mail are limited to the following:

length: 5 inches - 11 1/2 inches
width: 3.5 inches - 6 1/8 inches
thickness: .007 inches - .25 inches (enough to send a 20-page newsletter of 20-pound paper, folded once)

Bundling

Bundles of sorted letters must be secured with at least one rubber band across the width of the bundle (the shortest distance), and at least two rubber bands (one along the width and one along the length) if between 1-4 inches in thickness.

Each bundle should be prepared by following the steps 1-5 (Note that labels, rubber bands, and trays are provided free by the U.S.P.S. bulk mail center):

Step 1: Make bundles of letters with the same five-digit Zip code, if at least 10 share the same Zip code. Place a red "D" label in the bottom left corner of the first letter of each bundle.

Step 2: Make bundles of remaining letters with the same *first three* numbers in their Zip codes, if at least 10 share the same first three numbers. These bundles need not be sorted by Zip code within each bundle. Place a green "3" label in the bottom left corner of the first letter of each bundle.

Step 3: Make a bundle of remaining letters going to the same Area Distribution Center (ADC) if at least 10 share the same ADC. Place a pink "A" in the lower left hand corner of the first letter of each bundle. Note: The Postal Service in 1996 eliminated sorting by state and has substituted ADC sorting to make the mail move more efficiently. Contact the U.S. Postal Service for information about ADC groupings.

Step 4. Make a bundle of the remaining letters from the various ADCs, and place a tan "MS" label in the lower left corner of the first letter.

Tray Requirements

1. If there are 150 pieces or more with the same five-digit Zip code, they are placed in their own tray. The U.S.P.S. wants you to provide them with full trays. "Full" is defined as two-thirds full, so choose either a one-foot tray or two-foot tray in order to comply with this requirement. If you cannot provide a "full" tray at this step, combine the 5-digit tray with the 3-digit tray.

2. After completing step 1, if there are 150 pieces or more that have the first three digits in common, they are placed in their own tray. Do not combine the 3-digit pieces with the ADC pieces to create a full tray unless you are willing to pay a higher postage rate on the 3-digit pieces.

3. If, after completing steps 1 and 2, there are 150 pieces or more that go to the same ADC, they are placed in their own tray.

4. The remaining letters must be placed in a tray or left on top of the other trays.

5. Each bulk mail processing unit has a list of local Zip codes for which you can qualify for an even lower postage rate (12.1 cents per piece for 3-digits if at least 10 and 14.8 cents if less than 10 pieces to the same Zip). To qualify for this rate, these pieces must be separated out and placed in their own tray. Check with your local post office to obtain the Zip codes that qualify for this rate.

6. Trays must be enclosed by a tray sleeve and bound with polyethylene strapping. Strapping material can be purchased from a commercial office supply house.

The trays must be labeled appropriately to reach the correct destination. The Postal Service can provide correct tray labeling information.

The applicable postage must be deposited in the organization's postage account balance is not enough to cover the postage for the mailing. A mailing statement provided by the Postal Service that identifies the organization, its bulk mail account, and the number of pieces being mailed for each standard class category, must accompany each mailing.

The bulk mail operation is performed successfully by hundreds of for-profits and nonprofits alike every day. It can save thousands of dollars in postage compared to mailing every piece first class. It also saves the bother of affixing individual postage stamps. While it may appear intimidating at first, it becomes routine with practice.

In general, the Postal Service attempts to deliver standard class mail within ten days of receipt. Often, this mail is delivered just as expeditiously as first-class mail, although a 4-5 day time period for processing is not unusual. As a general rule, nonprofits should think twice before mailing anything standard class that absolutely *must* be received within 12 days after the organization delivers the mailing to the bulk mail center.

Only certain post office branches are equipped to process bulk mail. There are commercial services that specialize in processing bulk mailings. There are volunteer organizations that will offer to help nonprofit organizations do bulk mail, as well. The U.S. Postal Service has prepared a comprehensive publication titled *Preparing Standard Mail A,* updated January 1999. To order this publication (Publication 49), write to the U.S. Postal Service or contact your local post office.

Another U.S.P.S. Publication, *Quick Service Guide* (Publication 95), provides specifications for bar-coding and OCR-related mail preparation. The Postal Service will most likely require all bulk business mail to be bar-coded within a few years. It is recommended that nonprofit organizations review this publication before building a database for a mailing list.

A pre-addressed postcard for ordering most of the forms and booklets described in this section is included in the back of this book.

Tips:

- When creating a mailing list, it is useful to have the list in Zip-code order or to be capable of sorting it in Zip-code order. Otherwise, letters must be sorted by hand to take advantage of the bulk mail discounts.

- Most of the popular word processing programs will perform a Zip-code sort operation and create mailing labels, and virtually all of the database programs do. Many are capable of automatically inserting a bar code, which further reduces postage rates if printed in accordance with postal service regulations.

- Contact the U.S. Postal Service for help with bulk mail preparation or rates. A useful telephone number is:

  1-800-238-3150—National Customer Support Center
  U.S.P.S. Web site: http://www.usps.gov

Chapter 23
Nonprofits and Small Business Competition

> **Synopsis:** Some small business advocates have charged that nonprofits have unfair advantages when they compete in the sale of goods and services. Legislation and regulations to remove these advantages are a clear threat to the ability of the nonprofit sector to function effectively.

An issue has emerged on the agenda of Pennsylvania policy makers that could jeopardize the ability of many nonprofits to perform their vital missions. Tracing its beginning to the early 1980s, the issue of alleged unfair competition between nonprofits and small business earned its first stamp of legitimacy when the U.S. Small Business Administration issued a report in late 1983 entitled *Unfair Competition by Nonprofit Organizations with Small Business: An Issue for the 1980's.*

Small businesses had, until then, complained with muted voices that nonprofit corporations possessed advantages in the marketplace that hindered the ability of small businesses to compete. Among these advantages were said to be:

1. Tax exemptions—the most tangible benefit of nonprofits;
2. Reduced postage rates;
3. Tax deductions for those who contribute goods and services to nonprofit organizations;
4. Use of venture capital—the ability to use contributions and non-taxable surpluses for expansion, state-of-the-art equipment, and seed money for new activities that may compete with private enterprise;
5. "Captured referrals"— "sweetheart deal" arrangements between affiliated nonprofits that eliminate competition from non-affiliated businesses;
6. Use of plant, staff, supplies, and equipment donated or funded by grants to spur unrelated business enterprises that may compete with small business; and
7. "Halo effect"—referring to the willingness of the public to do business with a nonprofit because of the perception that the organization is serving the public good rather than being operated for a private profit motive.

During the 1970s, nonprofit corporations were becoming increasingly sophisticated in their efforts to generate revenue. These efforts accelerated during the 1980s when many social service nonprofits were hit by the loss of government funding during the retrenchment of domestic spending under the Reagan Administration. Nonprofit hospitals were a particular target of small business owners, who resented the establishment of laundry and pharmaceutical services that competed with them. Small business advocates continue to complain that Pennsylvania government has no effective mechanism to track funds that may be channeled between a nonprofit agency and its for-profit affiliates.

Also targeted nationally were YMCAs and their Jewish counterpart JCCs. Some of the YMCAs and JCCs began marketing their lucrative health club services to an "upscale" market segment to generate revenues to cross-subsidize services provided to their more needy clients. Such facilities were caught in a "Catch 22." If they charged less than the market rates, they were accused of undercutting small business by taking advantage of their tax exemptions and other advantages. If they charged the same or more than the private health clubs, they were accused of operating just as any other business and thus not deserving of any tax exemption. Private health clubs across the nation, through the guidance of their associations, participated in legal actions against several YMCAs and instigated reviews by local taxing authorities that were designed to challenge the historical tax-exempt status of these facilities. An effort by nine private health clubs in the Pittsburgh area to challenge the tax exemption of the Golden Triangle YMCA in Pittsburgh was partially successful (see Chapter 24).

Colleges and universities garnered the wrath of small business owners who objected to college bookstores selling television sets and refrigerators, selling surplus computer time, engaging in testing service businesses, establishing travel agencies, or otherwise entering markets in direct competition with small business.

These small business owners found a voice in the Small Business Administration. On July 27, 1983, the Small Business Administration's Office of Advocacy held a one-day symposium on this issue, and followed up the conference with a November report entitled *Unfair Competition by Nonprofit Organizations With Small Business: An Issue for the 1980's*. This report charged that "traditional 'donative' nonprofits, such as the Red Cross and the Salvation Army, which rely primarily on gifts and contributions for their operating revenue, are being replaced by 'commercial nonprofits'... which derive all or nearly all of their income from the sales of goods or services they produce." The report charged some of the nonprofit sector with creating an oversupply of goods, and charging significantly lower than the prevailing market rates as a result of exemptions from laws and regulations. The report concluded:

> "It is the responsibility of the Congress and the Executive Branch to make a systematic inquiry into whether these exemptions are still justified in light of the emergence of the commercial nonprofit sector."

Among other recommendations, the report called for:

1. A higher tax or outright prohibition on unrelated business activities by nonprofits;

2. Defining the definition of "substantially related" more clearly and narrowly for purposes of what constitutes an unrelated business;

3. Establishing a threshold above which a nonprofit engaging in unrelated business activities would lose its tax exemption; and

4. Eliminating the "convenience" exception for the payment of unrelated business income taxes.

Soon after the report was released, approximately 20 national business associations, many of which participated in the drafting of the 1983 SBA report, formed the "Coalition for Fair Business Competition" to lobby on behalf of business interests on this issue.

The issue of nonprofit competition with small business was among the most compelling of the issues reported by small business owners at the 1986 White House Conference on Small Business. Conference delegates designated it the number three issue on a list of 40 major concerns culled from a list of 2,232 proposed by small business owners nationwide. Legislation was introduced in several states in response to this conference.

Pennsylvania Background

On December 11, 1985, the Pennsylvania House of Representatives, by a vote of 195-0, passed a resolution introduced by Rep. Italo Cappabianca (D-Erie) three weeks earlier to establish a seven-member bipartisan Select Committee to Study Nonprofits. The stated purpose of the Select Committee was to "study tax-exempt nonprofit organizations engaged in the sale of goods and services within the Commonwealth, especially with regard to the impact on small business."

The Select Committee held 16 days of hearings between March and August 1986. On November 25, 1986, the Select Committee issued its final report, which included nine recommendations. The report concluded that it was impossible to judge whether there was unfair competition by nonprofits because of the paucity of information on nonprofits in Pennsylvania. The report stated that Pennsylvania law is filled with "many loopholes and exemptions with regard to reporting requirements."

Among the report's nine recommendations were the following:

- establish an entity within the Pennsylvania Department of Revenue to determine which nonprofits are engaging in activities beyond the realm of the purpose for which they were incorporated;

- require all Pennsylvania nonprofits to file their IRS tax exemption code number and most recent federal income tax returns with the Commonwealth;

- require all nonprofits to disclose their "affiliations" with other corporations;

- restrict nonprofit entities from performing commercial business ventures in a nonprofit environment that takes advantage of tax exemptions;

- require that surpluses of nonprofits be used to fund their tax-exempt purposes; and

- prohibit the commingling of nonprofit resources with those of any for-profit within the same organizational structure.

Many in the Pennsylvania nonprofit community expected that the attention on this issue had concluded with the publication and distribution of the final report. It was, in fact, only a prelude. On January 6, 1987, Rep. Cappabianca introduced another resolution, H. Res. 4, with 43 cosponsors, including the House Majority Leader at the time, the late James Manderino (D-Westmoreland). The new resolution proposed a nine-member bipartisan Select Committee to study the possibility of direct and unfair competition resulting from nonprofits charging fees for their services. It raised the issue of potential adverse impacts of such competition, including forcing small businesses out of business and eroding the tax base. H. Res. 4 was adopted on February 5, 1987, by a vote of 189-5, and another series of hearings was launched.

Institutions of Purely Public Charity Act—Section 8

The Institutions of Purely Public Charity Act, Act 55 of 1997, was enacted on November 26, 1997, and is the culmination of the decade-long struggle between Pennsylvania small businesses and nonprofit organizations. With some irony, this law was supported by the National Federation of Independent Businesses (NFIB), and the legislation, the top priority of Pennsylvania charities for nearly a decade, was unlikely to pass without this support from such an unlikely source. Section 8 of this bill includes modest restrictions on nonprofit operations that were negotiated between charities and the small business community leadership. The principal restriction is that "(A)n institution of purely public charity may not fund, capitalize, guarantee the indebtedness of, lease obligations of or subsidize a commercial business that is unrelated to the institution's charitable purpose as stated in the institution's charter or governing legal documents."

This restriction does not apply to existing business arrangements. There are three major exceptions. The first is if the business "is intended only for the use of its employees, staff, alumni, faculty, members, students, clients, volunteers, patients or residents." The second exception is if "the commercial business results in sales to the general public that are incidental or periodic rather than permanent and ongoing." The third exception is if the institution "is formally requested to do so by the Commonwealth or a political subdivision." The law also includes an exception applicable to the use of facilities to host groups for educational purposes. The Department of State is authorized to administer an arbitration system to adjudicate small business complaints. Those unsuccessful may appeal the arbitrator's decision to a court of common pleas. As of January 1999, this system was utilized just once, and the arbitrator threw out the initial complaint against the Ridley Park YMCA in Delaware County.

Federal Unrelated Business Income Tax (UBIT)

Federal law provides that nonprofit corporations pay federal taxes on unrelated business income. Corporations with at least $1,000 of such income are required to file a 990-T annually. Income is defined as unrelated if it is derived from a trade or business, is regularly carried on, and is substantially unrelated to the exempt purpose of the corporation. Income clearly exempt from UBIT includes that generated from activities performed by volunteers, that from selling merchandise received as gifts or contributions, and dividends, interest, royalties, and capital gains. Also exempt is income from business operations that are conducted for the "convenience" of an organization's members, students, patients, and staff, such as a hospital cafeteria or college bookstore.

The Internal Revenue Service reports that $502 million in UBIT was collected from 50,034 organizations in 1996, and $486 million was collected from 48,563 organizations in 1997.

Both the Congress and the Internal Revenue Service have been skeptical about whether charities should have a broad exemption from paying taxes on business income. The House Ways and Means Committee's Oversight Committee held a series of hearings in June 1987 on the issue of changing federal policy on unrelated business income taxes. The subcommittee followed up on its hearings by issuing a press release on March 31, 1988, describing policy options on changes to UBIT, many of which caused concern in the nonprofit sector. The options included suggestions to narrow the "substantially related" test for exempting organizations from UBIT, to repeal the "convenience" exception (which, for example, permits college bookstores and cafeterias to be tax exempt), to apply UBIT to fitness/health clubs unless the program is "available to a reasonable cross section of the general public such as by scholarship or by fees based on community affordability," and to apply UBIT to advertising income and allow deductions from UBIT only on direct advertising costs (a major concern to exempt nonprofits whose publications accept commercial advertising to defray expenses of the parent organization).

In March 1990, a revised report leaked from the subcommittee entitled *Summary of Main Issues in Possible Modification of Oversight Committee UBIT Options*. The draft proposal eliminated many of the controversial proposals that caused so much concern to nonprofits. While the "substantially related" test was retained in the proposal, the "convenience" exception was repealed. Most indirect and overhead expenses relating to advertising income would be deductible, but such expenses could not reduce net income by more than 80%. The subcommittee membership was unable to reach a consensus on UBIT proposals.

The Internal Revenue Service has aggressively audited some charities focusing on UBIT issues, and has taken charities to court to promote its policy of restricting UBIT exemptions. During the 1990s, the Internal Revenue Service expanded its attention to enforcement of UBIT, and developed policies with respect to some of the gray areas that were problematic to charities. Some cases involving the interpretation of what constitutes unrelated income were litigated. Several relatively recent decisions on generic UBIT issues have been decided in favor of charities. Three examples have been cases involving mailing list rental income, affinity credit card income, and income from bingo games.

Two cases involving whether mailing list rental income is considered subject to UBIT have resulted in victories for the challenged charity. The first involved the Sierra Club, which was heard by the 9th Circuit Court of Appeals. A subsequent case before United States Tax Court involving the American Academy of Ophthalmology also found that such income was not taxable. Tax Court also rejected the contention of the IRS that payments made to the Mississippi State University Alumni Association by a bank were royalty payments rather than business income, and thus are not subject to UBIT. Each of these three cases had fact-specific aspects that may not apply to every case of a charity generating revenues by renting their mailing lists or utilizing affinity credit card arrangements, and some caution needs to be taken in generalizing. However, the courts apparently have been reining in the IRS for a generally broad interpretation of what constitutes unrelated business income, and this is a positive trend for charities seeking unconventional methods to generate the revenue they need to provide their services. Another case, involving income from instant pull-tab bingo games, developed when the IRS determined that income from these games conducted by Women of the Motion Picture Industry and other 501(c)(3) and (c)(6) organizations was subject to UBIT. The tax code does provide for UBIT exception for most bingo game income, but the conditions are narrow and do not apply to the instant pull-tab games. Tax Court ruled in favor of the organizations.

A case decided in August 1996 in U.S. District Court involving the American Academy of Family Physicians determined that the organization's income from a group insurance plan offered to its members underwritten by a private insurance carrier was not subject to UBIT. Again, the facts of this case may not be typical of conventional agreements between an insurance carrier and an exempt organization, but the opinion of the court on the issue was a favorable development.

Differences Between Nonprofits and For-Profits

There are clear and fundamental differences between the operations and motivations of nonprofits and for-profits. The buildings of some types of nonprofit charities and their for-profit counterparts may, in some cases, be similar. For-profit and nonprofit hospitals, nursing homes, day care centers, and recreational/youth service facilities may have the same equipment and physical plants, and provide some of the same services. Yet these similarities often are exaggerated in an effort by some overzealous small business advocates to discredit the tax exemptions of those they perceive as competitors. The YMCAs in a growing number of communities particularly have endured vicious attacks from some private health club owners. In specific cases around the nation, these attacks have been given a credibility unsupported by the facts, and have resulted in the loss of tax-exempt status.

Among the differences between nonprofit charitable organizations and for-profits are the following:

1. A nonprofit charity is driven by its service mission philosophy rather than by the profit motive.

2. A nonprofit charity serves those who cannot afford to pay full costs.

3. Any excess revenue over expenditures is funneled back into the institution to further its exempt purpose.

4. The charitable institution likely will remain in the community even if it suffers financial losses.

5. The nonprofit charity is more accountable to its board for public service.

6. The nonprofit charity often will proactively look for ways to respond to community needs without regard to any profit motive.

7. A nonprofit charity may not compensate its employees higher than "reasonable" rates, as is evident from the successful prosecution of several television religious broadcasters who were paid exorbitant salaries and benefits.

8. A nonprofit charity's board of directors is typically comprised of unpaid community leaders motivated by public service and serving the unmet needs of the community rather than making a profit.

9. A nonprofit charity, because of its legal mission to serve rather than to make profits, often attracts thousands of hours of volunteer time and philanthropic contributions that further its purposes.

Recommendations for Nonprofits with Respect to Competition

1. Nonprofits should not publicly advertise products and services in a manner that underscores price competition with the for-profit sector.

2. Nonprofits should refrain from entering markets that are not substantially related to the mission of the organization, and should be prepared to pay unrelated business income taxes (UBIT) on income derived from activities not "directly" related, should this change in the law be approved.

3. Nonprofits should review their activities that could be construed as commercial, and identify all those that require the filing of a 990-T and payment of UBIT.

4. In exploring options for generating new agency revenue, nonprofits should be sensitive to meeting needs that are unmet by the for-profit sector rather than relying on undercutting the price of goods and services already being offered in the marketplace.

5. Nonprofits should support efforts to improve disclosure and accountability of the voluntary sector, and cooperate with expanded enforcement of laws governing this sector, so that the few nonprofits that are abusing the law do not stain the reputation of the entire sector.

6. Nonprofits should periodically review their bylaws and tax-exempt status purposes, and update these documents to reflect changing conditions.

Chapter 24
State and Local Tax Exemptions

> Synopsis: Many nonprofit charities have been subject to challenges to their state and local tax exemptions in recent years. Legislation was signed into law in 1997 to constrain the misinterpretations by taxing bodies of a Pennsylvania Supreme Court case that provided a judicial definition of institutions eligible for tax-exempt status.

Sales and Use Tax Exemption

Pennsylvania has a 6% sales and use tax on most goods and many services. There is an additional 1% sales tax collected in Philadelphia as a result of a 1991 state law, and in Allegheny County as a result of a 1994 state law. Many charitable nonprofit organizations are legally exempt from paying this tax on purchases for their use. Organizations that believe they qualify for exempt status need to submit this information when they file the PA-100 form with the Department of Revenue, and must file an REV-72 form. This tax exemption is for purchases by the organization and does not extend to items sold by such organizations during fundraising efforts, unless the sale qualifies as an "isolated transaction." Answers to the questions on the form with respect to tax-exempt status should be sensitive to the issues discussed later in this chapter.

Sales and Use Tax Charitable Exemption Application Form

Organizations seeking exemption from paying Pennsylvania sales tax must submit an REV-72 to the Department of Revenue. The form was last revised in December 1998, and it reflects both changes made in statute with the enactment of the *Institutions of Purely Public Charity Act* and negotiations with the charitable community to streamline the form and reduce burdensome requirements. This 12-page form is still unreasonably burdensome, according to representatives of Pennsylvania charities, and it is still possible that the form will be streamlined further once the department recognizes the difficulty charities will have in filling out this form. The form is divided into two major sections titled Registration Information and Financial Information. Registration information is subdivided into subsections labeled Institutional Information, Form of Organization, Organization Information, Affiliate Information, Officer Information, and Salary Information. The Financial Information section is subdivided into subsections labeled Basic Questions, Recipient Information, Goods or Services Provided, and Fundraising Activities. Institutional Information and Form of Organization are straightforward requests for general information about the institution.

Organization Information requests "a detailed description of the past, present, and planned future activities of the institution for a period of three years" including a description of how beneficiaries are selected. Affiliate information requires disclosure of the date of affiliation, percent of ownership, and other general information. Officer information requires disclosure of annual compensation, if any, for each officer, and other benefits and amounts of each. Salary information must be provided that discloses whether compensation is based in any way on the performance of the institution. The position, salary, and other compensation of the four highest paid individuals must be disclosed.

The financial data disclosure is quite extensive. Many of the questions track the various options for meeting the five-part HUP test found in Act 55 (see pages 222-224). Even if an institution clearly demonstrates that it meets one of these options for "donating a substantial portion of its services," the disclosure form requests detailed information about how the organization meets virtually all of the options. For example, applicants must disclose the percentage of individuals receiving goods or services from the institution who receive a reduction of fees of at least 10% of the cost of goods or services provided to them.

In addition to filling out the form, applicants must also provide a copy of their Articles of Incorporation, bylaws, any other governing legal document, most current financial statement (new organizations may submit a proposed budget), their most recent 990 annual federal tax return if they file one, and a copy of their IRS determination letter if they have one.

The Pennsylvania Constitution

Federal tax exemption status of an institution has no bearing on state exemption status policy. Article VIII, section 2(a) of the Pennsylvania Constitution provides the legal basis for the granting of tax exemptions in Pennsylvania. This section of the Pennsylvania Constitution provides that the General Assembly "may by law exempt from taxation" a narrow list of five types of institutions. Charitable institutions are among those potentially exempt, provided they are considered to be "institutions of purely public charity." See Appendix G for the full text of this section of the Constitution.

There is no definition of the term "institutions of purely public charity" in the Pennsylvania Constitution or in statute. Until now, the only guidance on this definition has been provided by the courts.

Pennsylvania Tax Exemption Law

The General Assembly has used the authority of the above section of the Constitution to provide tax exemptions to certain classes of institutions. The act of May 22, 1933 (P.L. 853, No. 155), known as the General County Assessment Law, as amended, provides that "...hospitals, academies, associations of learning, benevolence, or charity...founded, endowed, and maintained by public or private charity" are exempt from "all county, city, borough, town, township, road, poor and school tax." See Appendix G for the text of this act, which applies to counties of the first through third class [72 P.S. §5020-204(a)(3)]. A parallel law authorizes tax exemptions for such institutions in fourth through eighth class counties [72 P.S. §5453.202(a)(3)]. The act of March 4, 1971 (P.L. 6, No. 2, 72 P.S. §7204) provides an exemption from the state sales and use tax on "(T)he sale at retail to or use by (i) any charitable organization, volunteer firemen's organization or nonprofit educational institution..." See Appendix G for an excerpt from the text of these exemptions. State law (72 P.S. §7236) requires the organization seeking a tax exemption to affirmatively prove that it is entitled to an exemption.

Hospital Utilization Project v. Commonwealth of Pennsylvania (HUP v. PA)

Although the term "purely public charity" has not been defined with exactness under Pennsylvania law, case law has provided criteria establishing the parameters of a "purely public charity." In 1985, the Pennsylvania Supreme Court, after reviewing prior law stated:

> *"(It) may be safely said that whatever is gratuitously done or given in relief of the public burdens or for the advancement of the public good is a public charity. In every such case as the public is the beneficiary, the charity is a public charity. As no private or pecuniary return is reserved to the giver or any particular person, but all the benefit resulting from the gift or act goes to the public, it is a 'purely public charity,' the word 'purely' being equivalent to the word 'wholly'..."*

The court elaborated further that receiving revenues from recipients sufficient to keep the institution in operation, so long as this revenue does not go beyond self-support, does not affect its status as a purely public charity. This principle is consistent with current Pennsylvania statute as well.

In its summary, the court concluded that "an entity qualifies as a purely public charity if it possesses the following characteristics:

1. *advances a charitable purpose;*
2. *donates or renders gratuitously a substantial portion of its services;*
3. *benefits a substantial and indefinite class of persons who are legitimate subjects of charity;*
4. *relieves government of some of its burden; and*
5. *operates entirely free from private profit motive."*

The HUP case should have had little or no bearing on the granting or denial of tax exemptions by the Department of Revenue or local governments. There was no new legal doctrine made by the case, and the decision was entirely appropriate given the facts of the case. Yet it is evident from reading the above five criteria outside the context of the cases in which these were developed that they are basic and general. The terms are unclear if viewed in a vacuum. What does the term "legitimate subjects of charity" mean? Does it mean only the poor? What about the term "substantial portion of its services"? Does this mean 75% or 5%? Does the provision of money rather than "services" preclude an organization from meeting these criteria?

The HUP case does provide appropriate guidance on the intent and meaning of the court's definition of "institution of purely public charity." For example, the only mention of the term "legitimate subjects of charity" in the HUP case is a quotation from its previous decision in the *YMCA of Germantown v. Philadelphia* (1936) case. In seeking to define a "purely public charity," the Court wrote:

> Under this definition the characteristics of an organized charity are: *First whatever it does for others is done free of charge, or at least so nearly free of charge as to make the charges nominal or negligible; second, that those to whom it renders help or services are those who are unable to provide themselves with what the institution provides for them, that is, they are legitimate subjects of charity.*

Thus the term "legitimate subjects of charity" is broad enough to include those who use libraries and museums and attend symphony concerts.

The initial "judge" in a tax exemption case is usually the very unit of government that has the most to gain financially by the most narrow interpretation of tax-exempt status criteria. As has been demonstrated in several cases detailed below, these five criteria have been interpreted more narrowly than intended by the HUP decision, and in some cases, intentionally misinterpreted in order to maximize revenues for governmental units. Legislation was enacted by the General Assembly in 1997 to standardize the meaning of the HUP criteria.

Department of Revenue Sales and Use Tax Regulations

The text of the current regulation in force was published in April 1995 as a corrective reprint to the regulations published in the *Pennsylvania Bulletin* on December 24, 1994. These regulations have been administratively replaced with informal rules that implement Act 55, the *Institutions of Purely Public Charity Act* (see pages 222-224).

Recent Tax Exemption Cases of Interest

Case 1: St. Margaret Seneca Place

A Commonwealth Court opinion of February 20, 1992, sent shock waves throughout the Pennsylvania charitable community. A three-judge panel overturned a lower court decision that had determined that a 156-bed Allegheny County nursing home had activities consistent with all five HUP criteria and the three statutory criteria as well, and thus was entitled to a refund of its property taxes for 1989. Using the logic of the Commonwealth Court opinion, virtually no modern charity would be eligible for tax exempt status in Pennsylvania. The court determined that, contrary to the findings of the lower court, St. Margaret's did not meet a single one of the five HUP criteria. To do so, the court had to stretch the intent of the HUP criteria to a point of absurdity and, according to many experts, did so. For example, the facility's Medical Assistance caseload was 48.5% of admissions, and the home lost hundreds of thousands of dollars by providing charity care to subsidize the difference between costs and Medical Assistance reimbursement. The court determined that accepting MA patients was analogous to an airline charging lower costs to different classes of persons in order to fill its seats—and thus this was a general business practice and not charity. The facility lost on two of the five HUP criteria because its executive testified that the facility would rather have a paying patient than someone who could not afford to pay because—

"Given our current census and the number of Medicaid patients that we have now and the amount of charitable care that we are already providing, we would have to take the person who could afford to pay us something. We don't have unlimited resources in terms of funds to continue to take care of our deficits."

To rule that St. Margaret's was not eligible for tax-exempt status, Commonwealth Court had to find that the facility failed on only one of the five HUP criteria or three statutory criteria. In ruling that the lower court was wrong on its interpretation of the HUP test on every single criterion as well as the three-part statutory test, the Court had to blatantly ignore substantial factual data that supported the facility's position. Some analysts suggested that the intent of the opinion was not to dispassionately weigh the merits of the case but to provide a political message to all Pennsylvania charities.

St. Margaret's appealed the case to the entire Commonwealth Court. In its appeal, the facility pointed out many obvious errors and omissions made by the Court that even the most zealous anti-charity judge disregarding political considerations would not have ignored. In addition, the facility noted that one member of the three-judge panel, Dan Pellegrini, "formerly served as Solicitor of the City of Pittsburgh, and in that capacity was very active in attempts to remove exemptions of many previously exempt institutions." Lawyers for St. Margaret's suggested that Judge Pellegrini's participation in this case would provide for "potential bias or appearance of impropriety." The appeal was denied. In May 1992, the facility appealed to the Pennsylvania Supreme Court.

For some in the nonprofit community, the Commonwealth Court decision in the St. Margaret's case was, in one respect, a positive development. Because the rulings in the case were so clearly absurd, the opinion became a useful tool in educating members of the General Assembly and the public about why a statutory solution was necessary.

The Nonprofit Advocacy Network organized an effort by more than a score of state-wide nonprofit charitable associations to file an *amicus* brief in this case. NPAN officials argued that there has never been such an obvious miscarriage of justice as occurred in this case, and this represented the best opportunity for the Pennsylvania Supreme Court to once and for all end the misinterpretation of its own ruling in the HUP case. Several other *amicus* briefs were filed by individual associations.

On April 20, 1994, the Pennsylvania Supreme Court ruled 5-1 in favor of St. Margaret Seneca Place. The court repudiated virtually every finding of Commonwealth Court, noting that the nursing home did, indeed, meet all of the five HUP criteria. Of importance to many charities is the finding that obtaining revenue from government sources to finance charity care was not a disqualification for charitable tax-exempt status. Also, the court ruled that a charity need not provide services that are "wholly gratuitous," a standard advanced by the lower court that, in effect, would have disqualified almost every modern charity from exemption. However, the opinion did not clarify the terms of the five HUP criteria beyond that which was necessary as a result of the actual facts in the particular case before the court, and thus did not obviate the need for statutory clarification provided by legislation such as Act 55.

Case 2: PA Institute of Certified Public Accountants (PICPA)

In October 1993, the Pennsylvania Supreme Court denied a sales tax exemption to the PICPA's educational foundation. The court ruled that the organization failed to meet several of the HUP criteria, including that it did not benefit the general public. About 38% of those attending PICPA seminars were not members of the organization. The court did not agree with the organization that government would have had to provide the educational services provided by PICPA if the organization did not provide them. Prior to the decision in the St. Margaret Seneca Place case, the PICPA case caused substantial concern in the charitable community because of the extremely narrow interpretation of the court on the issue of public benefit and relief of government burden. Even when an educational program is available to all who are interested, the court failed to recognize that "an indefinite class of persons" is being served. As one legal analyst pointed out, "by extending the court's logic, one wonders whether a medical school, law school, art school, or any other focused form of education qualifies as benefiting 'an indefinite number of people.' "

Case 3: Golden Triangle YMCA

In 1986, the Golden Triangle YMCA in downtown Pittsburgh relocated. The City of Pittsburgh challenged the tax-exempt status of this facility, whose clientele consisted of many "upscale" health club members paying substantial annual fees. The Allegheny County Board of Property and Assessment, Appeals and Review ruled that the facility should be taxed on a seventh of its assessed value because one floor of the seven-story building was a state-of-the-art health and fitness club that, the board determined, was not being used for charitable purposes. Both the YMCA and local taxing bodies appealed the decision. The city and county argued that the entire facility should be taxable, and the YMCA contended that the 140-year YMCA exemption from taxation was still valid. On November 22, 1988, Allegheny County Court of Common Pleas Judge Ralph Smith, Jr., ruled that the Golden Triangle YMCA failed to meet any of the five HUP criteria, all of which must be met in order for a facility to be an "institution of purely public charity" and eligible for tax-exempt status under the terms of the Pennsylvania Constitution.

The YMCA appealed the case to Commonwealth Court. In an opinion handed down September 29, 1989, the three-judge panel vacated and remanded the decision of the Allegheny County Court of Common Pleas. Commonwealth Court ordered that the lower court perform a use-by-use analysis of each floor of the facility and determine the extent the building was being used for charitable purposes. An appeal filed by the City and County of the Commonwealth Court decision, which was clearly a victory for the YMCA, was denied by the Pennsylvania Supreme Court.

On May 18, 1990, the court approved a settlement among the parties for the YMCA to make payments in lieu of taxes. The settlement stipulated that a percentage of the building shall be considered taxable, ranging from 15% for 1986 and 1987 up to 40% of the building's assessed value for the tax years of 1991-1995. The agreement provided that—

> "(i) the City, the County, the School District and the Board recognize the charitable nature of the YMCA in providing services to the citizens of the City of Pittsburgh and the County of Allegheny and the children attending the schools of the School District, (ii) the YMCA denies and continues to deny that it is liable for any real estate taxes as well as other taxes, recognizes the City's, the County's and the School District's fiscal needs and (iii) the parties hereto desire to avoid further expense, inconvenience and distraction of litigation."

Case 4: St. Luke's Hospital

Lehigh County Common Pleas Court Judge Robert K. Young handed down a decision April 19, 1990, in the St. Luke's property tax case confirming that hospital's tax-exempt status. The decision affirmed that the tax-exemption was valid even though hospital income regularly exceeded expenses and most of its patient care was reimbursed. Judge Young ruled that St. Luke's met all five parts of the HUP test, and he established a formula for what constitutes "substantial" in the HUP test criterion "donate or render gratuitously a substantial portion of its services." The standard used by the judge was to require that the amount of uncompensated care be at least 75% of the amount of hospital "profit" (or 51% during a major construction program). The judge's definition of "uncompensated care" included bad debts, Medicare and Medicaid payment shortfalls, community education programs, and other costs advocated for inclusion in that term by the hospital industry. Despite the victory for St. Luke's, hospital officials for the 116-year-old facility filed an appeal, arguing that there may be some future circumstances where the facility might not be eligible for a tax-exemption under the court's formula, yet may still meet the criteria for exemption provided for by statute and the PA Constitution.

The local governments involved refused to accept the judge's ruling and petitioned the assessment board to again revoke the hospital's tax exemption. The board did so. In order to avoid more costly litigation after expending almost $300,000 in legal fees, St. Luke's surrendered to what some hospital officials characterized as "extortion." To avoid further challenges to its tax exemption, the hospital agreed to provide free drug testing of county inmates, build a fire station for the borough, do cholesterol screening and offer prenatal counseling to pregnant teens for the school district, and develop an Alzheimer's disease education program.

Case 5: Hamot Hospital

An Erie County Court of Common Pleas judge ruled on May 18, 1990, that the Hamot Medical Center was not eligible for tax-exempt status. Judge George Levin ruled that Hamot failed to meet four of the five HUP criteria, pointing out that the facility funneled more than $25 million in profits to its for-profit facilities for investment in a marina, real estate, and other for-profit ventures unrelated to medical care. Judge Levin also criticized the facility for having a profit-sharing plan for its employees, and for claiming that revenue it was unable to collect in court suits from those unable to pay their hospital bills constituted charity care.

Judge Levin's opinion included a finding that government receipts under a designed reimbursement system (e.g. Medicare and Medicaid) did not constitute maintenance by public charity.

While Hamot officials appealed to the Pennsylvania Supreme Court for relief, they concurrently initiated negotiations with municipal government officials to provide for a settlement out-of-court. Hamot officials in 1992 agreed to make $4 million in annual in-lieu-of-tax payments. In addition, Hamot initiated a corporate restructuring geared to improving its chances of becoming an institution of purely public charity eligible for future tax-exempt status.

Case 6: Butler County Children's Center

A Butler County Common Pleas Court judge ruled on August 23, 1990, that the Butler County Children's Center was not eligible for its tax-exemption. The judge acknowledged that of the 142 children in the Center's Head Start program, 129 paid no fee and the rest were assessed on a sliding scale fee fixed by the state. The program was funded by Title XX, the United Way, and from fees. The judge ruled that this center did not "donate or render gratuitously a substantial portion of its services" because only 13 of the 142 students in the Head Start program were free non-paying, non-subsidized students. The Head Start funding was "taxpayers' money expended by a private agency, not public charity in the pure definition of public charity." The logic of this decision escaped virtually all human service agency advocates who would assert that the model of the Butler County center is exactly the kind of institution deserving of tax-exempt status.

Case 7: Jewish Federation of Reading

The Pennsylvania Department of Revenue on March 3, 1989, denied an application from the Jewish Federation of Reading for a sales tax exemption. The Federation appealed the decision to the Department's Board of Appeals, which reaffirmed the previous decision of denial on October 31, 1989. A seven-page decision of the board of Appeals detailed the reasons for denial. One significant finding of the board was that the Jewish Federation failed to "advance a charitable purpose" because the beneficiaries of its charity were other agencies and organizations rather than the public. Such a ruling was a direct contradiction of a 1973 Commonwealth Court case in which the United Way of Philadelphia was deemed to be an "institution of purely public charity." In addition, the board ruled that the Jewish Federation failed to "donate or render gratuitously a substantial portion of its services" because it provided funding rather than services. This ruling also was considered to be a threat to the tax-exempt status of all "umbrella" fundraising organizations, such as United Ways and foundations/community chests. The Board of Finance and Revenue unanimously approved the Federation's appeal and the tax exemption was restored.

Case 8: Washington and Jefferson College

The Pennsylvania Supreme Court on November 20,1997 handed down a 5-1 decision upholding a September 1995 opinion by Commonwealth Court that Washington and Jefferson College was entitled to tax-exempt status as an institution of purely public charity (see page 265).

Case 9: Community Accountants

The Pennsylvania Supreme Court on March 29, 1996, issued a terse, one-page ruling in the Community Accountants sales tax case. The court upheld the decision of Commonwealth Court denying exempt status to the Philadelphia-based charity. The March 1995 decision of Commonwealth Court was problematic, because the standards used by the court to meet the HUP tests of "relieve government of some of its burden" and "an indefinite class of persons who are legitimate subjects of charity" were so narrow that few, if any charities could meet them. However, there are other decisions by the Supreme Court that provide enough guidance to prevent the Community Accountants standards from serving as a precedent for denying every charity's exemption. Also, the Community Accountants' function and mission is so different from that of most charities that many advocates for charities did not see this decision as necessarily having any major impact on how human service charities would be viewed by the courts with respect to meeting the five HUP criteria.

Case 10: Longwood Gardens

In the Longwood Gardens case (*Unionville-Chadds Ford School District v. Chester County Board of Assessment and Longwood Gardens, Inc.*) decided July 20, 1998 by a 6-1 vote, the Pennsylvania Supreme Court issued a strong opinion favorable to charities, but did not use Act 55, the *Institutions of Purely Public Charity Act*, as its template to judge whether the institution met each of the five HUP criteria.

Commonwealth Court had previously rejected the school district's claim that the term "legitimate subjects of charity" means only the poor, incapacitated, distressed or needy. Citing the 1878 case known as "Donohugh's Appeal" in which Philadelphia's public library was found to be tax-exempt, the Court embraced the interpretation that the term "legitimate subjects of charity" was intended to have a broader meaning that, in some cases, encompasses the entire public.

Also rejected was the argument made by the school district that the requirement that charities "relieve some of the burden of government" means that government would otherwise be required to provide what the charity is providing. Such an interpretation would, if left unchallenged, result in virtually all charities being unable to meet this prong of the HUP test, because there are few activities that government is legally required to perform. Instead, the court agreed with the conclusion of Common Pleas Court Judge Robert J. Shenkin that it was only necessary to show that the state and local government engaged in activities that were consonant with the mission of Longwood Gardens, and that there would be substantial costs to the public if Longwood Gardens' property had to be maintained by government rather than subsidized by a foundation.

The court rejected arguments that the fees charged to the public for admission, and for services provided by the facility's garden shop and restaurant, somehow tainted the institution's charitable status.

"Regardless of whether it shows a profit, the garden shop primarily advances and supports the institution's educational purposes through its sale of books and films on horticulture-related topics," the court stated in its opinion filed by President Judge James Gardner Colins. This perspective will be useful to many institutions who undergo challenges. Because few cases on charitable tax exemption advance to the Pennsylvania Supreme Court (the court has ruled on just three since the *1985 Hospital Utilization Project v. Commonwealth of PA* case), a softening of the position on this issue by Commonwealth Court is a welcome development to charities.

The court agreed with the trial court's interpretation that since the admission fees covered less than 30 percent of operating expenses, the institution donated or rendered gratuitously a substantial portion of its services.

Institutions of Purely Public Charity Act (Act 55)

After nearly a decade of bitter wrangling among the Administration, the General Assembly, local government groups, representatives of the small business community, and the voluntary sector, Pennsylvania's charities won a major legislative battle with enactment of Act 55, the *Institutions of Purely Public Charity Act*. As previously mentioned, the Pennsylvania Constitution permits the General Assembly to grant tax-exempt status to "institutions of purely public charity," but does not define this term. Through more than a century of case law, the courts have defined this term. Act 55 codifies into law the five criteria of the *Hospital Utilization Project v. Commonwealth of Pennsylvania* case decided by the Pennsylvania Supreme Court in 1985 that determine whether a charity is an "institution of purely public charity" and eligible for property and sales tax exemptions. For each of these five broad criteria, the new law provides measurable ways for charities to meet them.

Before Act 55, even a charity that met all five criteria could lose its exemption if a court determined that it did not meet a three-part statutory test found in the general assessment law of being "founded, endowed and maintained by public or private charity." Act 55 says that if a charity meets the five criteria relating to the constitutional definition, then it is considered to meet the three statutory criteria.

While all five criteria must be met to be considered an "institution of purely public charity," Act 55 provides options for how charities meet each of the standards. In general, all but sham charities should easily meet four of the five tests. First, to "advance a charitable purpose," a charity may accomplish "a purpose that is recognized as important and beneficial to the public and that advances social, moral or physical objectives." That is only one of the options for a charity to meet this criterion and is a catch-all for virtually every single one.

Second, the standard for "operating entirely free from private profit motive," with one exception, is, with one notable exception, restatement of existing Pennsylvania law that applies to all nonprofits. Act 55 adds that "compensation, including benefits, of any director, officer or employee, (may) not (be) based primarily upon the financial performance of the institution." This does not prohibit financial performance from being a factor, however, and should not be a problem for conventional charities. Act 55 adds a new requirement that organizations include in their Articles of Incorporation a provision that upon sale or dissolution, it is prohibited for any surplus funds to be used for private inurement of any person (see pages 23-24).

Third, the criterion that the institution "must benefit a substantial and indefinite class of persons who are legitimate subjects of charity" is defined in the bill in a manner that will not be a barrier for legitimate charities. "Legitimate subjects of charity" is defined as "those individuals who are unable to provide themselves with what the institution provides for them." This is a direct quote from the HUP case. Opponents of the legislation have long argued that legitimate subjects of charity means only the poor and the sick. The legislation explicitly rejects that interpretation. The new law clarifies that organizations other than charities, such as advocacy organizations, labor unions, fraternal organizations, and business organizations, may not qualify for exempt status.

Fourth, the standard to "relieve government of some of its burden" also explicitly rejects narrow interpretations of this criterion, and substitutes a broad standard that should not be problematic for legitimate charities. Some interpretations of this criterion have been so narrow that few, if any, charities could meet this test had the narrow interpretation prevailed.

Despite the broad, encompassing nature of these four criteria, it is still almost impossible for organizations that are not legitimate charities to pass all of these four tests, even if many non-charities are able to pass one or two. And what sets apart whether a charity is an "institution of purely public charity" or not is the definition of the fifth criterion, "donate or render gratuitously a substantial portion of its services."

Generally, this criterion is highly favorable to the charitable community. This law provides seven ways to meet this standard. The most likely way is for a charity to demonstrate that it "provides uncompensated goods or services that, in the aggregate, are equal to at least 5% of the institution's costs of providing goods or services." "Uncompensated goods or services" is defined broadly. For institutions with open admission policies (such as hospitals), the criterion can be met by providing uncompensated goods and services of at least 75% of the institution's net operating income, but not less than 3% of the institution's total operating expenses. Institutions that provide at least 5% of their goods or services wholly gratuitously can meet the standard, even if they cross-subsidize their operations by charging the other 95% more than the value of the goods and services provided wholly gratuitously.

Charities may include the reasonable value of volunteer assistance in their calculations of the donation of goods and service. Charities may average their data for the five most recently completed fiscal years. Theoretically, a charity could qualify under this definition by providing as little as 1% of its goods and services as charity.

Almost every legitimate charity should be able to meet the five-part standard of Act 55. What is not clear is whether the courts will agree that every definition of the five-part test is consistent with HUP. Unlike virtually every previous version of this legislation, the bill as enacted into law requires some charity to be done by the institution. Is the amount required enough? We won't know until the standard is tested in the courts, and a lot will depend upon which institution is the test case. The first exemption case to reach the Pennsylvania Supreme Court after enactment of this law, a challenge to the tax exemption of Longwood Gardens, resulted in a clear and convincing victory for charities. However, there was nary a reference to the provisions of Act 55 in the court opinion. Perhaps the Court will rely on the provisions of Act 55 once a case is initiated after the date of enactment.

There are other provisions of interest in the new law. For example, there is a section providing incentives for creating foundations to accept voluntary contributions from charities that will be funneled to local governments. Without this provision, local powerful local government interests would have maintained their opposition to the legislation, and may have successfully kept the bill bottled up in the Senate.

The burden of proof in local property tax cases is changed, providing a further barrier for local governments to challenge charities. There is a provision forbidding charities from starting unrelated businesses that compete with existing small businesses, although a loophole permits this "unfair competition" provided the charity gets a formal request from a political subdivision or the Commonwealth to do so. Existing businesses of charities that are considered "unfair competition" by the standards of the bill are not affected by the new law.

Institutions that do not register under the *Solicitation of Funds for Charitable Purposes Act* must begin to make filings with the Bureau of Charitable Organizations, including sending copies of their 990 annual tax returns. Charities must now disclose information about relationships to other organizations, and pay a $15 filing fee. These disclosure provisions evolved from an effort launched more than 12 years ago by Rep. Italo Cappabianca (D-Erie).

Local Government Action

Local governments across Pennsylvania have been reeling in recent years from a crossfire of negative trends that have severely restricted their ability to provide municipal services. Among these trends have been—

- cuts in federal government grants, other than for health care

- increases in state and federal mandates to provide services without additional funding

- despite a recent economic boom, the economies of some regions have lagged behind, and are experiencing an increase in the demand for services and decrease in tax base—exacerbated by the implementation of state and federal welfare reform laws

- the flight of the middle class to the suburbs

- the burgeoning increase in tax-exempt property

- the unwillingness of property owners to absorb additional tax increases

- the explosion of drug abuse, crime, AIDS, homelessness, and other social ills

Several Pennsylvania cities were emboldened by the experiences of Pittsburgh municipal officials who were able to increase revenues by requesting that charities make "voluntary" contributions in exchange for not requiring them to expend hundreds of thousands of dollars in resources and staff time to fight exemption challenges. Among them have been—

Erie: In December 1992, the assessment board in Erie sent notices to the owners of more than 300 tax-exempt properties informing them that the properties would lose their exemptions beginning in January and they should begin to pay property taxes. The board pledged to hold hearings sometime in 1993 to determine if the properties were truly tax-exempt. Those that were determined by the board to be tax-exempt would be provided refunds. In early 1993, representatives of affected charities began negotiating with the City Solicitor and School District Solicitor to reach out-of-court settlements. In the majority of cases, tax exemptions were restored. Many other institutions, however, agreed to make payments-in-lieu-of-taxes, including all four Erie-area hospitals. Some charities retained their exemptions as the result of a March 29, 1994 ruling by Common Pleas Court Judge George Levin.

Harrisburg: Early in 1993, Dauphin County officials sent tax bills to the four general hospitals in the county, and followed this up with tax notices to nursing homes the following year. Most of the nursing home bills were withdrawn following the decision of the Pennsylvania Supreme Court in the St. Margaret Seneca Place case, but litigation was still pending in one hospital case in 1999. The hospital cases were appealed to Common Pleas Court. In May and June 1996, Dauphin County Court of Common Pleas ruled that two of the hospitals failed to meet all of the HUP criteria, and thus were ineligible for exempt status. Commonwealth Court ruled in favor of two hospitals and against two others. The hospitals that lost appealed the decision, but a settlement was reached in which the hospital system that owns the two hospitals agreed to make payments-in-lieu-of-taxes to the school district, city, and county for five years.

Philadelphia: On June 30, 1994, the City of Philadelphia began the process of sending letters to many of its charitable institutions requesting voluntary payments-in-lieu-of-taxes and/or services-in-lieu-of-taxes of 40% of what they would owe in taxes without their exemptions, and announced that the city would challenge the exemptions of those that did not respond favorably. The rate was discounted to 33% for agreements made by December 1, 1994, and services could be provided for a third of the amount owed. Virtually every hospital agreed to participate, as well as several institutions of higher learning. The City sent scores of letters out to smaller human services agencies acknowledging that the City would not be requesting payments.

Why User Charges May Not Be the Answer

No reasonable ways exist to measure the public services that are directly utilized by charitable nonprofits.

Property taxes, by themselves or disguised as "user charges," neglect the factors by which these institutions have earned their tax exemptions in the first place. In accordance with state law, these institutions have been founded, maintained, and endowed by public and private charity. They are, for the most part, created to provide benefits to the community. The tax exemption provided to these organizations is a benefit that is returned to the communities many times over.

The amount of financial support accruing to municipalities by taxing charities is generally not believed to be substantial. At least one study done in Wisconsin showed that 67% of the state's tax-exempt property belonged to government, and that an additional 10% was owned by religious organizations. All of this property would continue to be exempt under legislative proposals to authorize municipalities to impose user charges on tax-exempt property. While the reduction in local property taxes that would result if such legislation were enacted would be negligible, the impact on the charities themselves would be real and would threaten their continued viability. By state law, all incremental revenue over expenses of these charities is returned to the operations of the organization. There is no profit that is distributed into private pockets. Thus, the payment of taxes would result in a limited set of options for charitable nonprofits, all of which are injurious.

The first option is that charities can decide that they are unable to continue operations, since the property tax payment required could be substantial in comparison to their total budgets. A second available option is to reduce services. A third option is to increase the cost of their services, but doing so often makes the service inaccessible to those who most need them.

In any one of these cases, the cost of reducing the activities of these charities is eventually borne by the community. That is why these organizations have been granted tax-exempt status in the first place—to assure that their total resources are dedicated to meeting community needs.

Even with tax-exempt status, times are tough for these institutions. Government support for many nonprofit charitable activities has substantially declined since 1981. Demographic trends—including the aging of our population, the increase in homelessness, drug abuse, single-parent families, domestic violence, children living in poverty, and the increasing economic necessity of two parents in the family working in order to make ends meet—have resulted in the demand for more free and subsidized services. Private enterprise has, in recent years, invaded the traditional turf of nonprofit human service agencies. In virtually every case, the for-profit business has marketed its services to garner the most lucrative market segment, siphoning away clients who generated incremental revenue that was used by the nonprofit charities to cross-subsidize services for the needy. By skimming off this market share, private enterprise has placed an additional burden on the charitable nonprofit sector.

Finally, economic instability in Pennsylvania has had an impact on not only an increase in service demand, but also a decrease in the revenue depended upon by charities, including fees for service and charitable contributions.

Justification For the Charitable Tax Exemption

There has been much discussion above about the legal basis for tax-exempt status in Pennsylvania. The Constitution provides that the General Assembly *may* by law exempt from taxation certain classes of institutions. That the General Assembly has done so is not something that the charitable community should take for granted. At any time, the General Assembly can pass legislation either revoking or restricting the extent to which this exemption is granted for "institutions of purely public charity." Thus it is imperative that charities continue to reinforce the public policy reasons why this exemption deserves to be protected and continued.

Some of the reasons are:

1. Charitable nonprofits augment and, in some cases, replace the role of government in responding to and preventing society's problems. Tax-exempt status is an acknowledgment that these organizations have been deputized to act in the public interest and to improve societal conditions rather than to serve any private interest. As a result, such tax-exempt

organizations have a special responsibility to assure that their programs and activities are consistent with these principles and that the level of accountability is on par with government.

2. Nonprofit charities have many advantages in responding to societal problems that are not available to government. Among them are:

    • Nonprofit charities can be galvanized to attack a problem much more quickly than can government. Those who disagree with this need only consider how long it took for government to act in responding to problems such as AIDS, homelessness, and drug abuse compared to individual nonprofit charities. Clearly, nonprofits can respond to problems before a political consensus is developed by either the public at large or by a legislative body. Charitable nonprofits can, in many cases, direct resources toward solving the problem without the typical government bureaucracy and lag time between the identification of a problem and the approval of a statute, budget, regulation, request-for-proposal (RFP), and the actual expenditure of funds to solve the problem.

    • Nonprofits can effectively and efficiently respond to and solve problems that are localized in nature. This is a politically difficult task to accomplish under our present governmental system. Our political system often requires that a problem be universal in nature before resources are allocated to it. Also, politics makes it more likely that government will be unable to target resources to solve a problem, because there is often a cost to obtaining the necessary votes to pass a law.

    • Nonprofits attract volunteers. Volunteers, both on boards and doing the actual work of the agency, include many who would not be attracted to government service and the restraints of government-affiliated organizations.

    • Nonprofits can provide services when government programs, because of a limit on tax revenues, cannot expand. Charitable nonprofits often fill the void between what government provides to those who are destitute and what the for-profit sector provides to those who can afford the market rate for services. These charities provide services to those caught in the middle, who are not "poor enough" for government entitlement programs, but yet would be denied services by the for-profit sector. By charging fees for services on a sliding scale, these nonprofits are able to serve many who would otherwise not be served. This permits government to concentrate on serving only the most needy, while private business serves those who can afford to pay market rates.

The entire public benefits from the improvement of society resulting from the activities of these organizations. The tax-exemption provided to charities is a cost to the entire public, but is only a small fraction of the public benefit accruing from these activities. Beyond the monetary benefit of this exemption, which permits these charities to commit *all* of their resources to the mission of the organization, there is a principle involved. The tax exemption is an acknowledgment that the public values this type of altruistic activity and has foregone the collecting of taxes. It makes a statement that these organizations play an important role in strengthening the safety net that government cannot offer by itself.

It is in the public interest to promote the health of these charitable organizations, because government could not perform their missions as creatively, efficiently, or as cost-effectively.

Tips:

- **To protect tax-exempt status, serve clients who cannot afford to pay the full costs of services, and make services accessible to some clients who cannot afford to pay anything for services.**

- **Periodically quantify the dollar amount of free and subsidized services provided to the organization's clients and to the public at large.**

- **If state and local tax-exempt status is desired, develop a careful and honest outline of how the organization meets each of the five HUP criteria. If staff feel that one of more of these criteria is problematic, then consider changing operations to reasonably meet these criteria.**

- **View or download Pennsylvania Department of Revenue tax forms at: http://www.revenue.state.pa.us**

Chapter 25
Property Tax Challenges: How To Respond

Synopsis: This chapter outlines the steps a nonprofit organization can take to be prepared should its tax exempt status be challenged.

Recent efforts across Pennsylvania to challenge nonprofits' property tax exempt status have produced a great deal of anxiety within the nonprofit community. Rumors abound; questions are raised; organizations are challenged; exempt status may or may not be retained.

The reasons behind these challenges are many and complex and, thus, are not likely to be addressed easily or quickly. It must be assumed that, for the moment, local governments and school districts will continue their attempts to obtain revenue from the nonprofit community. Nonprofit organizations must be prepared to respond. Organizations may choose from a number of responses: pay the tax bill (accept the loss of property tax-exempt status), negotiate a voluntary payment (retain exempt status) or fight to retain their full exemption. Though there is no single, easy or quick answer that can be offered in response to a challenge to tax-exempt status, there are a number of things that organizations can do to insure that the appropriate response is chosen— whether the choice is to negotiate a settlement or fight the challenge in court. **Each organization must determine for itself how to respond to such a challenge**.

Ultimately the nonprofit organization must be able to articulate its charitable nature through the provision of evidence that leaves no doubt as to its charitable status. Even a choice to negotiate a voluntary contribution is based upon the legitimacy of tax-exempt status. Should the charitable status of the nonprofit organization be overturned, responsibility for the entire tax burden is no longer at issue.

The evidence needed to prove the legitimacy of exempt status can be generated through a process that involves five components: education, planning, documentation, communication and collaboration. Each will be discussed below. After a brief summary, key questions that must be considered as part of each component are listed.

Education

The first step in preparing an appropriate response to a challenge to property tax-exempt status is to gather the knowledge to make the correct decision. Nonprofit organizations must educate themselves about this issue before a challenge is presented. Through training and discussion, both board and staff must understand the implications of the challenge for their own particular organization. For example, it is no longer enough to assume the mantle of "educational" or "health care" institution. Organizations must be able to articulate for themselves the reason their nonprofit health care organization is different from a for-profit health care organization. Another example might be: Why is a nonprofit day care center deserving of an exemption when a for-profit day care center is not?

This process of education is only accomplished through introspection, training and dialogue. Boards of directors and staff must involve themselves in a broad-based conversation in which every member and group understands the issue and its implications. Through this dialogue, the following kinds of questions need to be answered:

1. What has happened in our geographical area regarding tax exemption and nonprofits? What efforts have the taxing authorities initiated? What taxing bodies are actively involved?
2. Which organizations have been formally or informally challenged? How did they respond?
3. What decisions or outcomes have occurred thus far? Are any decisions pending, or in appeal?
4. Why does our organization deserve continued exemption? What is our expressed rationale for tax-exempt status?
5. Is there consensus among the board and staff as to these issues?

Planning

A natural outcome of knowledge is the ability to plan a response. As an organization understands the issues and their implications, decisions can be made as to appropriate strategies. The position of strength for a nonprofit organization is to be prepared for a challenge should one emerge. The goal in a planning process is to have necessary policies and procedures in place so that, if challenged, the normal difficulties associated with a tax challenge will not be exacerbated by indecision, bickering and in-fighting among and between board and staff. To have the time to make reasoned, deliberate decisions is critical; planning allows for this.

Some of the planning questions that need to be answered include:

1. If challenged, what would we do? Would we negotiate? Would we go to court? Who makes this decision?

2. How is the board's position expressed? Is there a policy or stated position?

3. Which board members are involved on a day-to-day basis? At what point does the full board need to be consulted?

4. What staff would be involved? Who would have direct responsibility for this issue?

5. What legal services would we need? What do we have available?

6. What financial resources would be needed? Where will we get dollars?

Documentation

Critical to any organization's successful response to a property tax challenge is the ability to provide both quantitative and qualitative information as to its charitable nature. It is not enough to simply say, "We serve poor people" or "We do good things for children." Everything an organization says about itself or its services must be proven.

The key aspect to this documentation is being able to meet the definition of a charity as defined by the courts in Pennsylvania. These criteria are as follows:

- advances a charitable purpose,
- donates or renders gratuitously a substantial portion of its services,
- benefits a substantial and indefinite class of persons who are legitimate subjects of charity,
- relieves government of some of its burden, and
- operates entirely free from private profit motive.

Some of the questions that need to be answered include:

1. Who are our clients? Who is our constituency? How many do we serve?

2. Who uses our services? What are their ages, their incomes?

3. Who are our donors? How much money do they give us? How many donors?

4. Who are our volunteers? How much time do they give us? What is the dollar value of their time?

5. Are our services responsive to the needs of the community? How do we know this? What information can we provide that shows our organization is responsive to changing needs?

6. Who receives which services? Who uses our programs, our community screenings, our educational programs?

7. If fees are charged, how are levels of payment determined? Is anyone turned away for lack of resources?

8. What levels of subsidy are available? How many people are subsidized? Where do the subsidies come from?

9. What is our policy regarding ability to pay? How do we communicate these policies?

10. If local taxpayers are not the direct receivers of our services, how do they benefit?

11. How is *local* government relieved of a burden?

Communication

Research revealed the discrepancy between the community's perception of nonprofit organizations and their financial realities. Yet "perception" can be argued to be "reality" in that what people believe to be true drives behavior and interactions. Therefore, effective communication between the nonprofit organization and its community is critical.

Questions to be considered include:

1. What messages do we, as an organization, communicate to the community?

2. Do our publications and advertising promote an image of inclusivity or exclusivity? Are we communicating, in written form, our charitable nature and mission?

3. Do we communicate issues of reduced fees, subsidies, scholarships? Would members of the community know of these policies?

4. If asked, would the community be able to express the benefits our presence offers? Would they agree that our organization deserves tax exemption? Would they agree that they are the direct or indirect recipients of our services and presence? How do we assess community perception?

Collaboration

The lack of collaboration among nonprofit organizations is viewed as a weakness in potential responses to a property tax challenge. There is tremendous power in the nonprofit sector; choosing to separate oneself from other nonprofit organizations because of some perceived uniqueness can be destructive to that power. This is not to argue that nonprofit organizations should create a single, unified response. Sharing of information and ideas, and efforts to collaborate, however, can be positive for several reasons.

First, collaboration engenders a sense of community across diverse nonprofit organizations. Second, it empowers a group that could easily become fragmented and divisive. Third, it increases knowledge and experience of younger, smaller organizations. Fourth, it communicates to local units of government the strength that can be mustered should nonprofit organizations become united on issues. Fifth, it fosters creativity and innovation within the nonprofit sector. Finally, it creates a knowledge base about this issue. Much of what we know thus far about these challenges to property tax status is anecdotal. More good data is needed to create effective, responsible policy. The nonprofit sector should be proactive in the creation of this data, not reactive. Good information helps to insure a position of power.

Questions to be considered include:

1. What are the issues that unite us across fields of activity, across dimensions of size and geography?

2. What do we as a sector gain through collaboration? What do we lose if we are divided?

3. In what kinds of activities, unrelated to tax exemption, might we collaborate?

4. How can we ensure the adoption of appropriate and effective legislation? What kinds of legislation will strengthen our position as nonprofit organizations?

5. Are there existing structures or organizations in which we can participate and join others on this issue?

Discussion

Many nonprofit organizations will find the questions listed above difficult to answer. Some organizations may find that they are not currently in a position to answer them adequately. For these organizations, this process of self-examination and discussion becomes critical—not only as a means to improve existing services and operations, but also as a means of preparation should exempt status be challenged. Yet any organization can benefit from this process of self-examination.

In considering *how* to respond to a property tax challenge, the most difficult part may be the removal of "blinders" and acknowledging that, warranted or not, the status of your organization may be challenged. Research has shown that many executives are not really interested in this issue until directly confronted with a tax bill. Chief executives often are surprised and dismayed by a challenge; they wonder how anyone could question their charitable status. Realizing that there are people and groups in your community who do question your charitable status can be a shock. For the smaller, more traditional charities, this may be especially true.

This is a hurdle that must be overcome. Nonprofit organizations and their boards of directors must understand that whether or not they are directly challenged, they will be affected. The manner in which all nonprofit organizations operate in the future will change as a result of these challenges.

To avoid the issue—to *not* plan a response—is the worst tactic an organization can choose. Through a process of discussion and education, planning, effective documentation and communication, and collaboration, a nonprofit organization can be well-prepared for a challenge. It is these organizations that will be in a position of strength when questioned by a local unit of government. It is these organizations that will be successful in defending their exempt status.

Yet more than being successful in a direct challenge to tax-exempt status, organizations may rediscover the "essence" of the nonprofit sector. Nonprofit sector scholar Jon Van Til (1993) writes,

> ... we might discover that the reason we exist is not to be "nonprofit," but rather to profit our communities and society in ways that families, governments, and corporations cannot. We might, in other words, discover the soul of a sector that has been lost by many contemporary nonprofits, blinded as they are by their quest to be both "business-like" and "tax-free."

Tips:

- **Hire legal counsel with experience handling tax exemption challenge cases, since the case law is so unusual in this area and is changing constantly.**

- **Prepare to answer how your organization meets each of the five HUP criteria.**

- **If challenged, consider not only appealing the exemption challenge, but appealing the amount of the assessment on the property.**

- **Keep up to date with relevant legislation, case law, and regulations on exempt status, since any judgments involving the feasibility and desirability of making a settlement with a local government will be colored by inaccurate or non-current information.**

NOTE: The strategies suggested in this chapter are based upon conclusions drawn from a research project conducted during the spring of 1994. Information presented here is a slightly modified version of the third chapter of a larger document summarizing this research entitled, *Responding to a Property Tax Challenge: Lessons Learned in Pennsylvania.* Copyright, Pamela J. Leland, Ph.D., ©1994. All rights reserved. Reprinted with permission.

Chapter 26
Mergers and Consolidations

> **Synopsis:** Mergers involving nonprofit organizations are increasingly common and require planning. There are steps that should be taken when planning for a merger between nonprofit organizations to meet legal requirements and promote a successful transition.

It wasn't too long ago that many nonprofit boards considered liquidation to be a preferable alternative to mergers. Considering the loss of identity was just too painful, and the term "merger" conjured up a vision of a corporate shark gobbling up weaker entities. Since then, mergers and consolidations among nonprofit organizations have become increasingly common, spurred in part by cost containment pressures that have been affecting the delivery of social services for several decades now, particularly in the healthcare industry.

Managed care, cuts in Medicare and Medicaid, DRG payments, and increased competition have been among the factors that have induced hundreds of nonprofit mergers among hospitals. There are increasing incentives for all nonprofit organizations to improve their efficiency and effectiveness. With the entry of for-profit organizations into providing services historically provided by nonprofits, competition for service dollars has increased. To create new sources of revenue, even staid nonprofits have become entrepreneurial and are offering services that may only be indirectly related to their core mission. Unwittingly, they may be siphoning off revenue from colleague agencies.

Factors That Trigger Merger Consideration

Among the events that trigger consideration of nonprofit mergers are:

- Organizations that deliver similar services recognize economies of scale can be achieved

- Organizations that are struggling financially seek a partner to stave off bankruptcy and liquidation

- National organizations may place restrictions on local affiliates, such as having a minimum asset level, technology capability, and service menu, which cannot be met without combining with another local affiliate

- Two nearby agencies find themselves engaging in destructive competition

- Changes in leadership capability, both staff and within the board, may trigger a strategic plan that recognizes an organization's inability to continue with the status quo

- Scandal or other ethical challenges in which merger or consolidation is seen as an alternative to liquidation

- Changes in the outside regulatory environment or economic environment (e.g. managed care) that make it more attractive to increase economic power to compete

- A loss of membership that makes it unfeasible to continue

- The agency's mission has been accomplished successfully.

Generally, the reasons for suggesting a merger can be divided into three categories.

Economic reasons: A merger will help the organization become more efficient, take advantage of economies of scale, increase its access to members and/or clients, help it raise more donations and grants, and contain costs. The non-renewal of a major grant that provided overhead expenses to the agency can threaten its continued existence. There is no longer the cash-flow necessary to continue the operation.

Programmatic reasons: Agencies recognize that there is a duplication of services with an unhealthy competition for the same clients. Or if not duplication, agencies recognize that combining administration and delivery of services that are provided to the same population of clients, can promote efficiencies.

Strategic reasons: An agency may be in a precarious state either economically or programmatically. Competition from for-profits or other nonprofits is becoming destructive, and funders are complaining. The board might be losing interest. A long-term CEO may be retiring and there is no one to take his or her place with the vision necessary to lead the organization. The staff is demoralized because of an ineffective CEO who cannot be removed for political reasons. The public or funders have lost confidence in the agency as a result of ethical lapses or a reputation for poor quality, or an agency in the outside environment is identified that, if a merger occurred, would create a strong synergy.

How to Begin

At a 1997 workshop session on nonprofit mergers sponsored by the Pennsylvania Association of Nonprofit Organizations, William Morgan of Performance Industries and Paul Mattaini of Barley, Snyder, Senft & Cohen distributed a list of areas to consider when contemplating a merger.

Among the issues they raise are—

- The importance of infusing key leadership with the view that merging is a viable option

- Whether the CEO will find a way to sabotage the merger because of ego

- Whether the merger will fit into the organization's mission

- Finding the right candidate to merge with, and finding the right staff (such as the attorney, accountant and consultant)

- Bringing together the two organizational cultures

- Handling the public relations and community relations aspects

Steps to Merger

1. The participating board should adopt a resolution in favor of the general principle of merging.

2. Each board should appoint a merger committee of board members and staff.

3 An outside, experienced merger consultant should be jointly hired to structure negotiations, with the cost shared by the participating organizations.

4 Meetings should be scheduled among the parties to discuss the goals of the merger, to determine whether merging is feasible and makes sense for all parties, and to negotiate, over time, the details, such as the change in the mission and values, new name, staffing, logo, merger budget, board selection, bylaws, personnel policies, location, and what happens to staff who are no longer needed.

Budgeting

Mergers cost money. There are likely to be legal fees, consultant fees, audit fees, personnel costs relating to layoffs, moving costs, the costs relating to covering the liabilities of the non-surviving corporation (which may be substantial, and be responsible for triggering the merger idea in the first place), and even printing new building signs, printing new stationery and business cards, and designing a new logo.

As David La Piana writes in *Nonprofit Mergers: The Board's Responsibility to Consider the Unthinkable,*

> "Although it is unlikely that the financial position of two merging organizations will immediately improve as a result of a merger, well-conceived and –implemented mergers can raise staff morale, better focus the organization's activities, and increase overall energy levels— that will help the new group tackle difficult problems. Thus, a successful merger can offer relief and renewed hope for nonprofit boards, staff, and donors, and, most importantly, benefit clients because of the greater energy, increased funding, and better management possible with a more

stable organization. In contrast, poorly conceived mergers may simply bring together two weak organizations that compound each other's problems."

Obstacles to Merger

Virtually every article about the difficulty of merging two or more organizations refers to the two scourges that often scuttle the best laid plans: "turf" and "ego." Many, if not most, mergers of nonprofit organizations involve a financially strong organization merging with an organization that is merging in order to stave off bankruptcy or liquidation. The surviving organization will have one chief executive, and it is often a traumatic and, at times, potentially humiliating experience for the chief executive of the non-surviving organization to hand over the reins of decision-making. It is not unusual for an otherwise "routine" merger to be derailed by petty squabbling over the name of the combined agency, the logo, or the office space that will be provided to the staff of the non-surviving agency.

Legal Requirements

Pennsylvania law spells out the procedures for mergers and consolidations that involve nonprofit corporations, and can be found in Title 15 of the Pennsylvania Consolidated Statutes (15 Pa. C.S.§§5921-5929). Chapter 79 of the Pennsylvania Nonprofit Corporation Law provides that corporate action is required for the merger, consolidation, or sale of substantially all of the assets of a nonprofit corporation.

A merger is defined as the combination of two or more corporations into one of them, designated as the surviving corporation. A consolidation involves a new corporation that is formed out of two or more existing corporations.

If a merger is carried out in accordance with the provisions of the Pennsylvania Nonprofit Corporation Law, it is considered a statutory merger. The effect of such a merger is that the merging corporations become a single corporation on the effective date of the merger. The existence of the corporations that merged is ended. All property and assets, debts and liabilities are transferred to the merged entity.

Pennsylvania law requires that a plan be put together setting forth the terms and conditions of the merger, how it will be carried out, and what changes will be made to the Articles of Incorporation. The plan must be adopted by the Board of Directors and submitted to the organization's members, if it has members, for a vote.

Draft Articles of Merger must be adopted, and must include the name and location of the registered office of the surviving entity, as well as the name and address of the registered office of each other party involved in the merger. The Articles must include the effective date of the merger.

Chapter 27
Introduction to the Year 2000 (Y2K) Problem

Synopsis: Nonprofit organizations should take steps to address the Y2K problem, which may affect their internal operations and society in general. There are resources available that will assist nonprofit organizations in responding to Y2K-related problems, and suggestions to minimize disruptions.

Just when you thought you were developing a stable list of donors, the world economy was beginning to recover, and your boss was hinting at a raise as a reward for your successful fundraising and marketing efforts, a looming crisis may keep you and your colleagues burning the midnight oil, literally, come December 31, 1999.

Nonprofit organization leaders are becoming increasingly more skittish about what has become known as the Y2K problem, also called the millennium bug or Year 2000 problem. There is good reason for this. Compared to their for-profit counterparts, nonprofit organizations are more likely to have older computer hardware and software that is not Y2K compliant. And nonprofits will be called upon to help clean up any mess caused by disruptions in food supplies, communication, transportation, and healthcare.

Purveyors of doom predict that some of the consequences of Y2K may be a cataclysmic world-wide depression, riots in the streets, airplanes falling from the skies, electric power shutting down in large cities, food supply disruptions, medical devices implanted into heart patients failing, and nonprofit charities facing public health and safety crises that government has failed to remedy.

Or Y2K may be the equivalent of the Kohotek comet—all sizzle and no steak. Perhaps the hundreds of consultants who sell Y2K fixes—hardware, software, and protocols to solve the problem—have exaggerated the consequences in order to hype the sales of their products and services.

More likely, it will fall somewhere in between. On March 2, 1999, the Senate's Y2K Committee released a report that suggested that there may be serious disruptions starting January 1, 2000. The Vice Chairman of the Committee, Sen. Christopher Dodd (D-CT), appearing on NBC's *Meet the Press* February 28, 1999. said it would not be unwise "for people to do a little stockpiling" of supplies that would last 2-3 days.

Some reliably estimate that businesses nationwide will be spending upwards of $600 billion to make their computer systems Y2K compliant. And these estimates do not include the billions of dollars worth of lawsuits that will surely follow in the event that individuals and corporations seek to recover damages if they are harmed by third parties as a result of Y2K issues. Estimates of potential Y2K-related lawsuits considered reliable by the Senate Committee have been in the range of $1 trillion.

As people change their behavior to avoid risk—avoiding airline flights and electronic financial transactions, squirreling away cash, stockpiling food and water—

these actions may create social and economic ripple effects even if there is not a single *direct* Y2K event.

Nonprofit organizations are routinely receiving forms from those that purchase their products requiring them to certify Y2K compliant systems are in place. What is this all about, anyway?

Definition of the Problem

In simple terms, Y2K refers to the issue of what will happen to computer systems and computer data on January 1, 2000. These computers may have an inability to recognize that January 1, 2000 is the day after December 31, 1999, and to process information accordingly. For almost four decades, time was recorded in computerese using just six digits—two digits each for the day, the month, and the year. This made perfect sense back when computer memory was expensive, and saving two digits had measurable cost savings associated with it. Punch cards, the data entry method of choice thirty years ago, had only limited space to record data, and each space was precious. Even more recently, computer programmers continued to use two digits for the year, expecting that their software would become quickly obsolete and be replaced. Also, it was easier to program in a two-digit year for purposes of printing out next to "19" in preprinted forms.

Some devices will function perfectly well on January 1, 2000, and then crash on February 29, 2000. This emanates from the fact that years divisible by 100 are generally not leap years, unless they are divisible by 400, as is the year 2000. Some software may not account for this fact. Additionally, some software recognizes the number 9999 as a special code rather than a date, so there may be Y2K problems surfacing this year as well.

It was taken for granted that the designation of 82, for example, meant "1982." On January 1, 2000, the computer will record the year as "00" and it is not clear whether this refers to "1900" or "2000."

This problem affects most mainframes and almost all older PCs. Every PC has an internal clock. After midnight on December 31, 1999, some will be set to 1900, some to 1980, some to 1984, and others to some other date.

For most nonprofits that depend on PCs, the extent of the Y2K problem that they can do something about is to test whether their computer's internal clock is Y2K-compliant. This means that the computer will operate correctly when the internal clock is set to every year from 2000 at least through 2009.

Why Nonprofit Organizations Should Be Concerned

Among the reasons are:

1. **Failure of internal computer systems**—Nonprofits using personal computers may have trouble billing delinquent accounts, keeping track of services provided

to their clients, calculating personnel benefits due their staff, and a myriad of other tasks performed by PCs that are taken for granted.

2. **Failure of government computer systems**—If government computers fail, nonprofit organizations will experience an overload of clients affected by a failure of government to provide income transfers and health benefits, in addition to potential law enforcement problems that will affect nonprofit service delivery.

3. **Weakness or meltdown in the world-wide economy**—Some predict a shutdown of public services; a failure of utilities to deliver gas, electricity, and water; a general banking system failure, and a cascade of events leading to a world-wide recession or depression. A weak economy usually results in a burgeoning of demand for nonprofit services at a time when people tend to donate less. The U.S. Senate's report expressed many concerns not only in the U.S., but also about the lack of mitigation of Y2K related problems in Africa, Latin America, and Asia, which could slow economic growth. The Senate report concluded that while there was no evidence that the United States would experience social or economic collapse, "some disruptions will occur and in some cases (these disruptions) will be significant." Other technologically-advanced countries, such as Germany, also have a lot of work to do to catch up on becoming immune from Y2K chaos.

4. **Failure of logic controllers and programmable logic controllers**—Many electronic devices use semiconductors to manage products such as fax machines, elevators, environmental controls, VCRs, security systems, and even coffee machines. Many of these have date-sensitive codes programmed into their chips. Those machines that have Y2K non-compliant chips may fail, or incorrectly operate.

5. **Failure of financial institution processes**—Some banks are even evaluating credit worthiness based on Y2K compliance in the computer systems of those applying for credit. This also affects other stakeholders of nonprofit organizations, such as the companies that support them and supply them. Accounts receivable may not be paid because a non-compliant computer will not recognize that the bill should be paid. Banks may not be able to process checks or handle other routine transactions.

6. **Fundraising disruption**—Businesses and their leaders may be so focused on Y2K problems that they may not be as able to share their money and time with charities, warns the United Way of America.

What To Do About the Problem

1. Stop buying hardware and software that is not Y2K compliant.

2. Don't permit organization staff to install software from home on your organization's computers. This is not only usually illegal because of licensing violations, but may harm your computers as well.

3. Educate your board, staff, and vendors about the Y2K problem, and document what your organization is planning to do to mitigate the potentially bad effects of it.

4. If your agency is large enough, appoint a staff person to have responsibility to deal with the problem, or hire an outside consultant. If your agency is small, purchase reliable, over-the-counter software that will test your computers and use it, following the directions provided with the software to backup critically-needed files.

5. Inventory all equipment and software that may be at risk, and query the manufacturers about whether it is Y2K compliant, and whether there is software that can be obtained to make it compliant, if not. Much of this information may be obtained at the vendor's web site.

6. Make sure that organizations you use to outsource services (such as payroll, taxes, personnel benefits) are Y2K compliant.

7. Backup critical data and store it in a safe place in case systems begin to fail. Don't simply back up your data on disk—if your computers fail, you may not be able to access the data on the disk. Store hard copies of critical information as well. Plan how you will respond in the event your organization's computers fail.

Y2K Internet Resources

There are lots of Y2K resources available that can be accessed for free on the World Wide Web, and targeted to the needs of nonprofit organizations. Among some of the more valuable are:

United Way of America
http://www.unitedway.org/year2000/

The United Way of America has prepared a comprehensive document on the Y2K problem, *The Year 2000 Challenge for United Ways*, targeted to its member agencies, but of use to all nonprofit organizations. It contains a solid background about the problem, recommendations on how to deal with it, and an appendix of resources, including manufacturer web sites and sample staff memos and letters to vendors. The latest version is dated July 1998. It can be downloaded free from the Internet in PDF format (which requires the use of an Acrobat Reader) or in Word 97.

The Cassandra Project
http://cassandraproject.org/home.html

The Cassandra Project is a nonprofit grass-roots advocacy organization founded in 1997 and named after a less-than-optimistic character from Greek mythology whose warnings about the future went unheeded. You can find a bulletin board and a chat room, and sample letters you can write to institutions such as local banks, power companies, hospitals, and local government agencies asking about their Y2K preparations and status of compliance. The group's founder, Paloma O'Riley, is the author of a guide for surviving the worst-case scenarios relating to Y2K called *Y2K Citizen's Action Guide*. It can be viewed and downloaded free at this site, although there is information as well about purchasing the hard-copy booklet. This is a practical handbook for preparing for any worst-case disruptions attributable to Y2K (and, perhaps, famine, flood, nuclear war, or global depression). It has tips for storing food and water; maintaining supplies; dealing with sanitation, communication, transportation, and power disruptions; handling emergencies and medical problems; and even provides advice for engaging in bartering if the financial system is severely disrupted.

CompuMentor
http://www.compumentor.org

Founded in 1987, CompuMentor bills itself as "the largest nonprofit computerization organization in the country." From the home page, click on "Y2K for Nonprofits." You can download the *CompuMentor Year 2000 Workbook for Nonprofits With the Year 2000 Worksheets* at this site. This workbook is described as a "do it yourself manual for people who are at least moderately comfortable with computers to undertake the Y2K Audit." There are also files of general interest about the Y2K problem.

The Nathan Cummings Foundation
http://www.ncf.org/ncf/publications/reports/y2k/intro/intro_contents.html

The Year 2000 Challenge: A Socially Responsive Way to Prepare for Disruptions in Computer-reliant Systems, a working document published October 28, 1998, is available free at this site. It explains the issue from the perspective of foundations, not only what they need to know about Y2K but what they should be doing about it. The document provides nine recommendations for foundation action.

UTNE Online
http://www.utne.com/y2k

UTNE is a private testing laboratory for hardware and software. You can download the free *YMARK20000 Year 2000 System Compliance Test* utility at this site, along with instructions and the technical information necessary to apply this test.

Independent Sector
http://www.indepsec.org/y2k.html

Independent Sector has devoted several useful pages on its site to Y2K. There are articles reprinted from the media, a list of 10 non-technical questions to nonprofit organization leaders should think about (*Preparing for Year 2000: Key Questions Every Philanthropic Leader Should Consider*), links to a database on Y2K product and software compliance information, links to community group action plans, and links to general Y2K information.

Penn State University Y2K Site

ftp://ftp.cac.psu.edu/pub/year2000   and
http://www.psu.edu/Year2000

This site, sponsored by Penn State University, has free software that can be downloaded by FTP and used to test your PC for Y2K compliance. Additional general information files can be found at the University web site.

As with any files that you download from the Internet, use common sense when taking any risks relating to viruses or other possibilities for crashing your computer and losing data.

Chapter 28
Quality Issues

Synopsis: Quality is as important, if not more so, to nonprofit organizations as for-profit businesses. Nonprofits need quality programs to compete for donations, clients, board members, workers, and political support.

Introduction

Many who govern and manage nonprofit organizations are increasingly finding their organizations subject to many of the same economic pressures as their for-profit counterparts. Their operations often resemble their for-profit competitors in both organizational structure and corporate culture. They are increasingly led by those trained in business rather than social work, and their mentality and style of administration often reflects this. Stereotypically, they often put the "bottom line" paramount above the needs of clients. One nonprofit CEO I spoke with recognized the inconsistency of trying to run a human service organization and retaining his "humaneness," while at the same time being forced to make rational business decisions, which meant the firing of "nice" people who were hurting the performance of his organization. He commented to me that his management credo was to be "ruthlessly altruistic."

In many cases, the products and services once provided solely by nonprofit, charitable organizations are now being provided by for-profits. One can often find health clubs, hospitals, schools, nursing homes, and day care centers—both for-profit and nonprofit—competing for clients on an equal basis within communities. When there is this direct competition, particularly in the delivery of human and educational services, cost is just one factor in a customer's decision. Quality of service is often even more important in a decision, and nonprofits that offer high-quality products and services obviously have a competitive edge. Those that can't offer quality may find themselves out of business.

Many thousands of other nonprofit organizations find themselves in a situation where they don't have direct economic competition from others providing the same service. There is only one United Way affiliate in each community, one Arts Council, one Arthritis Foundation, one AARP affiliate, and one Special Olympics affiliate. Except under unusual circumstances, it is unlikely that another organization will sprout up to directly challenge one of these. It would be easy to jump to the conclusion that having a monopoly of this nature would mean that quality and performance are not as important as they are to those with direct, head-to-head competition for providing a particular product or service. That conclusion would be flawed.

Why Quality is Important to Nonprofit Organizations

Quality is important to all nonprofit organizations, and none is immune from the consequences of neglecting quality. Charities rely on loyal customer support. Even if a nonprofit is not involved in direct economic competition, there is substantial competition for things that indirectly affect the viability of organizations. Among them are—

1. **Competition for government and foundation grants.** Most charitable nonprofits depend on grants to supplement any client fees they receive. Foundations are acutely aware of organizations with poor reputations with respect to skimping on service quality. No one wants to be associated with such an organization. It is no wonder that first-class organizations often have little trouble attracting funding, because everyone wants to be associated with them.

2. **Competition for private donations.** Would you make a donation to a charity that had a reputation of treating its clients like animals? Unless that organization is the Society for Prevention of Cruelty to Animals (SPCA), you are more likely to look elsewhere for a charity worthy of your donation.

3. **Competition for board members.** Why would anyone want to serve on a board of a second-class nonprofit and risk being condemned or otherwise embarrassed by the media, the political hierarchy, and clients? There are only so many skilled, committed civic leaders in each community who are willing to donate their time and expertise to serve on nonprofit boards, and it is clearly not attractive to serve on the board of a charity with a reputation for having poor quality.

4. **Competition for volunteers.** What can be said for board members goes double for service delivery and other volunteers. No one wants to be associated with an organization with a reputation for poor quality. Many volunteers see their volunteer work as a springboard for a career, and volunteering for a pariah in the community does not serve their interests.

5. **Competition for media.** The media play an important role in helping a nonprofit charity promote its fundraising, encourage clients to utilize its services, and improve employee morale. Poor quality can result in the media ignoring an organization or, worse, highlighting its shortcomings for the entire world to see.

6. **Competition for legislative and other political support.** Nonprofit charities have benefited from the support of political leaders, directly through the provision of government grants, and indirectly through the provision of favors such as cutting government red tape and legislation solving the problems of the agency and those of its clients. Political leaders are certainly not going to be responsive to an organization if they receive letters of complaint about the organization's poor quality.

7. **Competition for qualified employees.** Particularly during the current climate of low unemployment, quality nonprofits find that they have less employee turnover and find it easier to attract employees to fill vacancies and for expansion.

The consequences of having poor quality, or the reputation (public perception) of having poor quality, can result in the board of directors throwing up its hands and deciding to liquidate the organization. Or, in extreme cases, having the government step in and liquidate the organization. Imagine the aftermath of a child care agency that failed to perform a quality background check on an employee who later was found to be a child abuser. Or the hospital that failed to adequately verify that a staff member it hired was adequately board-certified.

As pointed out by Dr. John McNutt of Boston College's Graduate School of Social Work, most, if not all, states look at the community benefit provided by a nonprofit organization in considering whether it is eligible for nonprofit status in the first place. Quality and community benefit are inextricably linked.

In 1998, a scandal affected international agencies that raise funds for child welfare. Who knows how many millions of dollars will not be contributed to these agencies because some agency official did not feel it was important to inform donor sponsors that their sponsored child had died several years ago? With a public already conditioned as a result of the 1992 United Way of America scandal and the 1995 New Era Foundation scandal to be wary about charities, nonprofits need to be more vigilant about not only quality issues affecting the delivery of direct service, but about those that affect fiscal accountability as well.

The Cost of Poor Quality

The cost to organizations that have poor quality standards can be substantial. Read the newspapers and you can find many examples of the consequences of poor quality in nonprofit organizations. Owners of personal care boarding homes have failed to see the value of installing sprinkler systems and, as a result, have seen the loss of life and of their properties. Doctors have mistakenly removed the wrong kidney from a patient. Hospital maternity ward staff have given the wrong newborn to the wrong parents. The ramifications far exceed the financial loss and loss of prestige to the organization—human suffering for the clients and potentially huge, successful lawsuits against the nonprofit organization as a result of a preventable lapse in quality-related policies.

Quality in the Nonprofit Organization Context

For the typical nonprofit that doesn't deliver client services, quality should mean much more than the ability to answer the telephone on the first ring. It means having a newsletter without typographical errors. It means having an attractive, periodically updated Web site. It means spelling the names of donors correctly in substantiation letters. It means delivering on promises made to legislators for follow-up materials. It means having conferences where participants feel that they get their money's worth. It means assuring that each board member has the information necessary and appropriate to make governing decisions. It means that volunteers know in advance what is expected of them.

And for those that deliver direct human services, it means, among other things—

- treating each client with the dignity he or she deserves

- respecting confidentiality

- providing on-time services

- providing timely resolution to legitimate complaints

- providing services in a safe and secure setting

- providing services in a facility that is accessible, clean and functional

- delivering services provided by competent, trained personnel

- assuring that services provided meet high standards and respond to the clients' needs

- obtaining informed consent from clients before services are provided

- seeking constant feedback from clients to improve the delivery of services

- using advances in technology to improve communication between the organization and its clients.

Chapter 29
Change Management

> **Synopsis:** Change management strategies, such as Total Quality Management, Business Process Reengineering, Benchmarking, Outcome-Based Management, and Large Group Intervention, are potential ways to improve nonprofit organization quality and performance.

In the context of this chapter, "change management" does not refer to a prescription of getting rid of the people who run the organization. Rather, it is a menu of management strategies to change the philosophy of management to accomplish an objective or set of objectives such as, for example, improving efficiency and competitiveness, motivating employees and increasing their job satisfaction, or reducing absenteeism. In this sense, "change" is used as a noun rather than a verb.

There is general agreement among scholars, practitioners, and management experts that organizations must adapt to changing conditions to survive. Technology advances, markets change, the requirements and expectations of customers evolve, the needs of workers are altered as a result of demographics, economic conditions, and changes in culture, among other things.

Businesses, both for-profit and nonprofit, go out of business every day and this is attributable to many reasons. There may be an organizational scandal that causes the public to lose confidence or the government to take action against it. There may be quality lapses. The services provided by an organization may no longer be needed, or a competitor skims off a lucrative market share. The organization's operations may be too economically inefficient to support it. Government funding priorities or regulatory requirements may shift, leaving an organization in the lurch. The list of possible reasons goes on.

For years, the for-profit business community has utilized formal change management strategies to improve operations and keep organizations competitive and vibrant, improve efficiency, generate loyalty and maintain or expand support from their customers. It has only been recently that the nonprofit community, with healthcare institutions leading the way, started implementing some of these strategies. The material appearing here is based on my book, *Improving Quality and Performance in Your Non-Profit Organization*, which was published in January 1999. An order form can be found in the back of this book if you want to explore change management in more detail.

Among the most popular change management strategies being considered by nonprofit organizations are Total Quality Management (TQM), Business Process Reengineering (BPR), Benchmarking, Outcome-Based Management (OBM), and Large Group Intervention (LGI).

Total Quality Management

TQM is an innovative, humanistic, general approach to management that seeks to improve quality, reduce costs, and increase customer satisfaction by restructuring traditional management practices. It requires a continuous and systematic approach to gathering, evaluating, and acting on data about what is occurring in an organization. The TQM management philosophy includes the following:

1. It asserts that the primary objective of an organization is to meet the needs of its "customers" by providing quality goods and services, and to continually improve them. In the nonprofit organization context, customers include not only the direct recipients of services, such as clients, but the organization's board, elected and appointed government officials, the media, and the general public.

2. It instills in all organization members an *esprit de corps* that assures them that *having quality* as the number one goal is an important tenet. *All* organizational members are responsible for quality, even if it is related to an issue beyond the scope of his or her job. Eliminating the "it's not my job" mentality becomes an achievable organizational objective.

3. It continuously searches for ways to improve every activity, program, and process. It does so by constantly seeking feedback from its customers, and promoting suggestions from all sources, both externally and internally, on how to improve.

4. It rewards quality, not only internally, but from its suppliers. It recognizes that poor quality from its collaborators, be they suppliers or other organizations, affects the organization's quality.

5. It recognizes that staff must receive continuous training to improve their work performance.

6. It encourages all aspects of the organization to work as a team to solve problems and meet customer needs rather than competing against each other.

7. It empowers workers at every level, and permits them to be actively engaged in decisions that affect the organization, and to constantly look for ways to improve it.

8. It permits employees the opportunity to have pride in what they produce for the organization and to see the fruits of their labor measured in the quality of the service they provide rather than just having a paycheck.

9. It promotes a planning process that is geared toward continuously improving quality in *everything* the organization does.

In 1992, the United Way of America developed an award for nonprofit human service agencies, recognizing that quality improvement is just as important, if not more so, in charities as in private business. Known as the Excellence in Service Quality Award (ESQA), 501(c)(3) charities are eligible for four levels of recognition, with judging and criteria patterned after the Baldrige Award competed for by private corporations.

TQM principles are finding their way into nonprofit settings other than healthcare, such as community centers, arts organizations, and human services agencies. Focusing on the needs of the "customer" rather than on the "bottom line" is a value that the nonprofit sector should feel comfortable with compared to its for-profit counterparts. When a nonprofit organization's leadership becomes excited about TQM, it can become contagious, provided that the behaviors of the leaders are consistent with their words. When it "happens," those in a TQM environment notice the difference, whether they work there or benefit from the organization's services. Workers feel empowered. Clients notice a positive difference in staff attitudes. Everyone associated with the organization feels good about it.

Business Process Reengineering

If your heart stops beating and you keel over breathlessly, a professionally-trained medical professional often can revive you by administering CPR. But if it's your *organization's* heart that fails, BPR, administered by professionally-trained consultants or by those within an organization, is increasingly becoming the TLA ("three-letter acronym") of choice for cutting-edge managers BPR is a successor to TQM as the latest management bromide for reviving comatose organizations.

Business Process Reengineering is defined by Michael Hammer, BPR's leading guru, as "the fundamental rethinking and radical redesign of business processes to achieve dramatic improvements in critical measures of performance (cost, quality, capital, service and speed)."

The fanatical interest in Total Quality Management peaked in the 1980s, but its once pervasive influence seems to have waned in recent years. One of the reasons often given for its apparent decline in the United States is that the philosophy of slow, incremental, and continuous improvement is generally inconsistent with American culture. Perhaps this is so; American organizational leaders are perceived as more impatient to see tangible results of their business management interventions compared to their Asian, African, and European counterparts. They want to see quantum leaps of measurable improvement rather than the tortoise-paced improvement promised by TQM advocates. The tenure of many organizational leaders is short; several CEOs may come and go before TQM is fully implemented and showing results.

A major strategy involved with BPR efforts is to look at a business process that has many tasks that have been performed by several specialists. Then, the specialists are replaced with generalists (or the specialists are retrained to become generalists) who can handle all of the tasks of the process and have access to all of the information they need to perform *all* of the tasks.

BPR requires a new way of thinking. Unlike TQM, which requires the involvement of everyone in the organization, BPR is necessarily implemented from the top. It is the zero-based budgeting of business processes, contending that, at least theoretically, the past should have no bearing on what is planned for the future. It makes the assumption that organizations have evolved incrementally, reflecting a history of culture, tradition, technology, and customer needs that may not be particularly relevant today. BPR suggests that managers step out of the constraints of their current physical plant, work processes, organizational charts, and procedures and rules and look at how the work would be performed if they were starting from scratch.

BPR requires an organizational leader to step back and answer the question: If I were building this organization today from scratch, knew what I know now, had the technology and human resources that I have now, and the customer needs that I have now, would I still be doing things the same way? More often than not, the answer is a resounding "no!" In the nonprofit environment, this might mean redesigning data collection and reporting, client intake, billing, purchasing, and every other process.

In many cases, new technology is available that will enable efficiencies. For example, a human service agency may receive a telephone call from a client requesting even a minimal change in service as a result of some change in circumstances. The person answering the telephone may have to put the person on hold and call the client's caseworker, who has the client's case file. The caseworker may have to put the person on hold and check with the supervisor for a decision on whether to waive a rule, and the supervisor may have to meet with the caseworker to make the decision.

Following BPR, the person answering the telephone for the agency may be able to pull up the case file on a computer screen and be preauthorized to approve a change in services within a constraint programmed into the computer by the agency. Or the person answering the telephone may be able to give the caller technical advice on how to solve a problem by searching a "frequently asked questions" file on a computer screen that previously was routinely transferred to a technical specialist.

Another way of looking at this is that everyone in the organization is conventionally functioning solely on his or her part of a process rather than on the objective of the organization. The receptionist answers the telephone. The case manager holds the file for a particular set of clients. The supervisor makes decisions authorizing variances from agency rules. BPR permits a work process to change so that the true objective of the process—responding to the client's needs—does not require the intervention of several people in the organization. The revolutionary advances in information technology permit this.

With the use of networked computers and an educated labor force, it is possible for a single person to process and troubleshoot an entire order that previously may have required being passed serially from person to person in the organization, taking many days to complete. And the probability of an error under the old method multiplies the more hands are involved.

Among the major principles of BPR are:

1. Use modern technology to redesign work processes rather than work tasks, concentrating on permitting a single person to achieve a desired outcome/objective.

2. Let the worker who uses the output of a process also perform the process. For example, instead of having a purchasing department make purchases of pencils and paper clips for the accounting department and other departments, the accounting department orders its own pencils and paper clips and other "inexpensive and nonstrategic" purchases.

3. Let those in the organization who collect information be the ones who process it. For example, when the public relations department wants to send out its newsletter to a mailing list, it should be able to generate the mailing labels itself rather than having to make a request to a data processing department.

4. Treat organization resources that are decentralized as centralized, utilizing information technology to bring them together. A college with several satellite campuses, for example, could link its bursars so that a student making a payment at either the main office or a satellite campus would have the payment show up in the records of the registrars of all of the campuses.

5. Electronically link disparate parts of an organization to promote coordination.

6. Let those who perform the work make the decisions, thereby flattening the pyramidal management layers and eliminating the bureaucracy and delay that slows down a decision-making process.

7. Use relational databases and other technology to collect and store information only once, eliminating both redundancy and error.

Generally, BPR often enables a single person to perform all of the steps in a process by using information technology. One byproduct of BPR is that the need for many employees may be eliminated. This saves a lot of money for organizations. One downside is that it has the consequence of terrorizing a workforce.

Benchmarking

Benchmarking refers to studying how similar organizations to yours perform their business processes, and learning how to adapt those that are most efficient, innovative and successful. Obviously, no two organizations are alike, and there is no guarantee that copying something from another organization will automatically work well in your own. But certainly there is value in exploring how other organizations are performing some of the tasks your organization does, and discussing what efficiencies they may have found that would improve your business operations. For-profit organizations have been doing this in a formalized way for many years, and nonprofit organizations are only recently recognizing the value of benchmarking.

There are two types of benchmarking that nonprofit organizations might wish to consider. The first, internal benchmarking, looks at your organization and projects future goals, and includes a process by which employees are encouraged to meet performance targets. External benchmarking, on the other hand, tries to determine the "best practices" of similar organizations. Rather than reinventing the wheel, external benchmarking permits you to allocate minimal resources to finding how others have solved a problem, or have exponentially increased productivity with respect to some process, rather than having to discover that on your own. Many nonprofit organizations are not only willing to share this information, but are quite proud to do so. The fact that competition among nonprofit organizations is almost always either friendly or nonexistent promotes benchmarking in a manner that avoids some of the troublesome potential conflicts and ethical dilemmas in the for-profit context.

Jason Saul, writing in a chapter on benchmarking in *Improving Quality and Performance in Your Non-Profit Organization*, says that nonprofits should typically consider benchmarking three general categories: A **process** (such as screening job applicants or organizing inventory in a food bank), a **policy** (such as a salary structure or incentive plan), or a **program** (such as welfare-to-work or educational incentives).

The approaches taken to benchmarking include—

• technical approach (using computer models, statistics, spreadsheets, and other quantitative methods),

• committee approach (bringing in a team of experts from outside of your organization to gather data, and make judgments about what changes would be beneficial to the organization), and the

• survey approach (combining the above two models by creating a team of individuals from within the organization to identify which processes should be benchmarked, to define the measures, to define organizational performance, to obtain the "best practices" information, and implement these practices).

Saul, who is the author of a 1999 book on the subject (*Benchmarking Workbook for Nonprofit Organizations* published by Wilder Foundation Publishing), recommends a seven-step process for benchmarking, which includes self-assessment, measuring performance, assembling the team, data collection, evaluating practices, translating best practices, and continuously repeating the process.

Outcome-Based Management

To improve quality in a larger organization, simply adopting a progressive management philosophy such as TQM or BPR is not going to be enough in today's modern competitive business climate. As an organization grows, there are more pressures for accountability, not only internally from a board of directors, but from elected officials, government funders, foundation funders, individual donors and volunteers, and the public. Leaders of large organizations generally do not have the ability to visualize every aspect of their organization's operations and assess what is going on just by looking out their office windows, or by engaging in informal conversations with their staff and clients. The proverbial "one-minute manager" is an ideal construct that is not particularly well-suited to crystallizing the information a CEO needs to make judgments on how to allocate precious resources.

To accomplish the important task of assessing what is really going on within a large organization, most have a Management Information System (MIS) that permits the aggregation of data in a form that can be analyzed by a manager, enabling him or her to see trouble spots and make adjustments in operations and to generate reports required by the government, funders, auditors, and the board of directors.

For many larger nonprofits, particularly those that depend on government and foundation grants rather than private donations, the objective of "meeting clients' needs" has become a more formalized process. Times have changed within just the last decade or so. Traditionally, measures of organization performance for human service organizations were based on a model more appropriate for industrial processes, where raw materials were turned into finished products. In the language of industrial systems analysis, inputs (the raw material) were processed into outputs (the finished product). In adopting an analogous frame of reference to industry, the conventional thinking was that human service agencies took in unserved clients (input), provided services (process), and changed them into served clients (output). In this way of thinking, organizations improved their output by increasing the number of clients served.

An exciting new way of looking at the output of an agency is called outcome-based management (OBM) or "results-oriented accountability" (ROA). Most recently, results-oriented management and accountability (ROMA) has become the buzzword describing this general tool. OBM focuses on program outcomes rather than simply quantifying services delivered. Program outcomes can be defined as "benefits or changes for participants during or after their involvement with a program" (from *Measuring Program Outcomes: A Practical Approach, United Way of America)*. For example, an organization dealing with reducing drug abuse may have a stellar record of attracting clients through a flashy outreach program. It may be exemplary in convincing doctors in the community to donate thousands of hours of free services to the program, thereby reducing unit costs per client. It may have few complaints from the clients, who feel the staff are competent and treat them with dignity. An analysis of conventional data might indicate that there is little room for improvement. But, perhaps, no data is collected on whether those treated for drug abuse by the organization are successfully able to become independent, avoid future interactions with the criminal justice system, and rid themselves of the scourge of drug dependence for an extended period of time—all measurable outcomes for a successful substance abuse program. If most of these clients are back on the street and drug dependent, is that organization providing successful treatment even if drug abuse services are being provided? Are funders and taxpayers getting a fair return on their investment?

In the outcome-based management model, the number of clients served is an input. The output is considered to be measurements concerning the change in the condition of the clients after receiving the services. For example, if thousands of clients are served, but the conditions of the clients have not improved, then the outcome is zero, even if the services were provided 100% on time, every client received a satisfactory number of hours of services, and there were no client complaints. It no longer is indicative of the effectiveness and value of an organization to only collect data on how many clients sought services, how many of these were accepted into the client stream rather than being referred or turned down, how many hours of service were provided, and how much each service cost and was reimbursed. Outcome data together with the above process data is needed to measure the effectiveness and value of an organization.

In addition to a significant change in attitude about the accountability of the private nonprofit sector, the passage in 1993 of the *Government Performance and Results Act,* PL 103-62, changed the way federal agencies plan, budget, evaluate, and account for federal spending. The intent of the act is to improve public confidence in federal agency performance by holding agencies accountable for program results and to improve congressional decision-making. It seeks to accomplish this by clarifying and stating program performance goals, measures, and costs "up front." These changes were implemented beginning in September 1997.

For some organizations, the shift to outcome-based management will have modest cost implications. It may mean more data being collected from clients during intake. It may mean follow-up surveys to see what happens to clients after they have availed themselves of the organization's services. When this information is available, it is of extraordinary value to those who design, administer, and deliver those services.

What makes outcome-based management an easy sell to the human services sector is that it is common sense. What is the point of investing thousands, if not millions, of dollars of an agency's resources if the end result is not accomplishing what is intended by the investment—improving the lives of the agency's clients? Our human service organizations have been established to make people's lives better. When our organizations change their focus to concentrating on doing what it takes to make people's lives better compared to simply providing human services, then it is much more likely that this worthy goal can be accomplished successfully. This is compatible with the values of most in the sector, who often make financial sacrifices to make a difference in the lives of those who need human services.

In cases where the data show that an agency is successfully providing services, but those services are not having the intended effect on the clients, then the agency leadership should be the first to recognize that it is wasteful to continue business as usual. Outcome-based management is a powerful tool that allows organizations to allocate their precious resources to do the most good. If successfully implemented, it also can provide the ammunition to fight the increasing public cynicism about what is often perceived to be a poor return on investment of tax dollars, and provide a competitive edge to organizations that adopt it.

Large Group Intervention

Large Group Intervention (LGI) is the generic name given to a family of formal change management strategies that involve placing large parts of an organization, or even the entire organization, in simultaneous contact with one another to plan how the organization is going to change. Proponents and users of LGIs believe these methods are particularly well suited for organizations that are seeking to establish a shared vision of their future and to build a road to get there. Some LGI models are designed specifically for organizations that are seeking to change the way their work is done (e.g., through reengineering or business process redesign).

Although many different LGI models have been developed and are in current use, they generally have common origins and are rooted in similar principles. Among these principles are getting the "whole system" into interactive discussion, using a carefully designed mixture of communication elements, using processes designed to make effective use of participants' emotions as well as thoughts, and facilitating effective dialogue while validating differing perspectives.

Large Group Interventions are usually staged in a setting away from the workplace, where participants can focus on the objective at hand without the distractions of the normal work environment. Artificial boundaries within organizations, such as functional departments, are routinely and intentionally fractured to facilitate communication and participation. These boundaries often get in the way of addressing important needs of organizations. Strategies such as TQM and BPR, as well as strategic planning itself, demand that each member of the organization think about the needs of the entire organization rather than his or her piece of it. "Democratic," participatory efforts by organizations may facilitate their members to see beyond the borders of their individual organizational niche, and develop the spirit required to make TQM not simply a "program" but a working philosophy.

The general philosophy inherent in planning change is to recognize that there is resistance to change within organizations, and change is more likely to be successfully implemented when people affected can participate in the process, influence the process, and prepare for its consequences.

Much more than a device for overcoming psychological resistance, LGI is an effective approach to substantially improving the planned change and achieving more desirable results for the organization. One dimension of additional benefits is more effective communication about the changes planned. Plans become far less distorted when everyone affected is hearing the same message at the same time, rather than having it communicated through the grapevine, through regular hierarchical channels, or not at all.

Another advantage of LGI is that those affected by the changes can provide invaluable input. It is rare that a few layers of management (or a subset of the full breadth of functions) within an organization can have an adequately detailed grasp of the whole. In most change management strategies, those at the bottom of the hierarchy, who are usually the most aware of the "nuts and bolts" of current reality, are often frozen out of the planning process. Most LGI models bring in a broad base of stakeholders to brainstorm together and to weed out problems and unintended consequences that often are otherwise built into initial designs for change, because they are invisible to the traditionally unrepresentative group of staff involved in planning.

A third advantage of LGI is that it builds a diverse and broad base of support for planned changes. Useful in all cases, this advantage becomes particularly powerful when circumstances alter, planned changes need to be modified, and time is of the essence. Circumstances that otherwise could be expected to derail well-laid plans can be addressed by a robust and already-engaged subset of the organization. Plans are far more open to effective alteration mid-stream when developed via an LGI approach.

LGIs tend to bring together people from various hierarchical levels within the organization, who otherwise may have minimal direct interaction. Many organizational development experts believe that bringing large groups of organizational members together pays an additional dividend, which would not otherwise have been created, of creating positive social linkages among organizational members. Large Group Interventions create a new and different organizational bonding, which increases networks of informal communication within an organization and makes for more robust capabilities.

All of this can occur in a three-day period, significantly curtailing the process time of conventional change management planning.

Permitting workers affected by planning to participate in the planning process is one strategy to erode this resistance to organizational change, in addition to generating fresh ideas from people who have expertise as a result of doing their job every day. They may have shied away from making valid, responsible suggestions not only because "no one ever asked us," but because they may feel that their views are not important, or that management does not have an interest in listening to them.

Among the most popular models for LGIs are The Search Conference, Future Search Conference, and Real Time Strategic Change. For additional details about these interventions, consult the book *Improving Quality and Performance in Your Non-Profit Organization.*

Chapter 30
Recent Nonprofit Developments

Since the last edition of the *Pennsylvania Nonprofit Handbook* was published in July 1996, there have been major developments affecting Pennsylvania nonprofits. The purpose of this chapter is to provide a convenient summary of them.

1. *Institutions of Purely Public Charity Act* (Act 55) (see pages 222-224)

Governor Ridge signed this legislation into law on November 26, 1997, culminating a successful, decade-long lobbying effort by charities to codify clear, measurable standards for charitable tax-exempt status. The legislation is generally favorable to charities, and provides safe harbors for the amount of charity they must provide to meet the "donate or render gratuitously a substantial portion of its services" test, the most problematic of the five-part test set forth by the Pennsylvania Supreme Court in the 1985 case of *Hospital Utilization Project v. Commonwealth of Pennsylvania.* The law also places restrictions on the ability of charities to establish new commercial enterprises that compete with commercial businesses (see page 208). Almost immediately, this law was challenged in Commonwealth Court by some local government interests. The suit was dropped after initial court rulings on procedural matters appeared to be favorable to charities. While it is uncertain whether courts will use the provisions of this law to weigh the merits of tax exemption challenges by local governments, it has already had the effect of reducing these challenges. Act 55 also is being honored by the Pennsylvania Department of Revenue in its sales tax exemption determinations.

2. *Taxpayer Bill of Rights 2*—Intermediate Sanctions

The Taxpayer Bill of Rights 2 was signed into law by President Clinton on July 30, 1996. The principal purpose of this law is to punish individuals affiliated with charities and social welfare organizations who are participating in financial abuses, and to provide the government with a sanction other than simply revoking the charity's exemption status. The law also includes expanded public disclosure requirements for organization annual federal tax returns.

Previous law required charities to make their 990 tax returns available for public inspection, but did not require that copies be provided. The law was changed to require that if a person requests a copy of the 990 in person, it must be immediately provided for a reasonable fee for copying. If the request is made in writing, it must be provided for a reasonable copying and postage fee within 30 days. Organizations that make these documents "widely available," such as posting them on the Internet, are exempt, although they still must make the document available for public inspection. The law expands the disclosure that must be made on the 990, adding information about excess expenditures to influence legislation, any political expenditures, any disqualified lobbying expenditures, and amounts of "excess benefit" transactions.

The law increases the fine for failure to file a timely 990 from $10 per day to $20 per day, with a maximum of $10,000. Higher fines apply to organizations with gross receipts over $1 million.

Both state and federal law have prohibitions against "private inurement"—permitting a charity's income to benefit a private shareholder or individual. Legislation at the federal level to define what constitutes a prevalent form of private inurement and to refine the definition of a private shareholder was enacted to respond to alleged financial abuses by some organizations that were perceived as providing unreasonable compensation to organization "insiders."

To curb financial abuses, the law authorizes the IRS to impose an excise tax, 25% in most cases, on certain improper financial transactions by 501(c)(3) and 501(c)(4) organizations. The tax applies on transactions that benefit a "disqualified person," defined as people in positions to exercise substantial influence over the organization, their family members, or other organizations controlled by those persons. Disqualified persons include voting members of the board, the president or chair, the CEO, the chief operating officer, the chief financial officer, and the treasurer, among potential other officers and staff. The benefit to the disqualified person must exceed the value that the organization receives in order to be subject to the tax. To avoid problems, tax experts are advising organizations to treat every benefit to a director or staff person as compensation, and reflect these benefits in W-2s, 1099s, and in their budget documents. Seemingly innocent benefits, such as paying for the travel and lodging expenses for a spouse attending a board retreat or a health club membership for an executive director, may trigger questions about excess benefit. Luxury travel could be considered an excess benefit.

Compensation is considered reasonable if it is in an amount that would ordinarily be paid for similar services by similar organizations in similar circumstances. The term "compensation" is defined broadly, and includes severance payments, insurance, and deferred compensation. The draft regulations provide that a charity with less than $1 million in annual receipts can use salary data from five comparable charities in the same community as evidence that the compensation that charity provides is reasonable.

Most of the provisions relating to intermediate sanctions apply retroactively to September 14, 1995, the date the legislation was first introduced. Steep additional excise tax penalties, up to 200% of the excess benefit plus the initial 25% excise tax, apply for excess benefit transactions that are not corrected in a reasonable amount of time. An excise tax may also be applied to organization managers (a term which is meant to include an officer, director, trustee) who approve the excess benefit transaction in an amount of 10% of the excess benefit, up to $10,000 maximum per transaction.

Although these excise taxes apply to individuals and not to the organizations themselves, there is nothing in this law that prohibits organizations from paying the tax or purchasing insurance to cover an individual's liability for the tax penalty. However, if the organization does purchase this insurance, the premium must be considered compensation to the individual, and this insurance could become the basis for an excess benefit if total compensation to the individual, including this insurance, exceeds the fair market value that the person provides to the organization in exchange for the total compensation that person receives from the organization. It makes sense to consult an attorney knowledgeable about the *Taxpayer Bill of Rights 2* if there are any questions that would make an organization's directors and staff vulnerable to an IRS audit.

The Internal Revenue Service published draft regulations on this section of the Revenue Code in the *Federal Register* on August 4, 1998. The IRS intended to promulgate final regulations early in 1999, but announced a delay in these regulations until late 1999 or early 2000. The draft regulations can be viewed at the following web site:

http://www.access.gpo.gov/su_docs/fedreg/a980804c.html.The Taxpayer Bill of Rights 2 was signed into law on July 30, 1996. The principal purpose of this law is to punish individuals affiliated with charities and social welfare organizations who are participating in financial abuses. It provides the government with a sanction other than simply revoking the charity's exemption status. The law also includes expanded public disclosure requirements for annual federal tax returns.

3. Lobbying Reform (see Chapter 17)

The Pennsylvania General Assembly enacted a sweeping general reform of lobbying registration and reporting requirements in October 1998. Lobbyists now are required to register and submit their expense reports to the State Ethics Commission rather than to the Clerk of the Senate. Draft regulations to implement this law were published in the *Pennsylvania Bulletin* on January 30, 1999, and it is scheduled to be fully implemented by the fall of 1999.

4. Volunteer Protection Act

In July of 1997, President Clinton signed into law the *Volunteer Protection Act,* legislation designed to provide volunteers for nonprofits and governmental entities with a decreased standard of liability.

The law now provides a volunteer whose efforts on behalf of the organization resulted in harming others with a defense against civil lawsuits, unless that harm resulted from the volunteer's "willful or criminal misconduct, gross negligence, reckless misconduct, or a conscious, flagrant indifference to the rights or safety of the individual harmed by the volunteer." The decrease in the liability standard does not apply to volunteers causing harm while under the influence of drugs or alcohol, or while operating a motor vehicle.

The version signed into law differs from previous versions in that it lowers the standard of immunity for volunteers rather than for the charitable organizations providing the volunteer services. This law permits states to enact a law opting out of this new tort standard, although it is not likely that states will choose to do so.

Proponents of the legislation pointed to a survey that indicated that one in six potential volunteers refused to participate in volunteer work because of the fear of being sued.

5. Longwood Gardens Tax Exemption Challenge

The Pennsylvania Supreme Court ruled in favor of dismissing the property tax exemption challenge to Longwood Gardens on July 20, 1998, by a 6-1 vote, and issued a strong opinion favorable to charities. However, the court did not use Act 55, the *Institutions of Purely Public Charity Act*, as its template to judge whether the institution met each of the five HUP criteria. In a 21-page opinion, Commonwealth Court had systematically dismissed the narrow interpretations of each of the five HUP criteria advanced by the Unionville-Chadds Ford School District, and echoed interpretations of prior decisions by the Supreme Court and Commonwealth Court that were favorable to charities. The opinion establishes a solid foundation of case law that will assist the voluntary sector in defending unwarranted attacks on the tax-exempt status of legitimate charities, such as that which occurred in the Longwood Gardens case.

6. Legislation on Judicial Review of Mergers and Asset Transfers

An amendment added to S.B. 1153, state legislation designed to thwart a takeover bid by an out-of-state competitor of AMP, Inc., a popular, large Central Pennsylvania manufacturer, was introduced in the waning days of the 1998 legislative session. The legislation would require judicial review of transactions involving charities that involve the movement of charitable funds between charities, or between organizational entities resulting from merger, consolidation and sale of assets, dissolution or liquidation. The initiative raised concerns of Pennsylvania charities about the burdensome reporting requirements and court intervention.

7. State Tax Credit for Charitable Donations

Senate Finance Committee Chair Melissa Hart (R-Allegheny) introduced legislation in 1998 to amend the *Institutions of Purely Public Charity Act* (Act 55). The principal purpose of her bill, H.B. 1253, was to provide state taxpayers with a credit of up to 25% of the contributions they make to qualified "institutions of purely public charity." The bill was opposed by the Pennsylvania Association of Nonprofit Organizations (PANO) and much of the voluntary sector, including the organized religious community. Objections to enactment of the bill centered on its narrow focus. According to representatives of charities who testified before the committee, the bill would promote destructive competition among charities, confuse donors, reduce creativity by the sector, lower the quality of services provided by charities, mute meaningful and socially constructive advocacy activities of charities, and substantially increase the workload of state government. The legislation is likely to be reintroduced during the 1999 session of the General Assembly.

8. Department of Revenue's New Sales Tax Exemption Form

The Pennsylvania Department of Revenue began distributing its revised sales tax exemption application form to Pennsylvania charities at the end of 1998. Many charities are complaining that the new form is confusing, requires voluminous information and data only minimally relevant to whether they qualify for exempt status, obligates applicants to provide a much broader range of information than they reasonably expected, and requires a substantial increase in time and effort to apply or reapply compared to previous applications.

9. Washington and Jefferson College Tax Exemption Challenge

On November 20, 1997, the Pennsylvania Supreme Court handed down a 5-1 decision upholding a September 1995 opinion by Commonwealth Court that Washington and Jefferson College was entitled to tax-exempt status as an institution of purely public charity. The Court maintained its past practice of using its 1985 opinion in *Hospital Utilization Project v. Commonwealth of Pennsylvania* as the template to judge the tax exemption case before it. The 13-page opinion perfunctorily stated the evidence in favor of Washington and Jefferson College meeting all of the five HUP criteria—that it advanced a charitable purpose, donated or rendered gratuitously a substantial portion of its services, served a substantial, indefinite class of persons who are legitimate subjects of charity, relieved government of some of its burden, and operated entirely free from private profit motive. The standard used in this opinion to interpret the meaning of each of those five criteria is likely to make it substantially more difficult, if not impossible, for local governments to successfully challenge institutions of higher learning even if the courts do not honor the safe harbors of Act 55.

10. U.S. Postal Service Support of Philanthropy

Forty-thousand suggestions for new stamps arrive each year on the doorstep of the Postal Service's Citizens' Stamp Advisory Committee, and only about 30 of these are approved each year. In October 1998, the Postal Service issued a 32-cent stamp honoring philanthropy, with the line "Giving and Sharing: An American Tradition." In April 1998, the Postal Service announced that it would issue a 40-cent, first-class "Semipostal Stamp," in accordance with legislation passed by the Congress in 1997. Up to $60 million of the proceeds from sales of the stamp, after costs for postage, designing, and marketing are deducted, will be contributed to the National Institutes of Health and the Defense Department for breast cancer research. The sale of the stamp is expected to continue for at least two years and, if the experiment is successful, other charities will be petitioning for stamps supporting their causes.

Appendix A

Sample Articles of Incorporation Legal Notice

NOTICE IS HEREBY GIVEN that Articles of Incorporation were filed and approved by the Department of State and the Commonwealth of Pennsylvania, on (insert date), for the purpose of incorporating (insert name of corporation), under the provisions of the Pennsylvania Nonprofit Corporation law of 1988.

The corporation is incorporated under the Nonprofit Corporation Law of the Commonwealth of Pennsylvania, and the corporation does not contemplate pecuniary gain or profit, incidental or otherwise. The nature of the activities to be conducted and the purposes to be promoted or carried out by the corporation, shall be exclusively within the purview of Section 501(c)(insert) of the Internal Revenue Code of 1986, or the corresponding provisions of any subsequent tax laws of the United States. Without limiting the generality of the foregoing, the purposes of the corporation shall be: (insert).

Name of Corporation Secretary or Law Firm

Appendix B

SAMPLE BYLAWS (BASED ON THE BYLAWS OF THE PENNSYLVANIA JEWISH COALITION)

BYLAWS
OF
(INSERT)

ARTICLE I- CORPORATE NAME

1. The name of the corporation shall be (insert).

ARTICLE II - PURPOSE

1. The corporation shall have unlimited powers to engage in and do any lawful act concerning any and all lawful activity for which nonprofit corporations may be incorporated under *Pennsylvania Nonprofit Corporation law of 1988*, as amended, under the provisions of which the corporation is incorporated.

2. The corporation shall undertake such acts as it deems necessary to (insert purpose of the corporation).

ARTICLE III - OFFICES

1. The principal office of the corporation shall be located in (insert), Pennsylvania.

2. The corporation may also have offices at such other places as the Board of Directors may from time to time appoint or the activities of the corporation may require.

ARTICLE IV - SEALS

1. The corporate seal shall have inscribed thereon the name of the corporation, the year of its organization and the words "Corporate Seal, Pennsylvania."

ARTICLE V - MEMBERS

1. The corporation shall have no members. All powers, obligations and rights of members provided by law shall reside in the Board of Directors.

ARTICLE VI - DIRECTORS

1. The business and affairs of this corporation shall be managed by its Board of Directors. The number of directors shall not exceed (insert number). The minimum qualifications of members of the Board of Directors shall be (insert).

2. In addition to the powers and authorities by these Bylaws expressly conferred upon them, the Board of Directors shall have the maximum power and authority now or hereafter provided or permitted under the laws of the Commonwealth of Pennsylvania to Directors of Pennsylvania nonprofit corporations acting as a Board.

3. The Annual Meeting of the Board of Directors shall be held annually during the calendar year at such time and place as the Board of Directors shall designate in the notice of the meeting.

4. Regular meetings of the Board of Directors shall occur at least (insert) at such times and places as it shall designate from time to time.

5. Special meetings of the Board of Directors may be called by the Chairperson at such

times as the Chairperson shall deem necessary.

6. Written or personal notice of every meeting of the Board of Directors shall be given to each Director at least five (5) days prior to the day named for the meeting.

7. A quorum for the transaction of business shall consist of (insert). The acts of a majority of directors present and eligible to vote at a Board meeting shall be the acts of the Board of Directors. Any action which may be taken at a meeting of the Directors may be taken without a meeting, if the consent or consents in writing setting forth the action so taken shall be signed by at least a majority of all directors in office, and shall be filed with the Secretary of the corporation.

8. Except where inconsistent with law or these bylaws, corporate proceedings shall be governed by the latest edition of Robert's Rules of Order.

9. The Board of Directors may, by resolution adopted by a majority of the Directors in office, establish one or more committees to consist of one or more Directors of the corporation to report back to the Board on the matter(s) within the committee's jurisdiction. A quorum for the purpose of holding and acting at any meeting of a committee shall be a simple majority of the members thereof.

10. All Board members shall be nominated and elected to serve on the Board. The Board may designate one or more directors as alternate members of any committee, who may replace any absent or disqualified member at any meeting of the committee. In the absence or disqualification of a member of a committee, the member or members thereof present at any meeting and not disqualified from voting, whether or not he, she or they constitute a quorum, may unanimously appoint another director to act at the meeting in the place of any such absent or disqualified member. Each committee of the Board shall serve at the pleasure of the Board.

11. The Board of Directors may, by resolution adopted by a majority of the Directors in office, establish an Advisory Committee to advise and assist the Board of Directors in carrying out its responsibilities. The Advisory committee shall consist of (insert).

12. One or more persons may participate in a meeting of the Board or a committee of the Board by means of the conference telephone or similar communications equipment by means of which all persons participating in the meeting can hear each other. Participation in a meeting pursuant to this section shall constitute presence in person at such meeting.

13. The Board of Directors may declare vacant the office of a director if he or she is declared of unsound mind by the order of court or is convicted of felony, or if within sixty (60) days after notice of his or her selection, he or she does not accept such office either in writing or by attending a meeting of the Board of Directors, and fulfill each other requirements of a qualification as the Bylaws may specify.

14. Any Director or Officer of the corporation is authorized to receive reasonable compensation from the corporation for services rendered and for actual expenses incurred when authorized by the Board of Directors or its designee. No director of the corporation shall receive compensation merely for acting as a director.

ARTICLE VII - OFFICERS

1. The executive officers of the corporation shall be natural persons of full age, shall be chosen by the Board, and shall be a Chairperson, Vice Chairperson, Secretary, Treasurer and such other officers and assistant officers as the needs of the corporation may require. They shall hold their offices for a term of (insert) and shall have such authority and shall perform such duties as are provided by the Bylaws and as shall from time to time be prescribed by the Board. The Board of Directors may secure the fidelity of any or all such officers by bond or otherwise. There shall be no limit on the number or terms an officer can serve.

2. Any officer or agent may be removed by the Board of Directors whenever in its judgment

the best interests of the corporation will be served thereby but such removal shall be without prejudice to the contract rights of any person removed.

3. The Chairperson shall be the chief executive officer of the corporation; he or she shall preside at all meetings of the Directors; he or she shall have general and active management of the affairs of the corporation; shall see that all orders and resolutions of the Board are carried into effect, subject, however, to the right of the Directors to delegate any specific powers, except as may be by statute exclusively conferred on the Chairperson to any other officer or officers of the corporation. He or she shall execute all documents requiring a seal, under the seal of the corporation. He or she shall be EX-OFFICIO a member of all committees and shall have the general powers and duties of supervision and management usually vested in the office of Chairperson.

4. The Vice Chairperson shall act in all cases for and as the Chairperson in the latter's absence or incapacity, and shall perform such other duties as he or she may be required to do from time to time.

5. The Secretary shall attend all sessions of the Board and act as clerk thereof, and record all the votes of the corporation and the minutes of all its transactions in a book to be kept for that purpose; and shall perform like duties for all committees of the Board of Directors when required. He or she shall give, or cause to be given, notice of all meetings of the Board of Directors, and shall perform such other duties as may be prescribed by the Board of Directors or Chairperson, under whose supervision he or she shall be. He or she shall keep in safe custody, the corporate seal of the corporation, and when authorized by the Board, affix the same to any instrument requiring it.

6. The Treasurer shall have custody of the corporate funds and securities and shall keep full and accurate accounts or receipts and disbursements in books belonging to the corporation, and shall keep the moneys of the corporation in a separate account to the credit of the corporation. He or she shall disburse the funds of the corporation as may be ordered by the Board, taking proper vouchers for such disbursements, and shall render to the Chairperson and Directors, at the regular meeting of the Board, or whenever they may require it, an account of all his or her transactions as Treasurer and of the financial condition of the corporation.

7. Elections of officers shall be held every (insert) at the Annual Meeting of the Board of Directors.

ARTICLE VIII - VACANCIES

1. If the office of any officer or agent, one or more, becomes vacant for any reason, the Board of Directors may choose a successor or successors, who shall hold office for the unexpired term in respect of which such vacancy occurred.

2. Vacancies in the Board of Directors shall be filled in the same manner as provided for the designation of Directors in Article VI - Directors.

ARTICLE IX - BOOKS AND RECORDS

1. The corporation shall keep an original or duplicate record of the proceeding of the Directors, the original or a copy of its Bylaws, including all amendments thereto to date, certified by the Secretary of the corporation, and an original or a duplicate Board register, giving the names of the Directors, and showing their respective addresses. The corporation shall also keep appropriate, complete and accurate books or records of account which shall be reviewed on an annual basis. The records provided for herein shall be kept at either the registered office of the corporation in this Commonwealth, or at its principal place of business wherever situated.

ARTICLE X - FISCAL YEAR AND ANNUAL REPORT

1. The fiscal year of the corporation shall commence on (insert) and end on the following (insert).

2. The Board of Directors shall cause a report of the activities of the corporation to be prepared annually and sent to such persons as the Board of Directors shall determine.

ARTICLE XI - AMENDMENTS

1. The Board of Directors may alter, amend, suspend or repeal these Bylaws at any regular or special meeting called for that purpose, except as restricted by the *Pennsylvania Nonprofit Corporation law of 1988*, as amended.

ARTICLE XII - LIMITED LIABILITY OF DIRECTORS

1. A director shall not be personally liable for monetary damages as such for any action taken, or any failure to take any action, unless the director has breached or failed to perform the duties of his or her office under section 8363 of the Directors' Liability Act (relating to standard of care and justifiable reliance); and the breach or failure to perform constitutes self-dealing, willful misconduct or recklessness. The provision of this section shall not apply to the responsibility or liability of a director pursuant to any criminal statute; or the liability of a director for the payment of taxes pursuant to local, State or Federal Law.

Appendix C
Addresses of IRS Field Offices in a Sampling of PA Communities

Altoona:
Paine Webber Building
2nd Floor
1601 Eleventh Avenue
Altoona, PA 16601

Bethlehem:
Summit Bank One
Suite 700
1 Bethlehem Plaza
Bethlehem, PA 18018

Bradford:
Seneca Building
4th Floor, Room 417
2 Main Street
Butler, PA 16701

Butler:
Holly Pointe Center
Room 201
220 South Main Street
Butler, PA 16001

Cranberry Township:
Cranberry Corporate Center
213 Executive Drive
1st Floor
Cranberry, PA 16046

DuBois:
203 North Brady Street
DuBois, PA 15801

Erie:
1314 Griswold Plaza
Room 105
Erie, PA 16501

Harrisburg:
Federal Building
228 Walnut Street
Room 670
Harrisburg, PA 17108

Jenkintown:
Noble Plaza Building
4th Floor
801 Old York Road
Jenkintown, PA 19046

Johnstown:
Penn Traffic Building
Suite 200
319 Washington Street
Johnstown, PA 15901

King of Prussia:
601 S. Henderson Road
King of Prussia, PA 19406

Lancaster:
City Line Business Center #6
1175 Mainheim Pike
Lancaster, PA 17601

McKeesport:
Executive Building
1st Floor
332 Fifth Avenue
McKeesport, PA 15132

Media:
Rosetree Corp. Center
Building 1
1400 N. Providence Road
Suite 100
Media, PA 19063

Monroeville:
DeMarco-Durzo Building
2735 Mosside Blvd.
1st Floor
Monroeville, PA 15146

Philadelphia:
600 Arch Street
Room 1232
Philadelphia, PA 19106

Pittsburgh:
William S. Moorhead Federal Bldg.
Suite 1113
1000 Liberty Avenue
Pittsburgh, PA 15222

Reading:
1125 Berkshire Blvd.
Suite 180
Wyomissing, PA 19610

Scranton:
Suite 600
409 Lackawanna Avenue
Scranton, PA 18503

State College:
315 South Allen Street
Suite 316
State College, PA 16801

Washington:
Jefferson Court Plaza
Upper Level
162 West Chestnut Street
Washington, PA 15301

Wilkes-Barre:
Stegmaier Building
7 N. Wilkes-Barre Blvd.
Wilkes-Barre, PA 18773

Williamsport:
U.S. Court House & Federal Bldg.
2nd Floor
240 W. 3rd Street
Williamsport, PA 17701

York:
2801 Eastern Blvd.
York, PA 17402

Appendix D
Legal Journals for Advertising Articles of Incorporation Filing*

Adams County
Adams County Legal Journal
112 Baltimore St.
Gettysburg, PA 117325
717-334-1191

Allegheny County
Pittsburgh Legal Journal
400 Koppers Bldg.
7th Ave.
Pittsburgh, PA 15219
412-261-6225

Armstrong County
Armstrong County Legal Journal
Armstrong County Courthouse
Kitanning, PA 16201
412-543-2500

Beaver County
Beaver County Legal Journal
775 Fourth St.
Beaver, PA 15009
412-726-7622

Bedford County
Bedford County Legal Journal
c/o R. Martin Reity, Esq.
PO Box 440
Bedford PA 15522

Berks County
Berks County Law Journal
544-546 Court St.
PO Box 1058
Reading, PA 19063
610-375-4593

Blair County
Blair County Legal Bulletin
c/o Mrs. Roberta Hare, Jr., Editor
115 Logal Blvd.
Altoona, PA 16602
814-943-1496

Bradford County
Bradford County Law Journal
201 W. Lockhart St.
Sayre, PA 18840
717-888-2244

Bucks County
Bucks County Law Reporter
135 E. State St.
PO Box 300
Doylestown, PA 18901
215-348-9413

Butler County
Butler County Legal Journal
228 S. Main St.
Butler, PA 16001
412-285-1717

Cambria County
Cambria County Legal Journal
PO Box 338
Ebensburg, PA 15931
814-472-9530

Carbon County
Carbon County Law Journal
PO Box 6
Jim Thorpe, PA 18229
717-325-3097

Centre County
Centre County Legal Journal
Box 57
Bellefonte, PA 16823
814-355-5474

Chester County
Chester County Law Reporter
15 W. Gay St.
West Chester, PA 19380
215-692-1889

Clearfield County
c/o Gary A. Knaresboro, Esq.
101 S. 2nd St.
Clearfield, PA 16830
814-765-6555

Crawford County
Crawford County Legal Journal
PO Box 384
Meadville, PA 16335
814-332-6000

Cumberland County
Cumberland Law Journal
Roger M. Morgenthal, Esq., Editor
11 E. High St.
Carlisle, PA 17013
717-249-3022

Dauphin County
Dauphin County Reporter
213 N. Front St.
Harrisburg, PA 17101
717-232-7536

Delaware County
Delaware County Legal Journal
Bar Association Bldg.
Front & Lemon Sts.
PO Box 466
Media, PA 19063
610-566-6625

Erie County
Erie County Legal Journal
302 W. 9th St.
Erie, PA 16502-1427
814-459-3111

Fayette County:
Fayette Legal Journal
61 E. Main St.
Uniontown, PA 15401
412-430-1227

Franklin County
Franklin County Legal Journal
Ste. 210-212 Chambersburg Trust Bldg.
Chambersburg, PA 17201
717-263-9773

Greene County
Greene Reports
Courthouse
Waynesburg, PA 15370

Indiana County
Indiana Law Journal
c/o Donald R. Marsh, Esq.
307 Savings & Trust Co. Bldg.
Indiana, PA 15701
412-465-5651

Jefferson County
Jefferson County Legal Journal
316 Main St.
Brookville, PA 15825
814-849-1237

Lackawanna County
Lackawanna Jurist
205 Davidow Bldg.
Scranton, PA 18503
717-342-8089

Lancaster County
Lancaster Law Review
26 E. Orange St.
Lancaster, PA 17602
717-393-0737

Lawrence County
Lawrence Law Journal
c/o Lawrence Co. Government Center
New Castle, PA 16101
412-658-2541

Lebanon County
Lebanon County Legal Journal
Room 305 Law Library
Municipal Building
Lebanon, PA 17042
717-274-2801 ext. 2301

Lehigh County
Lehigh Law Journal
1114 Walnut St.
Allentown, PA 18102
215-433-6204

Luzerne County
Luzerne Legal Register
Room 23 Courthouse
Willkes-Barre, PA 18711
717-822-6712

Lycoming County
Lycoming Reporter
Lycoming County Courthouse
Williamsport, PA 17701
717-327-2258

Mercer County
Mercer County Law Journal
Jefferson Bldg.
19 Jefferson Ave.
PO Box 949
Sharon, PA 16146
412-342-6835

Mifflin County
Mifflin County Legal Journal
23 N. Wayne St.
PO Box 430
Lewistown, PA 17044
717-248-6751

Monroe County
Monroe Legal Reporter
c/o Michael R. Muth, Esq.
PO Box 786
Stroudsburg, PA 18360
717-424-7288

Montgomery County
Montgomery County Law Reporter
100 W. Airy St.
PO Box 268
Norristown, PA 19404
610-279-9667

Northampton County
Northampton County Reporter
155 S. Ninth St.
Easton, PA 18042
215-258-6333

Northumberland County
Northumberland Legal Journal
PO Box 126
Sunbury, PA 17801
717-266-7777

Philadelphia County
The Legal Intelligencer
1617 JFK Blvd., Ste. 960
Philadelphia, PA 19103
215-557-2300

Schuylkill County
Schuylkill Legal Record
Law Library
Schuylkill County Courthouse
Pottsville, PA 17901
717-628-1235

Somerset County
Somerset Legal Journal
PO Box 501
Somerset, PA 15501
412-445-4021

Washington County
Washington Co. Reports
523 Washington Trust Bldg.
Washington, PA 15301
412-225-6710

Westmoreland County
Westmoreland Law Journal
129 N. Pennsylvania Ave.
Greensburg, PA 15601
412-834-7260

York County
York Legal Record
137 E. Market St.
York, PA 17401
717-854-8755

*counties not listed do not have a legal journal

Appendix E

Regional Foundation Reference Collections provided by the Foundation Center

Bethlehem:
Northampton Community College
Learning Resources Center
4th Floor
3835 Green Pond Road
Bethlehem, PA 18017
(610) 861-5360

Erie:
Erie County Public Library
160 E. Front Street
Erie, PA 16507
(814) 451-6900

Harrisburg:
Dauphin County Library System
Central Library—Grants
Information Center
101 Walnut Street
Harrisburg, PA 17101
(717) 234-4976

Lancaster:
Lancaster Public Library
Adult Services Department
125 N. Duke Street
Lancaster, PA 17602
(717) 394-2651

Philadelphia:
Free Library of Philadelphia
Main Branch
1901 Vine Street
Social Science and History Dept.
Philadelphia, PA 19103-1189
(215) 686-5423

Pittsburgh:
Carnegie Public Library
Second Floor
4400 Forbes Avenue
Pittsburgh, PA 15213
(412) 622-1917

Pittston:
Economic Development Council of
  Northeastern, PA
1151 Oak Street
Pittston, PA 18640
(717) 655-5581 Ext. 251

Appendix F

Constitution of Pennsylvania

Article VIII, Section 1 and 2
TAXATION AND FINANCE

Uniformity of Taxation

Section 1. All taxes shall be uniform, upon the same class of subjects, within the territorial limits of the authority levying the tax, and shall be levied and collected under general laws.

Exemptions and Special Provisions

Section 2. (a) The General Assembly may by law exempt from taxation:

(i) Actual places of regularly stated religious worship:

(ii) Actual places of burial, when used or held by a person or organization deriving no private or corporate profit therefrom and no substantial part of whose activity consists of selling personal property in connection therewith;

(iii) That portion of public property which is actually and regularly used for public purposes;

(iv) That portion of the property owned and occupied by any branch, post or camp of honorably discharged servicemen or servicewomen which is actually and regularly used for benevolent, charitable or patriotic purposes; and

(v) Institutions of purely public charity, but in the case of any real property tax exemptions only that portion of real property of such institution which is actually and regularly used for the purposes of the institution.

(b) The General Assembly may, by law:

(i) Establish standards and qualifications for private forest reserves, agriculture reserves, and land actively devoted to agriculture use, and make special provision for the taxation thereof;

(ii) Establish as a class or classes of subjects of taxation the property or privileges of persons who, because of age, disability, infirmity or poverty are determined to be in need of tax exemption or of special tax provisions, and for any such class or classes and standards and qualifications, and except as herein provided may impose taxes, grant exemptions, or make special tax provisions in accordance therewith. No exemption or special provision shall be made under this clause with respect to taxes upon the sale or use of personal property, and no exemption from any tax upon real property shall be granted by the General Assembly under this clause unless the General Assembly shall provide for the reimbursement of local taxing authorities by or through the Commonwealth for revenue losses occasioned by such exemption;

(iii) Establish standards and qualifications by which local taxing authorities may make uniform special tax provisions applicable to a taxpayer for a limited period of time to encourage improvement of deteriorating property or areas by an individual, association or corporation, or to encourage industrial development by a nonprofit corporation; and

(iv) Make special tax provisions on any increase in value of real estate resulting from residential construction. Such special tax provisions shall be applicable for a period not to exceed two years.

(v) Establish standards and qualifications by which local taxing authorities in counties of the first and second class make uniform special real property tax provisions applicable to taxpayers who are long-time owner-occupants as shall be defined by the General Assembly of residences in areas where real property values have risen markedly as a consequence of the refurbishing or renovating of other deteriorating residences or the construction of new residences.

Appendix G

Excerpt from Act 2, Session of 1971

Part III
EXCLUSIONS FROM TAX

Section 204. Exclusions from Tax.—The tax imposed by section 202 shall not be imposed upon

The sale at retail or use of tangible personal property (other than motor vehicles, trailers, semi-trailers, motor boats, aircraft or other similar tangible personal property required under Federal laws or laws of this Commonwealth to be registered or licensed) or services sold by or purchased from a person not a vendor in an isolated transaction or sold by or purchased from a person who is a vendor but is not a vendor with respect to tangible personal property or services sold or purchased in such transaction: Provided, That inventory and stock in trade so sold or purchased, shall not be excluded from the tax by the provisions of this subsection.

***

The sale at retail to or use by (i) any charitable organization, volunteer firemen's organization or nonprofit educational institution, or (ii) a religious organization for religious purposes of tangible personal property or services: Provided, however, That the exclusion of this clause shall not apply with respect to any tangible personal property or services used in an unrelated trade or business carried on by such organization or institution or with respect to any materials, supplies and equipment used in the construction, reconstruction, remodeling, repairs and maintenance of any real estate, except materials and supplies when purchased by such organizations or institutions for routine maintenance and repairs.

***

The General Assembly of the Commonwealth of Pennsylvania hereby enacts as follows:

Section 1. Clause (3) of subsection (a) of section 202, act of May 21, 1943 (P.L. 571), known as "The Fourth to Eighth Class County Assessment Law," amended August 11, 1959 (P.L. 668), is amended to read:

Section 202. Exemptions from Taxation.—(a) The following property shall be exempt from all county, borough, town, township, road, poor, county institution district and school (except in cities) tax, to wit:

***

All hospitals, universities, colleges, seminaries, academies, associations and institutions of learning, benevolence or charity, including fire and rescue stations, with the grounds thereto annexed and necessary for the occupancy and enjoyment of then same, founded, endowed and maintained by public or private charity: Provided, That the entire revenue derived by the same be applied to the support and to increase the efficiency and facilities thereof, the repair and the necessary increase of grounds and buildings thereof, and for no other purpose: *Provided further, That the property of associations and institutions of benevolence and charity be necessary to and actually used for the principal purposes of the institution and shall not be used in a manner as to compete with commercial enterprise.*

***

Act 55 (Excerpt)

Note: The following is the section of Act 55, the *Institutions of Purely Public Charity Act*, which provides a measurable standard for meeting the "donate or render gratuitously a substantial portion of its services" test of *Hospital Utilization Project v. Commonwealth of Pennsylvania.*

(D) COMMUNITY SERVICE.—

(1) THE INSTITUTION MUST DONATE OR RENDER GRATUITOUSLY A SUBSTANTIAL PORTION OF ITS SERVICES. THIS CRITERION IS SATISFIED IF THE INSTITUTION BENEFITS THE COMMUNITY BY ACTUALLY PROVIDING ANY ONE OF THE FOLLOWING:

(I) GOODS OR SERVICES TO ALL WHO SEEK THEM WITHOUT REGARD TO THEIR ABILITY TO PAY FOR WHAT THEY RECEIVE IF ALL OF THE FOLLOWING APPLY:

(A) THE INSTITUTION HAS A WRITTEN POLICY TO THIS EFFECT.

(B) THE INSTITUTION HAS PUBLISHED THIS POLICY IN A REASONABLE MANNER.

(C) THE INSTITUTION PROVIDES UNCOMPENSATED GOOD OR SERVICES AT LEAST EQUAL TO 75% OF THE INSTITUTION'S NET OPERATING INCOME BUT NOT LESS THAN
 3% OF THE INSTITUTION'S TOTAL OPERATING EXPENSES.

(II) GOODS OR SERVICES FOR FEES THAT ARE BASED UPON THE RECIPIENT'S ABILITY TO PAY FOR THEM IF ALL OF THE FOLLOWING APPLY:

(A) THE INSTITUTION CAN DEMONSTRATE THAT IT HAS IMPLEMENTED A WRITTEN POLICY AND A WRITTEN SCHEDULE OF FEES BASED ON INDIVIDUAL OR FAMILY INCOME. AN INSTITUTION WILL MEET THE REQUIREMENT OF THIS CLAUSE IF THE INSTITUTION CONSISTENTLY APPLIES A FORMULA TO ALL INDIVIDUALS REQUESTING CONSIDERATION OF REDUCED FEES WHICH IS IN PART BASED ON INDIVIDUAL OR FAMILY INCOME.

(B) AT LEAST 20% OF THE INDIVIDUALS RECEIVING GOODS OR SERVICES FROM THE INSTITUTION PAY NO FEE OR A FEE WHICH IS LOWER THAN THE COST OF THE GOODS OR SERVICES PROVIDED BY THE INSTITUTION.

(C) AT LEAST 10% OF THE INDIVIDUALS RECEIVING GOODS OR SERVICES FROM THE INSTITUTION RECEIVE A REDUCTION IN FEES OF AT LEAST 10% OF THE COST OF THE GOODS OR SERVICES PROVIDED TO THEM.

(D) NO INDIVIDUAL RECEIVING GOODS OR SERVICES FROM THE INSTITUTION PAYS A FEE WHICH IS EQUAL TO OR GREATER THAN THE COST OF THE GOODS OR SERVICES PROVIDED TO THEM, OR THE GOODS OR SERVICES PROVIDED TO THE INDIVIDUALS DESCRIBED IN CLAUSE (B) ARE COMPARABLE IN QUALITY AND QUANTITY TO THE GOODS OR SERVICES PROVIDED TO THOSE INDIVIDUALS WHO PAY A FEE WHICH IS EQUAL TO OR GREATER THAN THE COST OF THE GOODS OR SERVICES PROVIDED TO THEM.

(III) WHOLLY GRATUITOUS GOODS OR SERVICES TO AT LEAST 5% OF THOSE RECEIVING SIMILAR GOODS OR SERVICES FROM THE INSTITUTION.

(IV) FINANCIAL ASSISTANCE OR UNCOMPENSATED GOODS OR SERVICES TO AT LEAST 20% OF THOSE RECEIVING SIMILAR GOODS OR SERVICES FROM THE INSTITUTION IF AT LEAST 10% OF THE INDIVIDUALS RECEIVING GOODS OR SERVICES FROM THE INSTITUTION EITHER PAID NO FEES OR FEES WHICH WERE 90% OR LESS OF THE COST OF THE GOODS OR SERVICES PROVIDED TO THEM, AFTER CONSIDERATION OF ANY FINANCIAL ASSISTANCE PROVIDED TO THEM BY THE INSTITUTION.

(V) UNCOMPENSATED GOODS OR SERVICES WHICH, IN THE AGGREGATE, ARE EQUAL TO AT LEAST 5% OF THE INSTITUTION'S COSTS OF PROVIDING GOODS OR SERVICES.

(VI) GOODS OR SERVICES AT NO FEE OR REDUCED FEES TO GOVERNMENT AGENCIES OR GOODS OR SERVICES TO INDIVIDUALS ELIGIBLE FOR GOVERNMENT PROGRAMS IF ANY ONE OF THE FOLLOWING APPLIES:

(A) THE INSTITUTION RECEIVES 75% OR MORE OF ITS GROSS OPERATING REVENUE FROM GRANTS OR FEE-FOR-SERVICE PAYMENTS BY GOVERNMENT AGENCIES AND IF THE AGGREGATE AMOUNT OF FEE-FOR-SERVICE PAYMENTS FROM GOVERNMENT AGENCIES DOES NOT EXCEED 95% OF THE INSTITUTION'S COSTS OF PROVIDING GOODS OR SERVICES TO THE INDIVIDUALS FOR WHOM THE FEE-FOR-SERVICES PAYMENTS ARE MADE.

(B) THE INSTITUTION PROVIDES GOODS OR SERVICES TO INDIVIDUALS WITH MENTAL RETARDATION, TO INDIVIDUALS WHO NEED MENTAL HEALTH SERVICES, TO MEMBERS OF AN INDIVIDUAL'S FAMILY OR GUARDIAN IN SUPPORT OF SUCH GOODS OR SERVICES OR TO INDIVIDUALS WHO ARE DEPENDENT, NEGLECTED OR DELINQUENT CHILDREN, AS LONG AS THE INSTITUTION PERFORMS DUTIES THAT WOULD OTHERWISE BE THE RESPONSIBILITY OF GOVERNMENT AND THE INSTITUTION IS RESTRICTED IN ITS ABILITY TO RETAIN REVENUE OVER EXPENSES OR VOLUNTARY CONTRIBUTIONS BY ANY ONE OF THE FOLLOWING STATUTES OR REGULATIONS OR BY CONTRACTUAL LIMITATIONS WITH COUNTY CHILDREN AND YOUTH OFFICES IN THIS COMMONWEALTH:

(I) SECTIONS 1315(C) AND 1905(D) OF THE SOCIAL SECURITY ACT (49 STAT. 620, 42 U.S.C. §§1396D(D) AND 1396N(C)).

(II) 42 CFR 440.150 (RELATING TO INTERMEDIATE CARE FACILITY (ICF/MR) SERVICES.

(III) 42 CFR PT. 483 SUBPT. I (RELATING TO CONDITIONS OF PARTICIPATION FOR INTERMEDIATE CARE FACILITIES FOR THE MENTALLY RETARDED).

(IV) THE ACT OF OCTOBER 20, 1966 (3RD SP.SESS., P.L.96, NO.6), KNOWN AS THE MENTAL HEALTH AND MENTAL RETARDATION ACT OF 1966.

(V) ARTICLES II, VII, IX AND X OF THE ACT OF JUNE 13, 1967 (P.L.31, NO.21), KNOWN AS THE PUBLIC WELFARE CODE.

(VI) 23 PA.C.S. CH. 63 (RELATING TO CHILD PROTECTIVE SERVICES).

(VII) 42 PA.C.S. CH. 63 (RELATING TO JUVENILE MATTERS).

(VIII) 55 PA. CODE CHS. 3170 (RELATING TO ALLOWABLE COSTS AND PROCEDURES FOR COUNTY CHILDREN AND YOUTH), 3680 (RELATING TO ADMINISTRATION AND OPERATION OF A CHILDREN AND YOUTH SOCIAL SERVICE AGENCY)

4300 (RELATING TO COUNTY MENTAL HEALTH AND MENTAL RETARDATION FISCAL MANUAL), 6400 (RELATING TO COMMUNITY HOMES FOR INDIVIDUALS WITH MENTAL RETARDATION), 6500 (RELATING TO FAMILY LIVING HOMES), 6210 (RELATING TO PARTICIPATION REQUIREMENTS FOR THE INTERMEDIATE CARE FACILITIES FOR THE MENTALLY RETARDED PROGRAM), 6211 (RELATING TO ALLOWABLE COST REIMBURSEMENT FOR NON-STATE OPERATED INTERMEDIATE CARE FACILITIES FOR THE MENTALLY RETARDED) AND 6600 (RELATING TO INTERMEDIATE CARE FACILITIES FOR AND 6600 (RELATING TO INTERMEDIATE CARE FACILITIES FOR THE MENTALLY RETARDED).

(VII) FUNDRAISING ON BEHALF OF, OR GRANTS TO, AN INSTITUTION OF PURELY PUBLIC CHARITY, AN ENTITY SIMILARLY RECOGNIZED BY ANOTHER STATE OR FOREIGN JURISDICTION, A QUALIFYING RELIGIOUS ORGANIZATION OR A GOVERN-MENT AGENCY AND ACTUAL CONTRIBUTION OF A SUBSTANTIAL PORTION OF THE FUNDS RAISED OR CONTRIBUTIONS RECEIVED TO AN INSTITUTION OF PURELY PUBLIC CHARITY, AN ENTITY SIMILARLY RECOGNIZED BY ANOTHER STATE OR FOREIGN JURISDICTION, A QUALIFYING

RELIGIOUS ORGANIZATION OR A GOVERNMENT AGENCY.

(2) THE INSTITUTION MAY ELECT TO AVERAGE THE APPLICABLE DATA FOR ITS FIVE MOST RECENTLY COMPLETED FISCAL YEARS FOR THE PURPOSES OF CALCULATING ANY FORMULA OR MEETING ANY QUANTITATIVE STANDARD IN PARAGRAPH (1).

(3) FOR THE PURPOSES OF CALCULATING THE NUMBER OF INDIVIDUALS FOR USE IN THE PERCENTAGE CALCULATIONS IN THIS SUBSECTION, EDUCATIONAL INSTITUTIONS MAY USE FULL TIME EQUIVALENT STUDENTS AS DEFINED BY THE DEPARTMENT OF EDUCATION.

(4) FOR PURPOSES OF THIS SUBSECTION, THE TERM "UNCOMPENSATED GOODS OR SERVICES" SHALL BE LIMITED TO ANY OF THE FOLLOWING:

(I) THE FULL COST OF ALL GOODS OR SERVICES PROVIDED BY THE INSTITUTION FOR WHICH THE INSTITUTION HAS NOT RECEIVED MONETARY COMPENSATION OR THE DIFFERENCE BETWEEN THE FULL COST AND ANY LESSER FEE RECEIVED FOR THE GOODS

OR SERVICES, INCLUDING THE COST OF THE GOODS OR SERVICES PROVIDED TO INDIVIDUALS UNABLE TO PAY.

(II) THE DIFFERENCE BETWEEN THE FULL COST OF EDUCATION AND RESEARCH PROGRAMS PROVIDED BY OR PARTICI-PATED IN BY THE INSTITUTION AND THE PAYMENT MADE TO THE INSTITUTION TO SUPPORT THE EDUCATION AND RE-SEARCH PROGRAMS.

(III) THE DIFFERENCE BETWEEN THE FULL COST OF PROVIDING THE GOODS OR SERVICES AND THE PAYMENT MADE TO THE INSTITUTION UNDER ANY GOVERNMENT PROGRAM, INCLUDING INDIVIDUALS COVERED BY MEDICARE OR MEDICAID.

(IV) THE DIFFERENCE BETWEEN THE FULL COST OF THE COMMUNITY SERVICES WHICH THE INSTITUTION PROVIDES OR PARTICIPATES IN AND THE PAYMENT MADE TO THE INSTITUTION TO SUPPORT SUCH COMMUNITY SERVICES.

(V) THE REASONABLE VALUE OF ANY MONEYS, PROPERTY, GOODS OR SERVICES DONATED BY A PRIMARY DONOR TO AN INSTITUTION OF PURELY PUBLIC CHARITY OR TO A GOVERNMENT AGENCY OR THE REASONABLE VALUE OF THE NET DONATION MADE BY A SECONDARY DONOR TO A PRIMARY DONOR. AS USED IN THIS SUBPARAGRAPH, THE FOLLOWING WORDS AND PHRASES SHALL HAVE THE FOLLOWING MEANINGS:

"NET DONATION." IN THE CASE OF A DONATION OF MONEY, PROPERTY OR IDENTICAL GOODS AND SERVICES MADE BY A SECONDARY DONOR, THE DIFFERENCE BETWEEN THE VALUE OF THE DONATION MADE BY THE SECONDARY DONOR AND THE VALUE OF THE DONATION MADE BY THE PRIMARY DONOR, PROVIDED SUCH VALUE IS POSITIVE.

"PRIMARY DONOR." AN INSTITUTION WHICH MAKES A DONATION OF ANY MONEY, PROPERTY, GOODS OR SERVICES TO AN INSTITUTION OF PURELY PUBLIC CHARITY.

"SECONDARY DONOR." AN INSTITUTION WHICH RECEIVES A DONATION OF ANY MONEY, PROPERTY, GOODS OR SERVICES FROM A PRIMARY DONOR AND THEN MAKES A DONATION BACK TO THAT PRIMARY DONOR WITHIN THREE YEARS OF HAVING RECEIVED SUCH DONATION.

(VI) THE REASONABLE VALUE OF VOLUNTEER ASSISTANCE DONATED BY INDIVIDUALS WHO ARE INVOLVED OR ASSIST IN THE PROVISION OF GOODS OR SERVICES BY THE INSTITUTION. THE REASONABLE VALUE OF VOLUNTEER ASSISTANCE, COMPUTED ON AN HOURLY BASIS, SHALL NOT EXCEED THE "STATEWIDE AVERAGE WEEKLY WAGE" AS DEFINED IN SECTION 105.1 OF THE ACT OF JUNE 2, 1915 (P.L.736, NO.338), KNOWN AS THE WORKERS' COMPENSATION ACT DIVIDED BY 40.

(VII) THE COST OF GOODS OR SERVICES PROVIDED BY AN INSTITUTION LICENSED BY THE DEPARTMENT OF HEALTH OR THE DEPARTMENT OF PUBLIC WELFARE TO INDIVIDUALS WHO ARE UNABLE TO PAY PROVIDED THAT REASONABLE AND CUSTOMARY COLLECTION EFFORTS HAVE BEEN MADE BY THE INSTITUTION.

(VIII) THE VALUE OF ANY VOLUNTARY AGREEMENT AS SET FORTH IN SECTION 7(C).

Appendix H
About the Author...

Gary M. Grobman (B.S. Drexel University, M.P.A. Harvard University, Kennedy School of Government) is special projects director for White Hat Communications, a Harrisburg-based publishing and nonprofit consulting organization formed in 1993. Mr. Grobman is a doctoral student at The Penn State University. He served as the executive director of the Pennsylvania Jewish Coalition from 1983-1996. Prior to that, he was a senior legislative assistant in Washington for two members of Congress, a news reporter, and a political humor columnist for *Roll Call*. He also served as a lobbyist for public transit agencies. In 1987, he founded the Non-Profit Advocacy Network (NPAN), which consists of more than 50 statewide associations that represent Pennsylvania charities. He currently is the Harrisburg Contributing Editor for *Pennsylvania Nonprofit Report* and the Internet site reviewer for the *International Journal of Nonprofit and Voluntary Sector Marketing*.

He serves on the Board of Directors of the Greater Harrisburg Concert Band as Vice President. He also served on the board of directors of the Citizen Service Project, and was the Treasurer of that 501(c)(3), which was established to promote citizen service in Pennsylvania. He is the author of *The Holocaust—A Guide for Pennsylvania Teachers* (1990), *The Non-Profit Handbook* (1996), *The Non-Profit Internet Handbook* (1998, co-authored with Gary Grant), and *Improving Quality and Performance in Your Non-Profit Organization* (1999).

For information about speaking engagements or consulting projects, contact Mr. Grobman at: **White Hat Communications, P.O. Box 5390, Harrisburg, PA 17110-0390. Telephone: (717) 238-3787; Fax: (717) 238-2090.**

About the PA Association of Nonprofit Organizations...

PANO offers information, technical assistance, public policy education, cost-saving programs and professional development opportunities to nonprofits across the Commonwealth. It is a 501(c)(3) nonprofit organization dedicated to helping Pennsylvania nonprofits operate efficiently and effectively. PANO can show how to improve management practices, increase the public's understanding of nonprofits and positively impact policies affecting nonprofits. PANO's members include executive directors, administrators, board members and staff of hundreds of nonprofit organizations of all types and sizes. PANO members receive advice on management, board and funding issues, money-saving insurance and management plans, up-to-date education and information services, advocacy with state government in Harrisburg, networking opportunities, information on philanthropic opportunities, and research and planning services. Your membership in PANO will increase your knowledge of nonprofit management and improve the efficiency of your organization like no other single investment, thanks to the services and information offered. For more information, use the postcard in the back of the book or contact PANO at: **PANO, 132 State Street, Harrisburg, PA 17101 (717) 236-8584.**

Appendix I
Pennsylvania Nonprofit Handbook
Reader Survey/Order Form

Return Survey To:
White Hat Communications
PO Box 5390
Harrisburg, PA 17110-0390

My name and address (please print legibly):

1. I would like to suggest the following corrections:

2. I would like to suggest the following topics for inclusion in a future edition:

3. I have the following comments, suggestions, or criticisms:

4. I would like to order ____ additional copies @$27.95 each plus $3.50 shipping and handling first book, $1 each additional book, plus $1.89 Pennsylvania sales tax for the first book and $1.74 for each additional book for Pennsylvania residents (total: $33.34 first book, $30.69 each additional book). Tax-exempt organizations may reduce this amount by the $1.89 sales tax if they include a copy of their exemption certificate from the Pennsylvania Department of Revenue. Note: Quantity discounts are available.

(use additional sheets if necessary)

Bibliography

A comprehensive bibliography for all aspects of nonprofit organization formation and operation can be found in a three-volume work:

Derrickson, Margaret Chandler, et. al. *The Literature of the Nonprofit Sector* (3 volumes), New York, NY: The Foundation Center, 1989.

Chapter 1/Chapter 2

Conners, Tracy D. (ed.). *The Nonprofit Organization Handbook.* New York, NY: McGraw-Hill Book Co., 1980.

Debnam, Robert J. *Handbook of Legal Liabilities for Nonprofit Executives.* Washington, DC: Rural America.

Hopkins, Bruce R. *Starting and Managing a Nonprofit Organization: A Legal Guide.* New York, NY: Wiley & Sons, 1989.

Kirschten, Barbara L. *Nonprofit Corporate Forms Handbook.* New York, NY: Clark Boardman Co., 1990.

Lane, Marc J. *Legal Handbook for Nonprofit Organizations.* New York, NY: Amacon, 1980.

Mancuso, Anthony. *How To Form Your Own Nonprofit Corporation.* Berkeley, CA: Nolo Press, 1990.

Mandel Center for Nonprofit Organizations. *Legal Issues in Nonprofit Organizations.* Mandel Center for Nonprofit Organizations Discussion Paper Series. Cleveland, OH: Case Western Reserve University, 1988.

Majmudes, Carol S. and Weiss, Ellen. (eds.). *Tax-Exempt Organizations* (2 vol.). Englewood Cliffs, N.J.: Prentice-Hall, 1988.

Ott, J. Steven and Shafitz, Jay M. *The Facts on File Dictionary of Nonprofit Organization Management.* New York, NY: Facts on File Publications, 1986.

Philadelphia Volunteer Lawyers for the Arts. *Guide to Forming a Non-Profit, Tax-Exempt Organization.* Philadelphia, PA: Philadelphia Volunteer Lawyers for the Arts, 1980.

Treusch, Paul E. and Sugarman, Norman A. *Tax-Exempt Organizations.* Philadelphia, PA: American Law Institute, 1983.

Whitaker, Fred A. *How to Form Your Own Non-Profit Corporation in One Day.* Oakland, CA: Minority Management Institute, 1979.

Chapter 3

Broadwell, Martin M. *Supervisory Handbook: A Management Guide to Principles and Applications.* New York, NY: Wiley, Inc., 1985.

Conners, Tracy D. (ed.). *The Nonprofit Organization Handbook.* New York, NY: McGraw-Hill Book Co., 1980.

Hopkins, Bruce R. *Starting and Managing a Nonprofit Organization: A Legal Guide.* New York, NY: Wiley & Sons, 1989.

Mancuso, Anthony. *How To Form Your Own Nonprofit Corporation.* Berkeley, CA: Nolo Press, 1990.

Ott, J. Steven and Shafitz, Jay M. *The Facts on File Dictionary of Nonprofit Organization Management*. New York, NY: Facts on File Publications, 1986.

Robert, III, Henry M. and Evans, William J. (eds.). *Robert's Rules of Order Newly Revised* (1990 Edition). Glenview, IL: Scott, Foresman and Co., 1990.

Conners, Tracy D. (ed.). *The Nonprofit Organization Handbook*. New York, NY: McGraw-Hill Book Co., 1980.

Chapter 4

Anthes, Earl, et. al. (ed.). *The Nonprofit Board Book*. Independent Community Consultants, West Memphis, Ark., Independent Community Consultants, 1985.

Bates, Don. *How to Be a Better Board Member: Guidelines for Trustees*. Voluntary Action Leadership (Winter 1983).

Black, Ralph. *What Do You Do With a Do-Nothing Board Member?* American Symphony Orchestra League (1987).

Brooklyn In-Touch Information Center. *Building a Board of Directors*. Brooklyn, NY: Brooklyn In-Touch Information Center, 1984.

————-*How To Conduct a Meeting*. 1988.

————-*How To Develop a Board of Directors*. 1988.

Conrad, William R. Jr. and Glenn, William E. *The Effective Voluntary Board of Directors: What is it and How it Works*. Chicago, IL: Swallow Press, 1983.

Duca, Diane J. *Nonprofit Boards: A Practical Guide to Roles, Responsibilities and Performance*. Phoenix, AZ: Oryx Press, 1986.

Hopkins, Bruce R. *Starting and Managing a Nonprofit Organization: A Legal Guide*. New York, NY: Wiley & Sons, 1989.

Independent Community Consultants. *The Nonprofit Board Book: Strategies for Organizational Success*. West Memphis, Ark: Independent Community Consultants, 1983.

Kirk, W. Astor. *Nonprofit Organization Governance: A Challenge in Turbulent Times*. New York, NY: Carlton Press, 1986.

O'Connell, Brian. *The Role of the Board and Board Members*. Nonprofit Management Series (#1). Washington, DC: Independent Sector, 1988.

———— *Finding, Developing and Rewarding Good Board Members*. Nonprofit Management Series (#2). Washington, DC: Independent Sector, 1988.

———— *The Board Member's Book: Making a Difference in Voluntary Organizations*. New York, NY: The Foundation Center, 1985.

Ott, J. Steven and Shafitz, Jay M. *The Facts on File Dictionary of Nonprofit Organization Management*. New York, NY: Facts on File Publications, 1986.

Chapter 5

Albert, K. J, editor. *The Strategic Management Handbook*. New York: McGraw-Hill, 1983.

Department. of Hospital Planning and Society for Hospital Planning. *Compendium of Resources for Strategic Planning in Hospitals*. Chicago, IL: American Hospital Association, 1981.

Armstrong, J. S. *The Value of Formal Planning for Strategic Decisions: Review of Empirical Research.* Strategic Management Journal (Ill, 1982:197-211).

Barry, Brian W. *Strategic Planning Workbook for Nonprofit Organizations.* St. Paul, Minn: Amherst H. Wilder Foundation, 1986.

Bryson, J. M. *Strategic Planning for Public and Nonprofit Organizations.* San Francisco: Jossey-Bass, 1988.

Mintzburg, Henry. *The Rise and Fall of Strategic Planning.* NY, NY: MacMillan, 1994.

Newman, W. H., Summer, C. E. and Warren, E. K. *The Process of Management.* Englewood Cliffs, NJ: Prentice Hall, 1982.

Pennings, J. M. *Organizational Strategy and Change.* San Francisco, CA: Jossey-Bass, 1985.

Peters, J. P. *A Guide to Strategic Planning for Hospitals.* Chicago, IL: American Hospital Association, 1979.

Rhenmann, E. *Organizational Theory for Long-Range Planning.* NY, NY: Wiley & Sons, 1973.

Steiner, G. A. *Strategic Planning: What Every Manager Must Know.* NY, NY: Free Press, 1979.

Chapter 6

Carver, John. *Boards That Make a Difference.* San Francisco, CA: Josey-Bass, 1990.

Chapter 7

Independent Sector. *Ethics and the Nation's Voluntary and Philanthropic Community.* Washington, D.C.

Josephson Institute of Ethics. *Making Ethical Decisions.* Marina del Rey, CA.

Chapter 8

Conners, Tracy D. (ed.). *The Nonprofit Organization Handbook.* New York, NY: McGraw-Hill Book Co., 1980.

Godfrey, Howard. *Handbook on Tax-Exempt Organizations.* Englewood Cliffs, NJ: Prentice-Hall, 1983.

Hansmann, Henry. *The Rationale for Exempting Nonprofit Organizations From Corporate Income Taxation.* New Haven, CT: Institute for Social Policy Studies, 1981.

Harmon, Gail and Ferster, Andrea. *"Dealing With the IRS."* Nonprofit Times (May 1988).

Hopkins, Bruce R. *Starting and Managing a Nonprofit Organization: A Legal Guide.* New York, NY: Wiley & Sons, 1989.

Kirschten, Barbara L. *Nonprofit Corporate Forms Handbook.* New York: Clark Boardman Co., 1990.

Larson, Martin A., and Lowell, C. Stanley. *Praise the Lord for Tax Exemption.* Washington, DC:

Robert B. Luce, 1969.

Mancuso, Anthony. *How To Form Your Own Nonprofit Corporation.* Berkeley, CA: Nolo Press, 1990.

Ott, J. Steven and Shafitz, Jay M. *The Facts on File Dictionary of Nonprofit Organization Management.* New York, NY: Facts on File Publications, 1986.

Skousen, Mark. *Tax-Free.* Merrifield, VA: Mark Skousen, 1982.

Stralton, Debra J. *"A Guide for Dealing With the IRS."* Association Management (August 1979).

Trompeter, Jean E. *"Formation and Qualification of a Charitable Organization."* Milwaukee Lawyer (Fall 1983).

Chapter 9

Brooklyn In-Touch Information Center. *How to Assess Board Liability. Fact Sheet for Nonprofit Managers* (#6). Brooklyn, NY: Brooklyn In-Touch Information Center, 1988.

Chapman, Terry S.; Lai, Mary L; and Steinbock, Elmer L. *Am I Covered For? A Guide to Insurance for Nonprofit Organizations.* San Jose, CA: Consortium for Human Resources, 1984.

Conners, Tracy D. (ed.). *The Nonprofit Organization Handbook.* New York, NY: McGraw-Hill Book Co., 1980.

Council on Foundations. *Directors and Officers Liability Insurance.* Washington, DC: Council on Foundations, 1983.

Davis, Pamela. *Nonprofit Organizations and Liability Insurance: Problems, Options and Prospects.* Los Angeles, CA: California Community Foundation, 1987.

Drucker, Peter F. *Managing the Nonprofit Organization.* New York, NY: Harper Collins, 1990.

Johnson, R. Bradley. *Risk Management Guide for Nonprofits.* Alexandria, VA: United Way of America, 1987.

Ott, J. Steven and Shafitz, Jay M. *The Facts on File Dictionary of Nonprofit Organization Management.* New York, NY: Facts on File Publications, 1986.

Peat, Marwick, Mitchell and Co. *Directors' and Officers' Liability: A Crisis in the Making.* New York, NY: Peat, Marwick, Mitchell and Co., 1987.

Chapter 10

American Institute of Certified Public Accountants. *Audits of Certain Nonprofit Organizations.* New York, NY: American Institute of Certified Public Accountants, 1981.

Brooklyn In-Touch Information Center. *How To Prepare a Budget.* New York, NY: Brooklyn In-Touch Information Center, 1988.

Conners, Tracy D. (ed.). *The Nonprofit Organization Handbook.* New York, NY: McGraw-Hill Book Co., 1980.

Drucker, Peter F. *Managing the Nonprofit Organization.* New York, NY: Harper Collins, 1990.

Gross, Jr., Malvern J. and Warshauer, William. *Financial and Accounting Guide for Nonprofit Organizations.* New York, NY: John Wiley, 1983.

Matthews, Lawrence M. *Practical Operating Budgeting.* New York: McGraw-Hill, 1977.

Olenick, Arnold J. and Olenick, Philip R. *Making the Non-Profit Organization Work: A Financial,*

Legal and Tax Guide for Administrators. Englewood Cliffs, NJ: Institute for Business Planning, 1983.

Ott, J. Steven and Shafitz, Jay M. *The Facts on File Dictionary of Nonprofit Organization Management.* New York, NY: Facts on File Publications, 1986.

Public Management Institute. *Bookkeeping for Nonprofits.* San Francisco, CA: Institute for Business Planning, 1983.

———- *Budgeting for Nonprofits.* San Francisco, CA: Institute for Business Planning, 1980.

Quint, Barbara Gilder. *Clear and Simple Guide to Bookkeeping.* New York: Monarch Press, 1981.

Ragan, Robert C. *Step-By-Step Bookkeeping.* New York, NY: Sterling Publications, 1987.

Sladek, Frea E. and Stein, Eugene L. *Grant Budgeting and Finance.* New York, NY: Plenum Press, 1981.

Vinter, Robert D. and Kikish, Rhea K. *Budgeting for Not-for-Profit Organizations.* New York, NY: Free Press, 1984.

Wacht, Richard F. *Financial Management in Nonprofit Organizations.* Atlanta, GA: Georgia State University, 1984.

Waldo, Charles N. *A Working Guide for Directors of Not-for-Profit Organizations.* Westport, CT: Greenwood Press, 1986.

Chapter 11

Anthes, Earl W. and Cronin, Jerry (eds.). *Personnel Matters in the Nonprofit Organization.* West Memphis, AR: Independent Community Consultants, 1987.

Anthony, Robert N. and Herzlinger, Regina E. *Management Control in Nonprofit Organizations.* Chicago, IL: Richard D. Irwin, 1975.

Becker, Sarah and Glenn, Donna. *Off Your Duffs and Up the Assets: Common Sense for Non-Profit Managers.* Rockville, NY: Farnsworth Publishing Co., 1988.

Borst, Diane and Montana, Patrick J. (eds.). *Managing Nonprofit Organizations.* New York, NY: Amacon, 1977.

Broadwell, Martin M. *Supervisory Handbook: A Management Guide to Principles and Applications.* New York, NY: Wiley, Inc., 1985.

Brown, James Douglas. *The Human Nature of Organizations.* New York, NY: Amacon, 1973.

Chruden, Herbert J. *Personnel Management.* Cincinnati, OH: South-Western Publications, 1976.

Conners, Tracy D. (ed.). *The Nonprofit Organization Handbook.* New York, NY: McGraw-Hill Book Co., 1980.

Drucker, Peter F. *Managing the Nonprofit Organization.* New York, NY: Harper Collins, 1990.

Goldberg/Rosenthal, Montgomery, Mc Cracken, Walker & Rhoads, and Paychex, Inc. *Accounting, Legal and Payroll Tax Guide for Nonprofit Organizations.* Philadelphia: Community Accountants, 1991.

Hopkins, Bruce R. *Starting and Managing a Nonprofit Organization: A Legal Guide.* New York, NY: Wiley & Sons, 1989.

Chapter 12

Bagley, Esq., Bruce. *Necessary v. Nosey—Guidelines and Strategies for Hiring.* PA Society of Association Executives' *Society News.* April 1996. pp. 20.

Gelatt, James P. *Managing Nonprofit Organizations in the 21st Century.* Phoenix, AZ: The Oryx Press, 1992.

Half, Robert. *On Hiring.* New York, NY: Crown Publishers, 1985.

Hopkins, Bruce R. *Starting and Managing a Nonprofit Organization—A Legal Guide.* New York, NY: Wiley & Sons; 1989.

Pennsylvania Human Relations Commission.*Pre-Employment Inquiries: What May I Ask? What Must I Answer?* Harrisburg, PA.

Rogers, Henry C. *The One Hat Solution—Rogers' Strategy for Creative Middle Management.* New York, NY: St. Martin's Press, 1986.

Thompson, Brad.*The New Manager's Handbook.*Burr Ridge, IL: Irwin Professional Publishing, 1995.

Chapter 13

Adams, Katherine. *"Investing in Volunteers: A Guide to Effective Volunteer Management."* Conserve Neighborhoods (1985).

Brown, Kathleen M. *Keys to Making a Volunteer Program Work.* Richmond, CA: Arden Publications, 1982.

Conners, Tracy D. (ed.). *The Nonprofit Organization Handbook.* New York, NY: McGraw-Hill Book Co., 1980.

de Harven, Gerry Ann. *"Fostering the Voluntary Spirit: Motivating People to Serve."* Fund Raising Management (March 1984).

Flanagan, Joan. *The Successful Volunteer Organization: Getting Started and Getting Results in Nonprofit, Charitable, Grassroots and Community Groups.* Chicago, IL: Contemporary Books, 1984.

Fletcher, Kathleen Brown. *The 9 Keys To Successful Volunteer Programs.* Taft Group: Rockville, MD., 1987.

Independent Sector. *Americans Volunteer, 1981.* Washington, DC: Independent Sector, 1982.

Lauffer, Armand and Gorodezky, Sarah.*Volunteers.* Beverly Hills, CA: Sage Publications, 1977.

London, Mark. *"Effective Use of Volunteers: Who, Why, When and How."* Fund Raising Management (August 1985).

McCurley, Stephen H. *"Protecting Volunteers From Suit: A Look At State Legislation."* Voluntary Action Leadership (Spring-Summer 1987).

O'Connell, Brian. *America's Voluntary Spirit.* New York, NY: The Foundation Center, 1983.

Rauner, Judy. *Helping People Volunteer.* San Diego, CA: Marlborough Publications, 1980.

Stafford, J. et. al. *Fundamentals of Association Management: The Volunteer.* Washington, DC: American Society of Association Executives, 1982.

Taylor, Shirley H. and Wild, Peggy. *"How to Match Volunteer Motivation With Job Demands."* Voluntary Action Leadership (Summer 1984).

Van Til, Jon. *Mapping the Third Sector: Volunteerism in a Changing Social Economy.* New York, NY: The Foundation Center, 1988.

Volunteer—The National Center. *New Challenges for Employee Volunteering.* Arlington, VA: Volunteer—The National Center, 1982.

Chapter 14

Conners, Tracy D. (ed.). *The Nonprofit Organization Handbook.* New York, NY: McGraw-Hill Book Co., 1980.

Kramer, Donald. *"Pa. Passes Solicitation Act With New Rules, Penalties."* Nonprofit Issues (December 1990).

Morgan, Lewis & Bockius. *"The Solicitation of Funds for Charitable Purposes Act."* Philadelphia: Morgan, Lewis & Bockius, May 1991.

Wickham, Kenneth. *Testimony Presented to House Finance Committee Regarding HB 2046 and HB 2047: November 1, 1989.* Harrisburg, PA: United Way of Pennsylvania, 1989.

Chapter 15

Conners, Tracy D. (ed.). *The Nonprofit Organization Handbook.* New York, NY: McGraw-Hill Book Co., 1980.

Dannelley, Paul. *Fundraising and Public Relations.* Norman, OK: Univ. of Oklahoma Press, 1986.

Des Marais, Philip. *How To Get Government Grants.* New York, NY: Public Service Materials Center, 1975.

Kletzien, S. Damon, ed. *Directory of Pennsylvania Foundations.* Springfield, PA: Triadvocates Press, 1990.

Margolin, Judith B. (ed.). *The Foundation Center's User Friendly Guide—Grant Seeker's Guide to Resources.* New York, NY: The Foundation Center, 1990.

Nelson, Paula. *Where to Get Money for Everything.* New York, NY: William Morris & Co., 1982.

Raybin, Arthur D. *How to Hire the Right Fundraising Consultant.* Washington, DC: Taft Group, 1985.

Seltzer, Michael. *Securing Your Organization's Future: A Complete Guide to Fundraising Strategies.* New York, NY: The Foundation Center, 1987.

White, Virginia (ed.). *Grant Proposals That Succeeded.* New York, NY: Plenum Press, 1983.

Chapter 16

Blum, Laurie. *The Complete Guide to Getting a Grant.* New York, NY: Poseidon Press, 1993.

Chelekis, George C. *The Action Guide to Government Grants, Loans and Giveaways.* New York, NY: Perigee Books, 1993.

Dermer, Joseph. *How to Write Successful Foundation Presentations.* New York, NY: Public Service Materials Center, 1984.

Dumouchel, J. Robert. *Government Assistance Almanac*. Washington, D.C.: Foggy Bottom Publications, 1985.

Educational Funding Research Council. *Funding Database Handbook*. Arlington, VA: Funding Research Institute, 1992.

Geever, Jane C. *The Foundation Center's Guide to Proposal Writing*. New York, NY: The Foundation Center, 1993.

Hillman, Howard and Chamberlain, Majorie. *The Art of Winning Corporate Grants*. New York, NY: Vanguard Press, 1980.

Margolis, Judith. *Foundation Fundamentals: A Guide for Grantseekers*. New York: Foundation Center, 1991.

_____ *The Foundation Center's User Friendly Guide: Grantseeker's Guide to Resources*. New York: The Foundation Center, 1992.

Smith, Craig W. and Skjei, Eric W. *Getting Grants*. New York: Harper and Row, 1979.

Chapter 17

Brandt, Sanford F. *Tax-Exempt Organizations' Lobbying and Political Activities Accountability Act of 1987: A Guide for Volunteers and Staff of Nonprofit Organizations*. Washington, DC: Independent Sector, 1988.

Caplan, Marc and Nader, Ralph. *Ralph Nader Presents a Citizen's Guide to Lobbying*. New York, NY: Dembner Books, 1983.

Conners, Tracy D. (ed.). *The Nonprofit Organization Handbook*. New York, NY: McGraw-Hill Book Co., 1980.

Gaby, Patricia V. and Gaby, Daniel M. *Nonprofit Organization Handbook: A Guide to Fundraising, Grants, Lobbying, Membership Building, Publicity and Public Relations*. Englewood Cliffs, NJ: Prentice-Hall, 1979.

Independent Sector. *Advocacy Is Sometimes an Agency's Best Service: Opportunities and Limits Within Federal Law*. Washington, DC: Independent Sector, 1984.

Mental Health Association. *A Layman's Guide to Lobbying Without Losing Your Tax Exempt Status*. Roslyn, VA: Mental Health Association. 1976.

Migdail, Rhonda G. *"Lobbying and Political Activities: What Every Nonprofit Should Know."* Nonprofit World Report 3 (May-June 1983).

Speeter, Greg. *Playing Their Game Our Way. Using the Political Process to Meet Community Needs*. Amherst, MA: University of Massachusetts, 1978.

Suhrke, Henry C. *" 'Political' Advocacy by Non-Profits."* Philanthropy Monthly (Feb 1983).

United States House of Representatives, Ways and Means Committee, Subcommittee on Oversight. *Tax Administration: Information on Lobbying and Political Activities of Tax-Exempt Organizations*. Gaithersburg, MD: U.S. General Accounting Office, 1987.

Webster, George D. and Krebs, Frederick. *Associations and Lobbying: A Guide for Non-Profit Organizations*. Washington, DC: Chamber of Commerce of the United States, 1979.

Chapter 18

Gates, Lowell, J.D. (Killian and Gephart). *Political, Lobbying and Grassroots Activities of 501(c)(3) Organizations.* LTC Legal Briefs; July 28, 1988.

Harvard Law Review. *Political Activities of Non-Profit Corporations;* May 1992.

Independent Sector. *Update on Permissible Activities of 501(c)(3) Organizations During a Political Campaign.* July 29, 1988.

Montgomery, Richard C. *Charitable Organizations and Prohibited Political Activities.* Pennsylvania Bar Association Quarterly; April 1992.

Wharton, Linda. *Guidelines for 501(c)(3) and 501(c)(4) Organizations Regarding Electoral Activities Under the Federal Tax Laws.* Memorandum of March 1, 1990.

Chapter 19

Committee to Defend Reproductive Rights of the Coalition for the Medical Rights of Women. *The Media Book: Making the Media Work for Your Grassroots Group.* San Francisco, CA: Committee to Defend Reproductive Rights, 1981.

Conners, Tracy D. (ed.). *The Nonprofit Organization Handbook.* New York, NY: McGraw-Hill Book Co., 1980.

Council on Foundations. *Communications and Public Affairs Guide.* Washington, DC: Council on Foundations, 1984.

Dannelley, Paul. *Fundraising and Public Relations.* Norman, OK: Univ. of Oklahoma Press, 1986.

Drucker, Peter F. *Managing the Nonprofit Organization.* New York, NY: Harper Collins: 1990.

Foundation for American Communication. *Media Resource Guide.* Los Angeles, CA: Foundation for American Communications, 1981.

Gaby, Patricia V. and Gaby, Daniel M. *Nonprofit Organization Handbook: A Guide to Fundraising, Grants, Lobbying, Membership Building, Publicity and Public Relations.* Englewood Cliffs, NJ: Prentice-Hall, 1979.

Green, Alan. *Communicating in the '80s: New Options for the Nonprofit Community.* Washington, DC: Benton Foundation, 1983.

Gross, Sallie and Viet, Carol H. *For Immediate Release: A Public Relations Manual.* Philadelphia, PA: Greater Philadelphia Cultural Alliance, 1982.

Ott, J. Steven and Shafitz, Jay M. *The Facts on File Dictionary of Nonprofit Organization Management.* New York, NY: Facts on File Publications, 1986.

Chapter 20

Gerwig, Kate. *Putting Your Mark on the Web.* NetGuide Vol. 3 No. 2 (February 1996) pp. 87

Gibbs, Mark and Smith. Richard. *Navigating the Internet.* Carmel, Indiana: Sams Publishing 1993.

Gilster, Paul. *The New Internet Navigator.* NY, NY: Wiley & Sons, 1995.

LaQuey, Tracy and Ryer, Jeanne. *The Internet Companion Plus.* Reading, MA: Addison-Wesley Publishing Co. 1993.

Manger, Jason J. *The Essential Internet Information Guide.* Berkshire, England: McGraw-Hill, 1995.

Chapter 21

Brown, Cherie R. *The Art of Coalition Building— A Guide for Community Leaders.* New York: American Jewish Committee, 1984.

Kahn, Si. *Organizing: A Guide for Grassroots Leaders.* Washington, D.C.: NASW Press, 1991 (Revised Edition)

MacEchern, Diane. *No Coalition, No Returns.* Washington, D.C.: Environmental Action.

Tydeman, Ann. *A Guide to Coalition Building.* Washington, D.C.: National Citizen's Coalition for Nursing Home Reform, 1979.

Chapter 22

Conners, Tracy D. (ed.). *The Nonprofit Organization Handbook.* New York, NY: McGraw-Hill Book Co., 1980.

Kirschten, Barbara L. *Nonprofit Corporate Forms Handbook.* New York, NY: Clark Boardman Co., 1990.

Mancuso, Anthony. *How To Form Your Own Nonprofit Corporation.* Berkeley, CA: Nolo Press, 1990.

Norsworthy, Alex (ed.). *The Nonprofit Computer Sourcebook.* Rockville, MD: The Taft Group, 1990.

Ott, J. Steven and Shafitz, Jay M. *The Facts on File Dictionary of Nonprofit Organization Management.* New York, NY: Facts on File Publications, 1986.

Chapter 23

Conners, Tracy D. (ed.). *The Nonprofit Organization Handbook.* New York, NY: McGraw-Hill Book Co., 1980.

Deja, Sandy. *"Nonprofit Organizations, Business Ventures, and the IRS: Your Guide to the Unrelated Business Income Tax Law."* Whole Nonprofit Catalog 6 (Spring 1988).

Dewan, Bradford N. *"Operation of a Business by Non-Profit Tax-Exempt Organizations."* Economic Development and Law Center (March-April 1986).

Gallaway, Joseph M. *The Unrelated Business Income Tax.* New York, NY: John Wiley, 1982.

Grobman, Gary. *"The Issue of Competition Between Non-Profit and For-Profit Corporations"* Harrisburg, PA: Pennsylvania Jewish Coalition, 1994.

Hopkins, Bruce. *"Hearings on Nonprofit 'Competition' ".* Nonprofit World 5 (Sept-Oct. 1987).

Kotler, Philip and Andreasen, Alan R. *Strategic Marketing for Nonprofit Organizations.* Englewood Cliffs, NJ: Prentiss-Hall, Inc., 1987.

Lehrfeld, William J. *"More Unrelated Business Tax Issues.* Philanthropy Monthly (October 1984).

Skloot, Edward (ed.). *The Nonprofit Entrepreneur.* New York, NY: The Foundation Center: 1988.

United States Congress, Joint Committee on Taxation. *Tax Policy: Competition Between Taxable Businesses and Tax-Exempt Organizations.* Gaithersburg, MD: U.S. General Accounting Office. 1987.

Wellford, Harrison and Gallagher, Janne. *The Myth of Unfair Competition by Nonprofit Organizations.* New York, NY: Family Service Association of America, 1985.

Chapter 24

Grobman, Gary. *"The Issue of Tax-Exempt Status for Pennsylvania Non-Profit Charities."* Harrisburg, PA: Pennsylvania Jewish Coalition, 1994.

National Council of Nonprofit Associations. *State Tax Trends.* Volume 2, No. 4; Summer 1994.

Wellford, Harrison and Gallagher, Janne. *The Myth of Unfair Competition by Nonprofit Organizations.* New York, NY: Family Service Association of America, 1985.

Chapter 25

Bookman, Mark. *Protecting Your Organization's Tax-Exempt Status.* San Francisco: Jossey Bass, 1992.

Gillespie, Catherine H. *Court Denies Tax Exemption for Nonprofit Nursing Home.* Nonprofit Issues, Philadelphia, PA: Montgomery, McCracken, Walker and Rhoads, March 1992.

Hopkins, Bruce. *The Law and Tax-Exempt Organizations, 6th edition.* New York: John Wiley and Sons. 1992.

Stepneski, Rob. *Rising Tax Pressure Hits Nonprofits.* NonProfit Times: April 1993.

Van Til, Jon. *Tax Exemptions Reconsidered.* NonProfit Times: June 1993.

Chapter 26

Cavadel, Joel. Nonprofit Mergers. Unpublished report on legal consideration relating to nonprofit mergers in Pennsylvania, 1996.

La Pinana, David. *Nonprofit Mergers: The Board's Responsibility to Consider the Unthinkable.* Washington, DC: Center for Nonprofit Boards, 1994.

Morgan, William, Mattaini, Paul and Doliner, Ann. *Is a Merger in Your Future?* Presentation to the Pennsylvania Association of Nonprofit Organizations (PANO), 1996.

Chapter 27

Anonymous. *The Year 2000 Challenge for United Ways.* Alexandria, VA: United Way of America, 1998.

Batchilder, Melissa. *Computer Bug Lurking for Nonprofits' Systems*. The Nonprofit Times. July 1998.

Greene, Stephen. *Preparing for the 2000 Bug*. The Chronicle of Philanthropy. v.XI, No. 4, December 3, 1998, p. 1.

Halpern, Charles, Friedman, Paul, and Korpivaara, Ari. *The Year 2000 Challenge: A Socially Responsive Way to Prepare for Disruptions in Computer-Reliant Systems*, New York: Nathan Cummings Foundation, 1998.

Levin, Amanda. *Are Hospitals Ready for Y2K?* National Underwriter (Property & Casualty/Risk & Benefits Management). v102 n40. Oct 5, 1998. p.9-10.

O'Riley, Paloma, et al. *Y2K Citizen's Action Guide. Minneapolis, MN: Utne Reader Books, 1998.*

Rea, Alan. *Frequently Asked Questions (FAQ) About the Y2K Problem.* http://unix.cc.wmich.edu/rea/Y2K/FAQ.html, 1998.

Chapter 28

Crosby, Philip B. *Quality is Free*. New York: McGraw Hill, 1979.

Garvin, David A. *Management Quality: The Strategic and Competitive Edge*. New York: Free Press, 1988.

Grobman, Gary. *Improving Quality and Performance in Your Non-Profit Organization*. Harrisburg, PA: White Hat Communications, 1999.

Martin, Lawrence. *TQM in Human Service Organizations*. San Francisco: Jossey-Bass, 1993.

Chapter 29

Bunker, Barbara Benedict and Alban, Billie T. *Large Group Interventions: Engaging the Whole System for Rapid Change.* San Francisco: Jossey-Bass, 1997.

Bunker, Barbara Benedict and Alban, Billie T. *What Makes Large Group Interventions Effective?* Journal of Applied Behavioral Science 28(4), 1992.

Carter, Reginald. *The Accountable Agency*. Thousand Oaks, CA: Sage Publications, 1983.

Creech, Bill. *The Five Pillars of TQM: How to Make Total Quality Management Work for You*. New York: Penguin Books, 1994.

Crosby, Philip B. *Quality is Free*. New York: McGraw Hill, 1979.

Deming, W. Edward. *On Some Statistical Aids Toward Economic Production. Interfaces*, v5, n4. Aug. 1975. The Operations Research Society of America and the Institute of Management Sciences, 1975.

Friedman, Mark. *A Guide to Developing and Using Performance Measures in Results-Based Budgeting.* Washington, DC: The Finance Project, 1997.

Greenway, Martha Taylor. *The Status of Research and Indicators On Nonprofit Performance In Human Services.* Alexandria, VA: United Way of America, 1996.

Hammer, Michael. *Reengineering Work: Don't Automate: Obliterate. Harvard Business Review,* July-Aug. 1990, pp. 104-112, 1990.

Hammer, Michael. and Champy, James. *Reengineering the Corporation: A Manifesto for Business.* New York: HarperBusiness, 1993.

Hammer, Michael and Stanton, Steven A. *The Reengineering Revolution: A Handbook.* New York: HarperBusiness, 1994.

Peters, Thomas J. and Waterman, Jr., Robert H. *In Search of Excellence: Lessons from America's Best-Run Companies.* New York: Harper and Row, 1982.

Richmond, Frederick and Hunnemann, Eleanor. *What Every Board Member Needs to Know About Outcomes.* Management and Technical Assistance Publication Series n2, Harrisburg, PA: Positive Outcomes, 1996.

Rouda, R. & Kusy, M., Jr. *Organization Development—The Management of Change. Tappi Journal* 78(8): 253 ,1995.

Steckel, Richard and Lehman, Jennifer. *In Search of America's Best Non-Profits.* San Francisco: Jossey-Bass, 1997.

Watson, Gregory H. *The Benchmarking Workbook: Adapting Best Practices for Performance Improvement.* Portland, OR: Productivity Press, 1992.

INDEX

Join the

Pennsylvania Association of Nonprofit Organizations

PANO is a 501(c)(3) nonprofit organization dedicated to helping Pennsylvania nonprofits operate efficiently and effectively. PANO can show how to improve management practices, increase the public's understanding of nonprofits, and positively impact policies affecting nonprofits.

PANO offers—

- ⌘ Advice on management, board and funding issues
- ⌘ Insurance and management plans that save you money
- ⌘ Up-to-date education and information services
- ⌘ Advocacy with the state government in Harrisburg
- ⌘ Networking opportunities with nonprofit staff and board members
- ⌘ Information on philanthropic opportunities
- ⌘ Research and planning

PANO's members include executive directors, administrators, board members, and staff of hundreds of nonprofit organizations of all types and sizes.

Your membership in PANO will increase your knowledge of nonprofit management and improve the efficiency of your organization like no other single investment, thanks to the services and information offered. For more information, use the postcard in the back of the book or contact PANO at:

PANO
132 State Street
Harrisburg, PA 17101
(717) 236-8584

PNR. . . Headlines the News

Philanthropy Experts Assess Climate in PA
by Winnie Atterbury, editor
Pennsylvania Nonprofit Report

Advancing Your Mission Through Marketing

Federal Budget Cuts & Policy Changes: Implications for Nonprofits
by Graham S. Finney

Salaries, Salaries, Salaries
by L. Martin Miller, CPA

Sweet Charity: How Sweet Must It Be for Tax-Exempt Status?
by Gary M. Grobman

Fifteen Ways to Nurture Donors
by Susan L. Walling, CFRE

How to Avoid Being Fined
by Karl Emerson, Director
Bureau of Charitable Organizations

Will Your 403(b) Plan Survive an Audit?
by J. Timothy Corle, Pension Consultant

What People Say About PNR

"Pennsylvania Nonprofit Report is an important contribution to communications in the nonprofit field."
Donald W. Kramer, Chair
Health, Education, Nonprofit Law Department,
Montgomery, McCracken, Walker & Rhoads

"Pennsylvania Nonprofit Report cuts the wheat from the chaff...keys in on important legislative issues and new funding sources and deadlines for us. It allows smaller nonprofits to spend time where it belongs—on their programs. It's the one periodical read by every member of the NGA staff."
Claire Power, Executive Director
Neighborhood Gardens Association

"I find the *Pennsylvania Nonprofit Report* to be an excellent source of current information on legislative and management issues.
Sheila M. Ross, Executive Director
Commonwealth Community Foundations

"Pennsylvania Nonprofit Report is great and packed full of very helpful information."
Louise Elkins, Director
Volunteer Center of United Way

"Strongly recommended reading! Atterbury's monthly *PNR* focuses on key issues and informational resources critical to the well-being of Pennsylvania's not-for-profit sector. Get it! Read it! You and your organization will benefit.
S. Damon Kletzien, Executive Editor
Directory of Pennsylvania Foundations 6th Edition

"I like the no-nonsense format and content. The publication recognizes that development is serious business and every issue has a few items I can act on immediately."
Suzette Baird, Director of Development
Presbyterian Children's Village

9923dm

16 x 12 =

Pennsylvania Nonprofit Report – 16 pages, 12 times a year.

News & Information that Saves You Time & Money

■ **Meet the Newest Funders**
Up to five profiles of newly formed foundations from the editor of the *Directory of Pennsylvania Foundations 6th Edition.*

■ **Funding Sources and Grants**
Timely listings of funding sources and new grant awards – regional and national.

■ **Management and Technical Assistance**
Acknowledged experts in nonprofit law, tax, accounting, fundraising, and human resources keep you on top of the issues.

■ **The Harrisburg Report**
Monthly reports direct from the state capitol.

■ **Special Features**
Surveys, Trends, People, Workshops & Seminars, Newsroom, Directory of Services, and more.

■ **Independent Reporting Since 1993**
from *PNR*'s correspondents throughout the state.

FREE BOOKS!
See special offer

" *PNR* is an important resource for people to know what's going on in Harrisburg. It disseminates timely and accurate information about the nonprofit sector, supplementing what we do here at PANO by pulling people out of their own regions to help them see the big picture statewide, and meet the challenges the sector is facing. "

Joseph Geiger, Executive Director
Pennsylvania Association of Nonprofit Organizations

PNR delivers the indispensable information that helps you get your job done, carry out your mission, develop leaders, recruit staff, plan programs, find new funding sources, and hone the budget – all for only $10 per month.

YES! I want a subscription to the *Pennsylvania Nonprofit Report*

Date_____

Because we know you'll be completely satisfied, we offer a complete 100% money-back guarantee. No questions asked.

Name_____ Title_____

Organization_____

City_____ State_____ Zip_____

Phone_____ Fax_____ e-mail_____

Signature_____

☐ Please send my one year subscription for $120 and my free book

☐ Please send my one year subscription, and all three books for $150

☐ Please bill me

*Order through **White Hat Communications** and receive a $10 discount on your subscription, or a $10 discount if you take advantage of the special offer! Call in or fax orders to White Hat Communications at: (717) 238-3787 (telephone) or (717) 238-2090 (fax). Or send a check to: White Hat Communications, PO Box 5390, Harrisburg, PA 17110. Note: This discount applies to check and credit card orders only.* 2EGROB

Improving Quality and Performance in Your Non-Profit Organization
by Gary M. Grobman

Managing non-profit organizations in the 21st century will be more challenging and sophisticated than ever before. ***Improving Quality and Performance in Your Non-Profit Organization*** provides an introduction to innovative, creative, and effective management techniques developed to totally transform your non-profit organization. Reap the benefits of the quality movement that is revolutionizing commercial and non-profit organizations, and make your own organization more competitive.

Read ***Improving Quality and Performance in Your Non-Profit Organization*** to learn how you can—

- respond to uncertainty and organizational turbulence
- reduce mistakes and infuse your staff with a quality ethic
- rebuild your work processes from the ground up
- find and implement "best practices" of comparable organizations

Improving Quality and Performance in Your Non-Profit Organization is a comprehensive, introductory guide to change management tools and strategies, including—

- Total Quality Management (TQM)
- Business Process Reengineering (BPR)
- Benchmarking/Best Practices
- Outcomes-Based Management (OBM)
- Large Group Interventions (LGI)

It also includes easy-to-read and practical applications of chaos theory and organization theory.

$16.95   5.5" x 8.5"   155 pages   Published January 1999   ISBN: 0-9653653-4-4

The Pennsylvania Nonprofit Handbook

5th Edition

by
Gary M. Grobman

Published by White Hat Communications with the cooperation of the Pennsylvania Association of Nonprofit Organizations

The Pennsylvania Association of Nonprofit Organizations' *Pennsylvania Nonprofit Handbook* is the most up-to-date and useful publication for those starting a nonprofit or for those already operating one. Published by White Hat Communications, the 5th edition features five new chapters prepared with your needs in mind.

This 309-page *Handbook* was originally published in 1992 with the help of more than two-dozen nonprofit executives and attorneys, and is now in its 5th edition. Each easy-to-read chapter includes a synopsis, useful tips, and resources to obtain more information. Pre-addressed postcards are included to obtain important government forms, instruction booklets, and informational publications.

This essential reference tool includes:

- Information about current laws, court decisions, and regulations which apply to PA nonprofits
- Practical advice on running a nonprofit, including chapters on communications, fundraising, lobbying, personnel, fiscal management, nonprofit ethics, and 20 other chapters
- Information on applying successfully for federal and state tax-exempt status
- How to write effective grant applications, hire and fire, Internet resources, and strategic planning
- **NEW!** Mergers and Consolidations
- **NEW!** Year 2000 Problem Planning
- **NEW!** Quality and Change Management

We know you will find *The Pennsylvania Nonprofit Handbook* to be an essential resource for you and your organization.

"The Pennsylvania Nonprofit Handbook will help you keep on track, with everything you need to know about starting up and running a nonprofit all in one volume. It is an extraordinary resource for those who already manage or serve on boards of nonprofits...it is a must reference guide for all nonprofit executives to have at their fingertips."

Joe Geiger, Executive Director, *PA Association of Nonprofit Organizations*

The Pennsylvania Nonprofit Handbook/Non-Profit Internet Handbook ORDER FORM:

Name_____ Organization_____

Address_____City_____State____Zip_____

#of PA Nonprofit Handbooks Ordered____ @$27.95 each $_____
#of Non-Profit Internet Handbooks Ordered ____ @$29.95 each $_____

Please charge: ❑Mastercard ❑Visa   **Shipping and Handling ($3.50 first book, $1 each add'l book) $_____**

Expiration Date_____   **6% PA Sales Tax* $_____**

Card Number _____**PA Nonprofit Report ($110/year/subscription) $_____**

Cardholder's Name (Print) _____   **TOTAL ENCLOSED $_____**

Cardholder's Signature _____

Billing Address (if different) _____   **Pre-payment must accompany all orders.**

* Enclose PA Dept. of Revenue tax-exemption certificate if exempt. Please allow three weeks for delivery.

For information about rush orders or quantity discounts, call (717) 238-3787

Make check or money order payable to: *White Hat Communications*.

Mail to: White Hat Communications, PO Box 5390, Harrisburg, PA 17110-0390

fax: 717-238-2090; http://www.socialworker.com/nonprofit/nphome.html   *pnh-5*

The Non-Profit Internet Handbook

by Gary M. Grobman and Gary B. Grant

The Non-Profit INTERNET Handbook is the definitive handbook for non-profit organizations that want to get the most out of the Internet. This is a valuable resource for:

- Non-profit organization executive staff
- Non-profit organization board members
- Those who fund non-profit organizations
- Those who contribute time and money to non-profit organizations.

The Non-Profit **INTERNET** *Handbook* includes:

- How to connect to the Internet
- How to do effective fund-raising and advocacy on the Internet
- How to develop your organization's World Wide Web site
- How to find information useful to non-profits on the Internet
- How to locate on-line sources of government, foundation, and private corporation grants.

Plus—
Reviews of more than 250 of the most valuable Internet sites for non-profit organizations!

Internet-related cartoons drawn by the internationally-acclaimed cartoonist Randy Glasbergen, creator of *The Better Half.*

The Non-Profit **INTERNET** *Handbook* is an essential reference publication for every non-profit organization.

$29.95 plus shipping.
ISBN 0-9653653-6-0   8½" x 11"
softcover   216 pages plus index

White Hat Communications, P.O. Box 5390, Harrisburg, PA 17110-0390 Phone: 717-238-3787 Fax: 717-238-2090

Telephone orders
(Mastercard or Visa):
717-238-3787
Fax orders: 717-238-2090
Online orders:
http://www.socialworker.com

ORDER FORM

PLEASE SHIP MY ORDER TO:

NAME _____

ADDRESS _____

ADDRESS _____

CITY/STATE/ZIP _____

TELEPHONE NUMBER _____

❏ Enclosed is a check for $_____ made payable to "White Hat Communications."

❏ Please charge my: ❏ MasterCard   ❏ VISA

Card # _____

Expiration Date _____

Name as it appears on card _____

Signature _____

Billing address for credit card (if different from above) _____

Billing City/State/Zip _____

Please send the following publications:

QUANTITY	TITLE		AMOUNT
_____	THE PENNSYLVANIA NONPROFIT HANDBOOK	$27.95	_____
_____	THE NON-PROFIT INTERNET HANDBOOK	$29.95	_____
_____	THE NON-PROFIT HANDBOOK, NATIONAL EDITION	$29.95	_____
_____	IMPROVING QUALITY AND PERFORMANCE IN YOUR NON-PROFIT ORGANIZATION	$16.95	_____
_____	PENNSYLVANIA NONPROFIT REPORT (One-Year Subscription)*	$110.00	_____
_____	PENNSYLVANIA NONPROFIT REPORT (3-book offer)**	$140.00	_____

SHIPPING $ _____

SUBTOTAL $ _____

PA SALES TAX (6%) $ _____

TOTAL DUE $ _____

Shipping charges: $3.50 first book/$1.00 each additional book in U.S.
Please contact us for rates on rush orders, other methods of shipping, or shipping outside the U.S.

PA Sales tax: 6% tax on books only for orders from Pennsylvania, unless accompanied by sales tax exemption certificate
*no sales tax on PNR subscriptions   **add $1.80 sales tax for this offer.

Federal EIN: 25-1719745

Send order form and payment to:
WHITE HAT COMMUNICATIONS
P.O. Box 5390-Dept. 2EB
Harrisburg, PA 17110-0390